"In this cultural moment when we are bombarded by many voices that seek to mold the soul, the timing and content of Fogleman's guide to the nature and act of Christian instruction couldn't be better. Herein is a most vital guide of instruction for whoever would instruct God's people."

—D. H. Williams
Baylor University

"With rare pastoral and theological insight, Alex Fogleman's *Making Disciples* shows why catechesis has such deep roots in Christian history, and how it can once again fuel the life of the church today."

—Thomas S. Kidd
Midwestern Baptist Theological Seminary

"The renewal of Christian catechesis is mission-critical to the church in late modernity—as it has been in epochs before. Expertly (and eloquently!) retrieving the treasures of catechetical wisdom from ages past, Alex Fogleman has provided us with a wonderfully wise and immensely practical guide to making disciples in the twenty-first century."

—Joel Scandrett
Trinity Anglican Seminary

"Most of us have followed a tour guide whose knowledge and love of a place captures our interest. Scholars can be like that, too. They open up a world hitherto unknown or unexplored by people outside the discipline. They do more than inform; they excite and inspire. Alex Fogleman has done exactly that in his book on catechesis, appropriately titled *Making Disciples*. He has clearly mastered the sources. The book is dense for that reason, but it reads lightly, helping readers stroll it as if on a pleasant hike. It demonstrates learnedness, yet it is surprisingly readable. It communicates a great deal of information, yet it never loses sight of the outcome, which is to apply catechesis to the church today. Fogleman's book is nothing short of a wonder. It should be on every pastor's reading list. I highly recommend it."

—Gerald L. Sittser
Whitworth University

"Catechesis or Christian formation never ends, for no believer is ever fully formed or wholly catechized. Alex Fogleman's *Making Disciples* is a persuasive presentation on the need for ongoing, robust catechesis in the Christian church. Such formation is not a luxury but a necessary and essential ingredient for any healthy congregation."

—Greg Peters
Nashotah House

"Alex Fogleman has written a book on catechesis that is also about so much more. Here we find out how to integrate faith, hope, and love; how to be deep both in Scripture and in sacrament; how to be a modern Christian who learns from the masters of Christian life, the church fathers; how to be a true disciple, filled with joy and wonder, who is able to share the faith in all circumstances; and how to value the catechetical tools and practices that Protestants, Catholics, and Orthodox Christians have developed. Read this book in order to learn how to catechize and, even better, in order to rejoice in the instruction and companionship of a master catechist."

—Matthew Levering
Mundelein Seminary

"Jesus calls the church to 'make disciples' by 'baptizing them in the name of the Father and of the Son and of the Holy Spirit and teaching them to obey everything that [he] commanded' (Matt 28:19–20). Yet discipleship does not just happen. As Tertullian, the second-century African church leader, contended, 'Christians are made not born.' Alex Fogleman provides an accessible account of the historic practice of making Christians, or catechesis, which guides new believers in the basic teaching of Christ (Heb 6:1–2). This book not only offers a rich account of the ancient tradition, but it also shows how to cultivate a robust catechetical practice in our churches today to make disciples."

—Curtis W. Freeman
Duke Divinity School

Making Disciples

Catechesis in History, Theology, and Practice

Alex Fogleman

William B. Eerdmans Publishing Company
Grand Rapids, Michigan

Wm. B. Eerdmans Publishing Co.
2006 44th Street SE, Grand Rapids, MI 49508
www.eerdmans.com

Published 2025
Printed in the United States of America

30 30 29 28 27 26 25 1 2 3 4 5 6 7

ISBN 978-0-8028-8385-8

Library of Congress Cataloging-in-Publication Data

A catalog record for this book is available from the Library of Congress.

For James, Thomas, William, and Charlie:

May your lives be founded on the Rock

"Everyone then who hears these words of mine and does them will be like a wise man who built his house on the rock. And the rain fell, and the floods came, and the winds blew and beat on that house, but it did not fall, because it had been founded on the rock."

—Matthew 7:24–25

Contents

Foreword

Saint Augustine's *City of God* famously contrasts the heavenly and earthly cities. Two opposing desires determine their respective identities: "We see then that the two cities were created by two kinds of love: the earthly city was created by self-love reaching the point of contempt for God, the Heavenly City by the love of God carried as far as contempt of self" (14.28). Our desires tell us where we belong, the heavenly or the earthly city.

Western civilization increasingly unmoors itself from the heavenly city by orienting its desires on this-worldly things. This direction of our desires—or, as the fathers would have called them, our passions—ultimately stems from self-love (*autophilia*). It is a cultural reorientation of desire that doesn't just happen; it is supported by a massive catechetical endeavor. Social media, especially (though not exclusively), shape the hearts and minds of the next generation for compliant membership in the earthly city.

The effectiveness of the earthly city's catechesis is evident both in missiological catechesis (tempting those who belong to the heavenly city) and in liturgical catechesis (reinforcing secular habits through numerous customs and rites). This two-pronged approach means that the earthly city catechizes not primarily by conveying information but by misdirecting the desires of our hearts.

Alex Fogleman's *Making Disciples* serves as a most welcome countercatechesis. Recognizing the power of our culture to catechize, he rightly insists: "Even more important than learning new ideas, though, Christians need an education of the heart—a formation of desire. We need not only to *know* God but to *love* God, too." He explains that for the early church, catechesis was a "pedagogy of enchantment" and an "education of desire."

Saint Augustine was, first and foremost, a teacher who tried to direct and shape the desires of people for the City of God. Augustine speaks of catechumens who arrive at the final stages of their catechetical training as *competentes* or coseekers. Fogleman quotes the bishop of Hippo addressing his catechumens as follows:

> Your very name—*competentes*—signifies that you are longing for the kingdom and aiming at it with all the energy of your minds. What else, after all, are *competentes* but people asking together? . . . And what is this one thing that you are asking and longing for? . . . "One thing have I asked from the Lord, this will I seek; to dwell in the house of the Lord all the days of my life . . . to contemplate the delight of the Lord, and to be protected by his temple" (Ps. 27:3–4).

A good catechist recognizes in his catechumens people who, together with (*com*) him, ask, seek, and long for (*petentes*) the face of God.

Fogleman, solidly rooted within patristic theology, never makes the mistake of pitting desire over against knowledge, or heart over against head. Since the passions bypass the mind, the earthly city denigrates the intellect as it attempts to shape our animal instincts. Augustine and other church fathers never accepted such denigration of the mind, and Fogleman rightly calls, therefore, for an approach that integrates faith (doctrine), hope (spirituality), and love (morals). The church fathers treated creation as a school and recognized that memory, as a function of the mind, is basic to our knowledge of God. At the end of the day, the intellect (knowledge) and the will (love) are one and the same, for they find their point of unity within the simplicity of God.

I have just now highlighted the careful nuance and balance of Fogleman's approach to knowledge and love. But this is just one example of the numerous exceptional qualities of this book. Fogleman offers a compact yet thorough treatment of the history of catechesis. He explains how basic Christian teachings (about the Trinity, eschatology, creation, salvation, conversion, and the church) affect our approach to catechesis. And he offers perceptive practical insights in how, today, we might embark on what he calls the "craft of catechesis." Its nuance, wide-ranging character, and ecumenical sensitivity make this book a must-read in seminary education, and it will be equally useful for pastors and lay teachers as well.

Most importantly, perhaps, Fogleman recognizes the high calling of catechesis. It refocuses our attention upon our heavenly end. After all, the City of God is a *heavenly* city, and its catechesis trains people in preparation for eternal heavenly citizenship. Catechesis in continuity with the tradition—and with patristic thought in particular—prepares students and teachers alike for the vision of God.

Alex Fogleman's *Making Disciples* does what it advocates: it imitates God's own pedagogy. In the incarnation, God comes down to us catechumens in the lowly depths of the earth for the sake of raising us up to heavenly heights. That, argues Fogleman, should be the structure of all Christian catechesis: "In Christ, the fullness of divine love comes down and the Spirit draws us into the divine presence through adoption in the Son. In catechesis, the fullness of God's teaching comes down and dwells in simple words and phrases, in food that can be chewed and swallowed, so that catechumens can be fed with God's very own life." *Making Disciples* does exactly this: offering catechetical food that can be chewed and swallowed, it renews our strength for the upward journey in Christ.

Hans Boersma
Saint Benedict Servants of Christ Professor in Ascetical Theology
at Nashotah House Theological Seminary

Abbreviations

ACW	Ancient Christian Writers
ANF	*Ante-Nicene Fathers*
FC	Fathers of the Church
LCL	Loeb Classical Library
NPNF[1]	*Nicene and Post-Nicene Fathers,* Series 1
NPNF[2]	*Nicene and Post-Nicene Fathers,* Series 2
PG	Patrologia Graeca
PL	Patrologia Latina
WSA	Works of Saint Augustine for the 21st Century

Introduction

Founded on the Rock

Many of us sense something deeply amiss in the church today. We feel adrift, cast about. We look for solid footing, but the ground keeps shifting under our feet. We have different ideas about why this is so, different stories about how we got here. And it's important to tell those stories. We need to diagnose the malaise that makes us feel, as Walker Percy put it, "lost in the cosmos." We need to tear down the idols that dehumanize and destabilize. But if there's a time to tear down, as the book of Ecclesiastes says, there's also a time to build (Eccles. 3:3).

Catechesis is about building. It's about building deep foundations in our lives, families, churches, and communities. The chief cornerstone of this building is the rock of Christ—there's no other foundation than this (Eph. 2:20; 1 Cor. 3:11; 1 Pet. 2:6). But what does it mean for our lives to be founded on Christ? What does it mean to become living stones built up as a spiritual house for holy worship (1 Pet. 2:5)? To lay deep foundations so that when the floods rise and the rains pour, the house remains steady because it was "founded on the rock" (Matt. 7:25; cf. Luke 6:48)?[1] That's the question this book asks. That's what catechesis is about.

The fourth-century bishop Cyril of Jerusalem put it like this: "Imagine catechesis as a building. Unless we bind and joint the whole structure together, piece by piece, we will have dry rot and leaks, and all our prior work will be wasted. Stone must be laid upon stone in proper sequence, the corners aligned, and the rough edges smoothed over: only then will the complete structure arise."[2]

1. Unless otherwise indicated, biblical quotations come from the English Standard Version.

2. Cyril of Jerusalem, *Procatechesis* 11, in *Lectures on the Christian Sacraments*, trans.

Catechesis is the craft of laying foundations for mature discipleship on the chief cornerstone of Christ. It's about becoming rooted and grounded in love (Eph. 2:17), about becoming apprentices who take up their crosses and follow Jesus. It anticipates a time when we'll no longer teach one another because the new law will be written on our hearts, because we'll all together drink from the fount of divine wisdom (Jer. 31:33).

So what is catechesis? My working definition is this: *catechesis is basic but comprehensive instruction in what Christians believe, hope, and love.*

First, catechesis is *basic*. It is about teaching the fundamentals of the faith. It's simple but not simplistic, intelligent but not intellectualist, practical but not pragmatic. It focuses less on current fashions and hot topics and more on the basic building blocks of thinking, praying, and living as a Christian. It is distinct from evangelism in that it goes beyond the proclamation of the gospel. But it's also distinct from preaching in that it does not presume a basic foundation in Christian doctrine and practice. Catechesis gives us a grammar for living the Christian life, a sturdy framework for lifelong discipleship. And because it's basic, it's also countercultural. This doesn't mean that catechesis is hostile or reactionary. But because it deals with fundamental narratives and beliefs, it strikes at the heart of our culture's unspoken beliefs about the good, the true, and the beautiful. It rubs against the grain of the world's core narratives and identity. In catechesis, we dig beneath the surface to clear out the rot that's crumbling our foundations.

Second, catechesis is *comprehensive*. It's not just about doctrine; nor is it just about prayer or just about ethics or just about the Bible. Catechesis is a way of seeing the whole in one glimpse. It's like viewing a large-scale painting in an art gallery—one of those enormous wall-sized images you can't take in all at once. Catechesis sees the whole before the parts. It gives an all-encompassing view of Christ through the refracted vision of faith, hope, and love.

Faith, hope, and love here are shorthand for three essential and interconnected aspects of the Christian life. Faith refers to doctrine or belief—the intellectual aspect of Christianity, the life of the mind. Hope is shorthand for the affective, *desiring* aspect; it's about prayer and spirituality, or how we relate to God. Finally, love invokes the ethical or moral life; it's about what we do and how we live in the world.

Typically, these aspects are expressed through three texts that form the main building blocks of many catechisms: the Apostles' Creed, the Lord's

---

Maxwell Johnson (Crestwood, NY: St. Vladimir's Seminary Press, 2017), 74–75 (translation mine). I discuss this passage in chapter 9 below.

Prayer, and the Ten Commandments. The creed summarizes what Christians believe to be true about reality; the Lord's Prayer encapsulates Christian spirituality and our hope for eternal fellowship with God; and the Ten Commandments offer a template for learning to live the Christian moral life.

We can picture the relationship as a threefold Venn diagram with catechesis at the center.

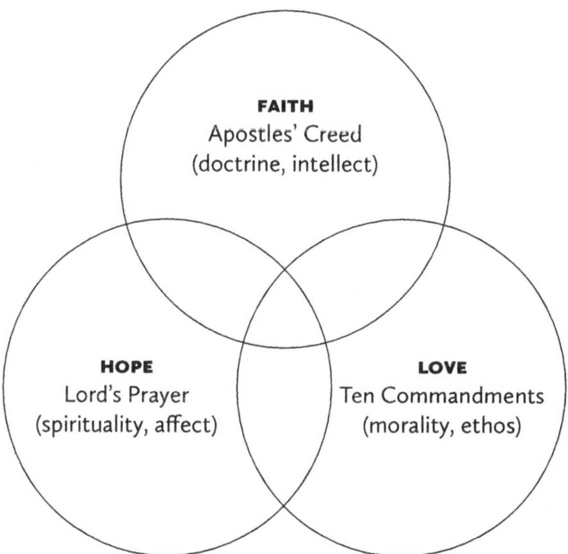

Together, these three components make up catechesis. And just like with good Trinitarian theology, these three are one: faith, hope, and love are distinct but indivisible. If we leave any one out, we get a distorted and truncated faith:

- Faith without doctrine is mushy and insubstantial. It's fast food for starving souls, and it leads to heresy and schism.
- Faith without prayer is dogmatism or moralism. It's theology PhDs or do-gooders who don't know how to talk with Jesus.
- Finally, faith without ethics—without love—is a clanging bell (1 Cor. 13:1). We may know the right answers; we may pray piously. But we walk right past Jesus on the street, begging for a cup of a water.

So we want to hold these three together, but we also want to be clear that *catechesis* is not the same thing as teaching a *catechism*. A catechism is a text—a tool for teaching. Catechesis is a practice, an art, a way of life. It's the craft of discipleship. Catechesis draws together faith, hope, and love to provide a foundation for loving God with all our heart, soul, mind, and strength. It involves the whole body of Christ and aims at nothing less than our final transformation in beholding the crucified and risen Lord. "We are God's children now," as 1 John puts it, "and what we will be has not yet appeared; but we know that when he appears we shall be like him, because we shall see him as he is" (1 John 3:2)

Why This Book?

For many reasons, catechesis has gone out of fashion, especially in evangelical circles. That may be something Roman Catholics or Lutherans do. Presbyterians may still cite the *Westminster Catechism*. But for most Christians, catechesis is a foreign or forgotten concept. *Cata-what?*

We have other things instead: evangelism, mission, small groups, Bible studies, Sunday school, Alpha. Not bad things, of course, but not catechesis. None do the foundational, ground-laying work that catechesis does. None give a basic but comprehensive introduction to the faith.

Catechesis is an urgent task for every age, but each age has its unique challenges. In the Reformation, for example, Catholics and Protestants disagreed vehemently about the nature of justification, but they did so because they shared much in common about basic issues like the doctrine of creation and the Trinity. Catechesis accordingly involved teaching the faithful *against* other Christian traditions with an emphasis on the doctrines that divided them. In North America today, the situation is different. Christians are grounded in the gospel of the American Dream rather than the gospel of the risen Christ. They live by the creed of expressive individualism rather than the creed of Nicene faith. Alan Jacobs has emphasized the many and various ways that "culture catechizes."[3] We're inundated with algorithmically calculated messages that shape our beliefs and desires in powerful ways. And churches that lack a robust countercatechesis are unable to provide any real alternative. We're left skimming the surfaces, formed by a secular vision of reality in a largely uncontested way.

We need a comprehensive model of Christian formation that addresses the challenges, and we need to re-form Christians who may have never been taught the basics of the faith. Even more important than learning new ideas, though, Christians need an education of the heart—a formation of desire. We

3. See, for example, Alan Jacobs, "Dare to Make a Daniel," *Homebound Symphony*, September 19, 2018, https://tinyurl.com/5bv2a6un.

need not only to *know* God but to *love* God, too, and to love our neighbors as ourselves. We need a kind of education that can strengthen our understanding of the faith *and* enable us to have a living encounter with the crucified and risen Lord. We need a retrieval of Christian catechesis.

In the early church, catechesis mostly referred to the instruction of new Christians before baptism. In some cases, it could last two to three years, and it was remarkably effective in helping converts make the difficult transition from a pagan way of life to a Christian one. Catechesis involved a process of conversion along with teaching the content of the faith. It was a dramatic theological, spiritual, and social transformation that entailed detachment from the dominion of darkness and the embrace of a radically new existence in the world.

As I will develop the concept in this book, catechesis can refer to teaching the faith at any stage of life in a way that builds the foundations of faith, hope, and love. Catechesis isn't just for children or those brand-new to the faith. Catechesis is for *all* Christians, for *all* of life. Pastors can no longer assume, if they ever could, that showing up on Sundays is any sound indication of biblical or theological literacy. We need to reimagine theological and spiritual formation for the whole body of Christ.

You might be thinking: This sounds too hard. It sounds too demanding; the bar is too high. Well, yes and no. On the one hand, yes: catechesis is hard. It is demanding. But only in the ways that following Jesus is *always* hard. Discipleship is costly because Jesus bids us nothing less than to come and die, as Bonhoeffer famously put it. (Though the cost of *nondiscipleship*, as Dallas Willard added, is even costlier.) And this is all the more difficult in a culture that is hard at work to distract us from the abundant life Jesus offers. It *is* hard to slow down and introduce hurried and harried people to the true rest that Jesus makes available. It *is* hard to make space in our hectic lives to patiently work through people's deep pains and questions without giving pat answers.

But on the other hand, the burdens of catechesis are easy and its yoke is light. Catechesis doesn't require adding *one more thing* to an already overloaded schedule and burned-out staff. It doesn't require expensive operational budgets or elaborate technical expertise. It simply requires attending to what's happening in front of us: What is the Spirit doing here? How is Christ already catechizing us? Beginning catechesis is as simple as gathering a few fellow travelers on the Way and seeking God together through thinking, praying, and trying to follow Jesus wherever he leads. And it turns out: many people actually *want* this. I hear over and over, "I've been a Christian my whole life, and no one's ever walked me through this before!" Furthermore, if they don't find a comprehensive vision for life in Christ, they'll look for it elsewhere. People are searching for a life of deep meaning and purpose, and we sell the gospel short when we offer a mere religious hobby.

It's not that catechesis is too hard. It's that we've forgotten how essential it is for the health and vitality of the church and the lives of its members. I'm convinced that retrieving catechesis is one of the most urgent tasks for our time, with the power to build up the church in powerful, Spirit-filled ways. As one of my catechetical heroes, J. I. Packer, once put it, "where wise catechesis has flourished, the church has flourished."[4] I'm willing to bet he was right.

How to Use This Book

If catechesis is about laying foundations, this book is a first point of entry for those seeking an apprenticeship in the craft of disciple making. My hope is to inspire you with a fresh vision for catechesis in your church and to equip you with the tools you need to begin.

We often think of education in terms of monologue or dialogue, talking *to* students or talking *with* them. Or we view education as engineering—"learning by design." If we just establish the right conditions, we'll get ready-made results. But there's another approach that I think better captures what we're after. One of my favorite theologians, Gregory of Nyssa, says that learning faith happens in the "workshop of virtue."[5] This is education as apprenticeship. Think of the way medical students learn the art of medicine. They read books about the human body and carefully study biology and other scientific disciplines. But they also follow the doctor around, visiting patients, taking notes, and generally doing what they see the doctor doing. The way is learned by walking. It is its own kind of discipleship.

The same thing happens in other fields: learning to repair cars, for example, or learning to be an artist. Education as apprenticeship occurs through an ongoing cycle of study, reflection, and praxis. The philosopher Michael Polanyi called this "tacit knowledge"—silent rather than spoken, implicit rather than

4. J. I. Packer and Gary Parrett, *Grounded in the Gospel: Building Believers the Old-Fashioned Way* (Grand Rapids: Baker Academic, 2010), 184.

5. Gregory of Nyssa, *On Virginity* 32. I owe this metaphor more generally to Lee Nelson, himself a master catechist and craftsman. And I learned about it in Gregory of Nyssa from Morwenna Ludlow, "Making and Being Made: Some Preliminary Thoughts on Craft-Education as a Model for Christian Formation," *Studies in Christian Ethics* 33, no. 1 (2019): 3–14. Finally, this metaphor is also ably deployed in Kevin Vanhoozer and Owen Strachen, *The Pastor as Public Theologian: Reclaiming a Lost Vision* (Grand Rapids: Baker Academic, 2015), chap. 4: "Artisans in the House of God."

explicit.[6] It allows the student to experience reality differently. The doctor can sense things in a patient's body that I cannot, though we have the same physical phenomena before us. The car mechanic hears a humming in the motor that I can't hear. The artist sees lines and colors that are lost on me.

If catechesis is an apprenticeship in the craft of discipleship, who are the master craftsmen who can guide us? In this book, we'll be learning from many of the past masters of church history, but especially from those grand masters of the early church. I have in mind especially those Christian teachers and pastors who lived in the first five centuries of the church's life, when catechesis was first developed and received a vibrant force of energy. When Christians in later periods sought a renewal of catechesis, they often looked to church fathers like Irenaeus, Tertullian, Cyril of Jerusalem, Ambrose, Gregory of Nyssa, John Chrysostom, Ephrem the Syrian, Augustine, and others for support, and I will do the same. The church fathers built a powerful practice of catechesis that was remarkably effective in helping those new to the faith become rooted and grounded in Christ. I hope to introduce you to these writers in a way that helps you not only learn more about them but also pick up on their intuitions and sensibilities for instructing believers in the foundations of faith.

The readers I have in mind are students training for ministry, clergy seeking to form the hearts and minds of believers new and old, and lay leaders with a call to serve the church through teaching. I hope I've left a few good rabbit trails in the footnotes for interested readers, but I've mostly kept the main text clear of scholarly minutiae. I am also writing for those involved in the growing classical education movement who would like to see more interaction between our churches and schools. We are seeing wide-scale transformations in education today, especially theological education, which are making it imperative for the church to reclaim its teaching office. Churches cannot simply cede this task to other teaching institutions, settling instead for merely hosting vibrant "worship experiences." The recovery of catechesis is one way that we can confront what Mark Noll termed the "scandal of the evangelical mind."[7]

While I write from an Anglican background, I have a broader ecclesial audience in mind: one that is small-*e* evangelical and small-*c* catholic; one that

6. Michael Polanyi, *The Tacit Dimension* (Chicago: University of Chicago Press, 1966). For a more recent account of this approach to knowledge, see Matthew Crawford, *The World beyond Your Head: On Becoming an Individual in an Age of Distraction* (New York: Farrar, Straus & Giroux, 2015).

7. Mark A. Noll, *The Scandal of the Evangelical Mind* (Grand Rapids: Eerdmans, 1994). The scandal being that . . . there is no evangelical "mind."

is, in Robert Webber's phrase, "ancient-future." This will become clear in the weight I place on early Christians who wrote before the major divisions that separate Catholics, Orthodox, and Protestants today. Regardless of how we view these writers as ecclesiastically authoritative, I take it as a given that they offer a rich treasure trove that belongs to the whole church, and which we neglect only to our peril.

Wherever you find yourself, my hope is that you come away with a renewed trust in the God who catechizes each of us. While we have much good work to do, it is Jesus Christ who is both the one foundation and the master builder. It is he who works in us to will and to work for his good pleasure (Phil. 2:13), making known to us his heavenly Father through the illumination of the Holy Spirit. It is by his grace that even now catechesis shares in that final end where we know God directly, beholding his glory face-to-face. My prayer for you in the end is that you may have strength "to comprehend with all the saints what is the breadth and length and height and depth, and to know the love of Christ that surpasses knowledge, that you may be filled with all the fullness of God" (Eph. 3:18–19).

Now, let's get building.

A Brief Catechetical Glossary

The language of catechesis may be unfamiliar to some, but it's both biblical and traditional, and well worth recovering. It carries an important set of assumptions that mark it out as a distinct form of Christian instruction. Of course, the practice of catechesis is more important than the language. Regardless, it may be helpful to lay out how various forms of the catechetical word family are used.

"Catechesis" comes from the Greek term *katēcheō*, which means to teach or instruct. Etymologically, it's related to words that have to do with sound or hearing, which we can recognize in English words like "echo" and "acoustic." It literally means something like to "re-sound" or "sound from above." The following are several variations on this word.

- *Catechesis* – The art of instructing new believers in the faith, with a view toward comprehensive instruction in the basic tenets of belief, spirituality, and ethics.
- *Catechize* – The verbal form of the word meaning to teach or instruct with reference to the basic but comprehensive foundation laying of catechesis.
- *Catechetical* – The adjectival form of the word: we may refer to catechetical teaching or catechetical texts.
- *Catechumenate* – The process or period of time devoted to the instruction of catechumens. In the early church, this period could last from one to three years, or even several decades. By the fourth century, the catechumenate concluded with an intense time of training during the season of Lent, just before Easter when baptisms took place. Following this was a brief period called "mystagogy," meaning "leading into the mysteries," when instruction focused on the sacraments and other rites of the church that were reserved only for the baptized.
- *Catechist* – One who teaches the basic doctrines of the faith in catechesis. This may be an ordained minister or a layperson. It may be an official designation in a church or an informal one. Some churches have a process of licensing lay catechists, both to equip the catechist and to ensure that the catechist's teaching is in alignment with the church's official doctrines and practices.
- *Catechumen* – One who is instructed, a hearer. In the early church, a catechumen was affiliated with the church but not yet a baptized member. In some traditions, the term may refer to someone who has been baptized but is undergoing formal instruction for official mem-

bership. It can also be used informally to refer to those receiving catechetical instruction in the faith.

- *Catechetics* – The study of catechesis. The book you're reading is, properly speaking, a work of catechetics. It is writing or instruction on the topic of catechesis.
- *Catechism* – A text used in catechesis. Catechisms proliferated in the Reformation and in the following centuries, ranging from short texts easily memorized by children to multivolume university lectures. Today, Luther's *Small Catechism* and *Large Catechism* are beloved by many Lutherans, as are the *Westminster Shorter Catechism* and *Heidelberg Catechism* by certain Presbyterian and Reformed Christians. In 1993, the Roman Catholic Church published *The Catechism of the Catholic Church*, the first universally standard catechism since the sixteenth century. There are not any comparably universal Eastern Orthodox catechisms, though several regional ones have appeared over the centuries, such as the Catechism of Platon II of Moscow (1765) or the Catechism of St. Philaret of Moscow (1823). Many Orthodox see the catechism format as a Western scholastic genre that is out of step with Eastern sensibilities.
- *Confession of Faith* – A short text or creedal statement that lays out the essential beliefs of a church tradition. In some contexts, a catechism is roughly equivalent to a confession of faith, but there are important differences. Confessions and creeds state a church's essential doctrines and beliefs, and they are intended to outline what is required to belong to a particular church. A catechism, by contrast, is meant for more educational purposes. Obviously there is overlap, but a catechism is more like a curriculum than a creed.

1

The Beginning and End of Catechesis

Around the year AD 400, a weary priest named Deogratias, who lived in the city of Carthage, wrote to one of the leading bishops of his day with a problem: his catechesis was utterly boring. Having to go over the same basic doctrines and rehearse the same basic stories year after year eventually wore on him. He was boring himself, and he was sure it was rubbing off on his catechumens.

In response, that leading bishop, who would become one of the most illustrious of the early church fathers, Augustine of Hippo, wrote a profound meditation called *On Catechizing the Uninstructed*. Augustine understood the challenges his correspondent faced. Anyone who's read the *Confessions* or the *City of God* knows that Augustine was a brilliant thinker and writer. Like a professional marathon runner training with a novice, it was no doubt difficult for Augustine to slow down and keep pace with newer Christians. As Augustine put it in his response to Deogratias, those whose thoughts soar to the heights of heaven can have a hard time coming down and "delaying over each slow syllable in the plains far below."[1]

Augustine gave Deogratias several practical suggestions. He taught him how to tell the biblical story, to ask good questions, and to gauge people's motives for wanting to become Christian. He gave advice for what to do when people seemed tired or distracted. But with such practical suggestions, Augustine also offered a pointed reflection on the God who catechizes us. To address practical issues, Augustine turned to theology.

Augustine especially pointed to the incarnation. However far we may think we come down to speak to newcomers, Christ comes down to an infinitely

1. Augustine, *On Catechizing the Uninstructed* 10.15, in *Augustine of Hippo: Instructing Beginners in Faith*, trans. Raymond Canning (Hyde Park, NY: New City, 2006), 91.

greater degree. Whatever distance lies between our high-minded thoughts and the catechumen's simple questions, the distance between Christ as the *form of God* and Christ as the *form of the servant* (Phil. 2:6–8) is infinitely greater. Saint Paul himself modeled this approach: though he seems "out of his mind" (*exestēmen*) to some, he speaks in his "right mind" (*sōphronoumen*) to those of simple understanding (2 Cor. 5:13).

Augustine compares this incarnational catechesis to the way a mother bird chews up food to nourish her young. The food doesn't change in substance but is adapted to a form the baby bird can receive. Augustine concludes by telling Deogratias that if he delights in thinking and reading, he can delight all the more in the downward ways of love: For "the more love goes down in a spirit of service into the ranks of the lowliest people, the more surely it rediscovers the quiet that is within when its good conscience testifies that it seeks nothing of those to whom it goes down but their eternal salvation."[2]

For Augustine, the movement of Christ's incarnate love is the foundation of Christian catechesis. The downward movement of humility and vulnerability, of nurture and feeding, is essential to Augustine's theology of catechesis.

The most important thing about catechesis is to know the triune God who catechizes us. To know God as a loving Father who teaches his children, to know Christ as the divine Wisdom and Truth of God, and to know the Spirit as the one who "sanctifies us in truth" (see John 17:17) is the basis for our whole understanding of catechesis. Irenaeus of Lyons puts this dynamic well in a remarkable description of baptism in the triune name:

> The baptism of our regeneration takes place through these three articles, granting us regeneration unto God the Father through His Son by the Holy Spirit: for those who bear the Spirit of God are led to the Word, that is to the Son, while the Son presents [them] to the Father, and the Father furnishes incorruptibility. Thus, without the Spirit it is not [possible] to see the Word of God, and without the Son one is not able to approach the Father; for the knowledge of the Father [is] the Son, and knowledge of the Son of God is through the Holy Spirit, while the Spirit, according to the good-pleasure of the Father, the Son administers, to whom the Father wills and as He wills.[3]

2. Augustine, *On Catechizing the Uninstructed* 10.15 (Canning, 93).

3. Irenaeus of Lyons, *On the Apostolic Preaching* 7, trans. John Behr (Crestwood, NY: St. Vladimir's Seminary Press, 1997), 44.

This passage illustrates the importance of Trinitarian theology for our understanding not only of baptism but also of catechesis. It is not just that catechesis imitates Jesus's style of teaching. Catechesis retraces the incarnation of the eternal God who reaches down to the depths of human being and raises us up to divine heights. Pope John Paul II once wrote: "throughout sacred history, especially in the Gospel, God Himself used a pedagogy that must continue to be a model for the pedagogy of faith."[4] Catechesis imitates the divine pedagogy of the God who guides his beloved children to the full maturity of human nature realized in Christ.

Catechesis is not a merely human project with this-worldly goals. We don't invent catechesis for our purposes. The goal isn't simply to make the world a better place or help our children be productive members of American society. Catechesis is about grounding believers in the knowledge and love of God, revealed in the Scriptures through Christ's body, the church, and it aims for nothing less than eternal fellowship in the vision of God. The triune God is the beginning and end of catechesis.

The Pedagogy of God

Scripture uses many images to describe God. He is King, Lord, Creator—yes. But God is also a teacher. More specifically, God is a *fatherly* teacher. God teaches from a place of abundant love for his children. Of course, God is by nature beyond gender. The divine nature is not male or female. Yet God is revealed in Scripture using the language of fatherhood to indicate something about his character. By attending to the revealed language of fatherhood, I follow the church fathers in seeing this language as an analogical image that reveals God as the Father of Jesus Christ, the Son of God by nature, in whom the Holy Spirit unites us to Christ as adopted sons and daughters by grace, who call upon God as "our Father."

We first meet God in the Scriptures as a fatherly teacher. God gives Adam and Eve guidance for human flourishing and warns them about the way that leads to death. The Psalms and Prophets go on to depict God as a teacher to his son Israel. In the book of Isaiah, God reveals himself this way:

4. This comes from his *Catechesi Tradendae*. For a recent set of essays based on this theme, see Caroline Farey, Waltraud Linnig, and Sr. M. Johannah Paruch, eds., *The Pedagogy of God: Its Centrality in Catechesis and Catechist Formation* (Steubenville, OH: Emmaus, 2011).

> "I am the LORD your God,
> who teaches you to profit,
> who leads you in the way you should go." (Isa. 48:17).

He is the one who "taught Ephraim to walk" (Hos. 11:3). The psalmist declares, "Blessed is the [one] whom you . . . teach out of your law" (Ps. 94:12, 10; see also Pss. 25:4–12; 71:7). God is a teaching father who leads his children—his beloved child—in the way of life.

Sometimes, though, the pedagogy is painful. The book of Hebrews, drawing on Proverbs 3, points to Israel's pedagogy in the wilderness as a paradigm for Christian hardship. After recounting the great "cloud of witnesses" in Hebrews 11, the author exhorts the audience to look to Christ, "the founder and perfecter of our faith," as the chief model of patient endurance (Heb. 12:1–2). Hebrews then points to Proverbs 3 as a reminder of the "discipline of the Lord":

> "My son, do not regard lightly the discipline (*paideia*) of the Lord,
> nor be weary when reproved by him.
> For the Lord disciplines the one he loves,
> and chastises every son whom he receives."
> (Heb. 12:5–6, quoting Prov. 3:11–12 LXX)

Hebrews especially highlights this word "discipline" (*paideia*), explaining that it is only reserved for God's own "child."[5] In other word: no *paideia*, no sonship. A lack of discipline would mean God did not really care for his beloved son. Though painful in the moment, such discipline yields "the peaceful fruit of righteousness to those who have been trained by it" (Heb. 12:11).

God's primary medium of teaching is through the law. The Hebrew word for law, *torah*, simply means teaching or instruction. It is a pedagogical term as much as a legal one. God gives *torah* to provide his beloved child with the true knowledge of who he is, how to worship him, and the right way to live a life of holiness and virtue. Old Testament wisdom literature provides a wealth of material for helping cultivate a love of such instruction. God's law is "perfect," "trustworthy," "radiant," and "pure"—more precious than gold and sweeter

5. See chapter 2 below on the concept of *paideia* in the ancient world. For a helpful study of the Hebrews passage along these lines, see Chad Spellman, "The Drama of Discipline: Toward an Intertextual Profile of *Paideia* in Hebrews 12," *Journal of the Evangelical Theological Society* 59, no. 3 (2016): 487–506.

than honey. The psalmist can speak of teaching, relationship, and reverence in the same breath:

> Teach me your way, O Lord,
>   and I will walk in your truth;
>   unite my heart to fear your name. (Ps. 86:11)

If the law is the medium of teaching, the temple and the home are where it happens. The temple was not only a place of worship for the Israelites but also a place of study and learning. The reading and exposition of the law was a chief focus for corporate gathering. In one of Isaiah's visions, we see a vision for the whole world learning the instruction of the Lord:

>   And many peoples will come and say,
> "Come, let us go up to the mountain of the Lord,
>   to the house of the God of Jacob;
> that he may teach us concerning his ways
>   and that we may walk in his paths."
> For out of Zion shall go the law,
>   and the word of the Lord from Jerusalem. (Isa. 2:3)

Throughout the Scriptures, God is revealed as a loving father who teaches his beloved son to walk in the way of the Lord, to follow the path that leads to life and light.

The Wisdom of the Word

The pedagogy of God goes deeper, however. The incarnation itself reflects God's instruction of his children. In the incarnation, God accommodates to our level of understanding, like a father speaking to an infant child in ways that child can understand. The Greek term for this accommodation is *synkatabasis*, which literally means "coming-down-with." In the fourth century, John Chrysostom defined it like this: "It is when God appears and makes himself known not as he is, but in the way one incapable of beholding him is able to look upon him. In this way God reveals himself proportionally to the weakness of vision of those who behold him."[6] God knows our capacities and limitations. He meets us in

6. John Chrysostom, *On the Incomprehensible Nature of God* 3.15 (FC 72:101). For a thorough exploration of this theme in Chrysostom, see David Rylaarsdam, *John*

ways that we can understand. The fourth-century theologian Athanasius of Alexandria put it this way: "As a good teacher who cares for his students always condescends (*synkatabainōn*) to teach by simpler means those who are not able to benefit from more advanced things, so also does the Word of God."[7]

And the reason God accommodates himself in the incarnation is so that we can become "accommodated" to God in return. We're not meant to remain babbling infants but are to grow up into the fullness of life with God. God is "accommodated to our capacity," John Calvin wrote, "so that we may understand it." And though our capacity in its finite nature cannot understand God in his true essence, "once we begin to conceive of God as he truly is, we will only want to accommodate ourselves to him."[8] This expresses in a different way what Athanasius famously wrote when he claimed, "God became man so that man might become God."[9] While God's nature is beyond every level of human comprehension, God has given us everything we need for life and godliness, including the divine promises through which we may become "partakers of the divine nature" (2 Pet. 1:4).

> He raises the poor from the dust
>   and lifts the needy from the ash heap,
> to make them sit with princes,
>   with the princes of his people. (Ps. 113:7–8)

God reaches down like a loving father, meets us where we are, and lifts us to his presence. This is the way of the divine pedagogy. This is the way God teaches his children as their true Father.

In his earthly ministry, Jesus was by all accounts an extraordinary teacher. His use of parables, examples, humor, and proverbs both attracted crowds and provoked enemies. He taught as one "who had authority" (Matt. 7:29), and his audience recognized that his teaching was not like that of other rabbis. They were right: This wasn't just another rabbi or prophet. This was God at work. This was divine pedagogy in action.

Chrysostom on Divine Pedagogy: The Coherence of His Theology and Preaching (Oxford: Oxford University Press, 2014).

7. Athanasius, *On the Incarnation* 15, trans. John Behr (Crestwood, NY: St. Vladimir's Seminary Press, 2011), 65.

8. John Calvin, *Sermons on the Ten Commandments*, trans. Benjamin W. Farley (Grand Rapids: Baker Books, 1980), 77 (translation altered).

9. Athanasius, *On the Incarnation* 54 (Behr, 107).

The Gospel of John makes the crucial point that Jesus is the Word, or Logos, of God. The word *logos* in Greek has a wide range of meanings: "word," "logic," "mind," "rationality," "structure," "principle," "reason." And the use of this term to identify Christ as the Son of God in John 1:1 is highly significant. It means God's ways in the world are ordered. Things are not made at random, without thought, but are based upon a logical plan—the Logos himself. Christ is God's wisdom: "the power of God and the wisdom of God" (1 Cor. 1:24). Wisdom, especially in the book of Proverbs, names God's creative and care-filled action in the world. Wisdom is a way of speaking of prudence, understanding, and discernment. Wisdom offers sound counsel and judgment. Wisdom encompasses not only logic and reason but also a wise way of life. Wisdom is about living well, not just living, and it guards against the foolishness that leads to death. Above all, wisdom leads to *beatitude,* or true happiness.

> Blessed is the one who listens to me [Wisdom]. . . .
> For whoever finds me finds life
>   and obtains favor from the LORD,
> but he who fails to find me injures himself;
>   all who hate me love death. (Prov. 8:34–36)

Wisdom is about truth, but truth in service to life, goodness, happiness, and blessing. Wisdom is God's way of being manifest in the world so that we can be caught up into God's very own life.

The Sanctification of the Spirit

But how do we know Christ as the Word and Wisdom of God? And what might it mean to know this not only as a true thing about the world but also as the very condition of our lives, the actual reality of our existence? Here, we can turn our attention to the Holy Spirit, the third person of the Trinity. In baptism, the Spirit unites us to Christ and enables us to share in the Son's own knowledge of the Father, his own relationship as Son. And as the Spirit continues the work of transformation in our lives, we grow into an ever-greater knowledge and love until "we all, with unveiled face, beholding the glory of the Lord, are . . . transformed into the same image from one degree of glory to another. For this comes from the Lord who is the Spirit" (2 Cor. 3:18).

The Holy Spirit is coequal with the Father and the Son, sharing fully in the life of the Trinity. The Spirit is God's creative, life-giving, and resurrecting power (Gen. 1:1; Pss. 33:6; 104:30; Rom. 8:11) and is especially identified with the work of sanctifying or holy making—hence the title Holy Spirit. Because the Spirit makes people holy, the Spirit is truly God, because only God can make people holy.

Part of the Spirit's work of "making holy" is giving true knowledge of the Lord to God's people, or what the prophet Isaiah calls the Spirit of the Lord:

> And the Spirit of the LORD shall rest upon him,
> the Spirit of wisdom and understanding,
> the Spirit of counsel and might,
> the Spirit of knowledge and the fear of the LORD. (Isa. 11:2)

In the Gospel of John, the Holy Spirit is identified as the "Spirit of truth" (John 14:17; 15:26; 16:13). Paul prays for the Ephesians, "May [Christ] give you a spirit of wisdom and of revelation in the knowledge of him, having the eyes of your hearts enlightened" (Eph. 1:17–18). The Spirit intercedes for us with sighs too deep for words when we do not know how to pray as we ought (Rom. 8:26). To the Corinthians, Paul writes that only the Spirit of God "comprehends the thoughts of God" and that Christians "have received not the spirit of the world, but the Spirit who is from God, that we might understand the things freely given us by God" (1 Cor. 2:11–12). The Spirit from *God* is one that truly is God: this is what gives believers true knowledge of the wisdom of God.

But what kind of knowledge is this? What is the character of this "in-spirited" knowledge? The Spirit's knowledge is given, first, to glorify Christ. In Jesus's farewell discourse in the Gospel of John, we read that "when the Spirit of truth comes, he will guide you into all the truth" (John 16:13). But what exactly does this mean? It means: "[The Spirit] will not speak on his own authority, but whatever he hears he will speak, and he will declare to you the things that are to come. He will glorify me, for he will take what is mine and declare it to you. All that the Father has is mine; therefore I said that he will take what is mine and declare it to you" (John 16:13–15).

The Spirit exhibits the kind of humility we see in the kenotic love of Jesus in the incarnation. The Spirit points not to himself but to Christ, and this is so that we can share all that the Father has given to the Son.

Second, the knowledge of the Spirit is the bond of love, both among one another and with Christ. The Spirit's knowledge is participatory; it is a mode of knowing rooted in the Christian's abiding in Christ through the church. Saint Augustine understood Romans 5:5 to say that God's own love, which Augustine identified with the Holy Spirit, is poured out in our hearts, and this is what enables us to love God and one another. God activates and energizes the believer's love by imparting the gift of the Holy Spirit to his people, which is why the Spirit is identified with "abiding" in Christ: "We know that we abide in him and he in us," 1 John says, "because he has given us of his Spirit" (1 John 4:13). The Spirit, then, makes the knowledge of Christ present and active in the believer. The Spirit is God's gift of himself; it is the knowledge of God's own life imparted to us. In the mutual bonds of love in Christ, the Spirit is the sanctifying knowledge of God.

Finally, the Spirit gives knowledge through the Christian's transformation in Christ. Why can't everyone recognize Christ as true God? Many Christians throughout the centuries would point to passages like Matthew 5:8: "Blessed are the pure in heart, for they shall see God." To see God is not just like seeing other kinds of things in the world. It requires a transformation of mind and body. We see God in and through purified hearts. We see God through sanctified vision, proceeding from glory to glory (2 Cor. 3:17–18). The transforming work of sanctification allows us with unveiled faces to know, love, and glorify God through the Holy Spirit.

Our transformation in the Spirit begins in baptism and grows over time. The fourth-century theologian Didymus the Blind wrote this: "The Holy Spirit as God renovates us in baptism, and in union with the Father and the Son brings us back from a state of deformity to our pristine beauty and so fills us with his grace that we can no longer make room for anything that is unworthy of our love; he frees us from sin and death and from the things of the earth; makes us spiritual men, sharers in the divine glory, sons and heirs of the Father. He conforms us to the image of the Son of God."[10] Catechesis, on this view, belongs to the spiritual transformation by which the Spirit sanctifies the hearts and minds of believers, enabling them to see God through their dynamic transformation in Christ.

Schooled for the Vision of God

The doctrine of the Trinity is as much about our reconciliation with God as it is about learning certain propositions about the divine nature. And so it already contains the seeds for a flourishing practice of catechesis rooted in the being of God.

10. Didymus the Blind, *On the Trinity* 2.12, cited in Thomas Finn, *Early Christian Baptism and the Catechumenate: Italy, North Africa, and Egypt* (Collegeville, MN: Liturgical Press, 1992), 217–18. This is a great collection of primary sources related to catechesis in the early church.

One of the outcomes of the heated debates about the Trinity in the fourth century was a much clearer perception that Christ and the Holy Spirit are "consubstantial" (of one substance) with the Father. They are not lower-level, semi-divine actors in a great chain of being but coequal in divinity, power, and glory. When we confess Christ as the Word and Wisdom of God and the Spirit as the Sanctifier in Truth, there is no diminishment of divinity. Christ is true God of true God, very God of very God. The Spirit is the Lord and Giver of Life.

The implications for catechesis are nontrivial. Christ, though equal to God, came down to the lowest rungs of the pedagogical ladder, meeting us where we are, just starting to climb. And yet, what we find in the humble Christ is not a kind of "dumbed-down" theology but one who is truly God. The Holy Spirit, in turn, reveals to us that this crucified criminal is none other than the eternal Word and transforms us into an ever-greater reflection of the divine image. God doesn't delegate the catechesis of new believers to substitutes who do the grunt work for him. God himself comes down to us.

If we think of Christ or the Holy Spirit as subordinate deities or lower-level messengers, our knowledge of God will never actually be true knowledge of God. There will always be a "real God" lurking in the background, and we won't be able to say with confidence that if we've seen Jesus, we've seen the Father (John 14:9). By confessing the Son and Spirit as fully divine with the Father, we come to see Christ's *humanity* as a true mediation of God, whom we know through the illumination of the Spirit. The Spirit enables us to recognize Jesus as indeed the fullness of Godhead dwelling bodily (Col. 2:9).

Our transformation by the Spirit into the likeness of Christ, the true image, happens now only in part. Its final goal awaits in the age to come. We understand things now, Saint Paul writes, in riddles and enigmas (1 Cor. 13:8). We know God through prayer in the Spirit as a kind of "learned ignorance," wherein the Spirit teaches us to pray with sighs too deep for words (Rom. 8:25–27). We groan in prayer with a desire for something beyond our comprehension, something beyond the limits of this world. In learning to pray in the power of the Spirit, we are stretched out to hope for something beyond what we can ask or imagine.

In the end, faith turns to sight. Our hope lies in the vision of God face-to-face, and so the telos of catechesis is eternal beatitude in the vision of God. In the meantime, we are schooled for this vision in worship. Saint Augustine described Christian worship as the highest form of wisdom. For human beings, he wrote, "wisdom (*sapientia*) is the same as worship (*pietas*)."[11] This is not just any

11. Augustine, *Enchiridion* 1.1 (WSA I/8:273).

pious activity, however. For Augustine, worship is rooted in the person and work of Christ and manifests in faith working through love (Gal. 5:6). It begins in faith and culminates in the vision of God that constitutes our highest happiness:

> When a mind is filled with the beginning of that faith that works through love, it progresses by a good life toward vision, in which holy and perfect hearts know that unspeakable beauty, the full vision of which is the highest happiness. This is without doubt what . . . we must hold first and last, beginning with faith and ending with vision. This is what the whole body of doctrine amounts to. The sure and proper foundation of the Catholic faith is Christ, as the apostle says, *For no one can lay any foundation other than the one that has been laid; that foundation is Jesus Christ* (1 Cor. 3:11).[12]

Learning to know God, in short, is inseparable from learning to love God. Both belong on the journey to our truest happiness in communion with God.

The God who is Father, Son, and Holy Spirit is the ground and logic of Christian catechesis. In Christ, the fullness of divine love comes down and the Spirit draws us into the divine presence through adoption in the Son. In catechesis, the fullness of God's teaching comes down and dwells in simple words and phrases, in food that can be chewed and swallowed, so that catechumens can be fed with God's very own life.

Without a robust grounding of catechesis in the Holy Trinity, we are left to the whims of our own ideas about what catechesis is and what it's for. We become transmitters of religious ideas rather than participants in the divine economy. Catechesis becomes instruction in the Bible or Christian theology rather than a part of the pedagogy of God. We will not always need to teach one another, but for now, God has arranged the world so that we depend on each other, so that we learn from one another the wonderful love of God. By beginning with the Trinity as the model and mode of our catechesis, we can see, if only a little less dimly, how God is leading his children to the glorious home our hearts are longing for.

12. Augustine, *Enchiridion* 1.5 (WSA I/8:274–75; translation altered).

2

The Rise of Catechesis in the Early Church

If the divine origins of catechesis lie in the triune God, its beginnings in the created world lie in the Great Commission: "Go therefore and make disciples of all nations, baptizing them in the name of the Father and of the Son and of the Holy Spirit, teaching them to observe all that I have commanded you" (Matt. 28:19–20). Here in brief are the core features of catechesis: mission, initiation, and instruction. The disciples were to take this command as far as the known world, not just to Judea and Samaria but "to the end of the earth" (Acts 1:8). This meant that they would meet people who had never heard of Jesus, much less the story of Israel and its unique theological and moral perspectives. But more than simply telling others about Jesus, they were called to make other disciples who would likewise walk in the way of the Lord. Indeed, Jesus's earliest followers were simply called "people of the Way" (see Acts 9:2; 19:9, 23; 22:4; 24:14, 22).

Making disciples in the early church involved a converting education. It included initiation through baptism in the triune name, and it included a guided process of teaching and instruction to help newcomers follow the way of Jesus. This converting education aimed at more than simply adding on to a basically good foundation. It meant building a new one.

In this chapter, we focus on the history of catechesis in the early church.[1] Despite many variations and differences across time and geography, the early church developed a remarkably coherent practice of catechesis that brought

1. On the rise of catechesis in the early church, see Alex Fogleman, *Knowledge, Faith, and Early Christian Initiation* (Cambridge: Cambridge University Press, 2023); Gerald Sittser, *Resilient Faith: How the Early Christian "Third Way" Changed the World* (Grand Rapids: Brazos, 2019), esp. chap. 9; and Stephen O. Presley, *Cultural Sanctification: Engaging the World like the Early Church* (Grand Rapids: Eerdmans, 2024), esp. chap. 1.

together the three key elements outlined in the introduction: learning how to think (doctrine), how to pray (spirituality), and how to live (ethics). Catechesis initiated newcomers into a new social and indeed cosmic imaginary.[2] It created citizens of a new kingdom, a fellowship of disciples empowered by the Spirit to bring the gospel to the ends of the earth. As a converting education, catechesis drew newcomers into "a whole pattern of learning to think, feel, and live well as a holy people."[3]

Teaching and Learning in the Ancient World

Early Christianity was born in the cradle of two great cultural traditions, the Jewish and the Greco-Roman, both of which shared many common convictions about the nature of education. Both traditions agreed that education was about more than learning facts and content. Education was about a way of being human, a cultural inheritance, a tradition—often encapsulated by the Greek term *paideia*.[4] Education included important commitments to truth claims, but also how to regulate the emotions and live virtuously. Greeks and Jews agreed that thinking well was inseparable from right affections and actions.

For the Israelites, however, education was more than just passing on a cultural tradition. It was vital to their covenant with God. They passed on the law to the next generation to remain faithful to the God who had rescued them from Egypt, and this included doctrines, rituals, prayers, and ethical teachings. Central to Jewish education was the teaching that there is only one God, which came with a host of related beliefs: that the one God had created the world good, that God had made humankind in his image, that Israel was elected to be a light to the world, and that the final end of human life was fellowship with God in a state of resurrection. These doctrinal teachings, in turn, entailed a way of life together. Israel was called to a distinctive social and ethical life

2. I borrow the term "social imaginary" from Charles Taylor's *Modern Social Imaginaries* (Durham, NC: Duke University Press, 2003). But the ancient context also has in view a much more expansive "imaginary," which would include angels, demons, and other spiritual forces that the New Testament refers to as principalities, powers, thrones, and dominions (Col. 1:16; Eph. 1:21).

3. L. Gregory Jones, "A Dramatic Journey into God's Dazzling Light: Baptismal Catechesis and the Shaping of Christian Practical Wisdom," in *Knowing the Triune God: The Work of the Spirit in the Practices of the Church*, ed. James J. Buckley and David S. Yeago (Grand Rapids: Eerdmans, 2001), 166.

4. See the classic treatment of this theme in Werner Jaeger, *Paideia: The Ideas of Greek Culture*, 3 vols. (Oxford: Oxford University Press, 1939–1944).

precisely because they were made in the image of God. They were called to be holy because the Lord their God was holy (Lev. 19:2). Many of these aspects of Jewish education were adopted in early Christian catechesis.

Early Christians were also heir to the great legacy of Greco-Roman culture, including the philosophical traditions of Plato, Aristotle, and the other major wisdom traditions of antiquity. By the first century AD, Greek and Roman philosophers had been asking and debating life's biggest questions for centuries: What is the good life, and how does one attain it? While the various schools approached these questions differently, they agreed that philosophy meant pursuing *eudaimonia*, which we might translate as "ultimate happiness" or "true flourishing." *Eudaimonia* was much more than simply feeling happy in the truncated modern sense of the term. For the ancients, *eudaimonia* meant living as humans are ultimately meant to live. It meant "living in accord with nature, in harmony with our deepest aspirations as human beings."[5] Such was the goal of ancient philosophy.

They also agreed that the path to *eudaimonia* was impossible apart from living virtuously. Virtue was understood as the form of the good life in the lives of individuals and communities. Students of philosophy in the ancient world learned virtue in many ways, from learning moral and metaphysical truths to undertaking spiritual disciplines like fasting and contemplation. But the primary way they learned virtue was by imitation, or *mimesis*. By imitating the lives of virtuous people, especially one's teacher, students of philosophy learned to become true "lovers of wisdom" (*philo* = love; *sophia* = wisdom).

Put another way, ancient philosophy was, as Pierre Hadot has famously termed it, "a way of life."[6] The goal was transformation through a series of applied spiritual exercises, including dialogue, study, attention, meditation, and memorization. Little by little, these exercises enabled, as Hadot puts it, "the indispensable metamorphosis of the inner self."[7] Philosophy sought to heal disordered passions that inhibited virtue and set students on the course to true wisdom and flourishing.

5. Robert Louis Wilken, *The Spirit of Early Christian Thought: Seeking the Face of God* (New Haven: Yale University Press, 2003), 273.

6. See Pierre Hadot, *Philosophy as a Way of Life: Spiritual Exercises from Socrates to Foucault* (Malden, MA: Blackwell, 1995).

7. Hadot, *Philosophy as a Way of Life*, 83.

Education in the New Testament

Early Christians absorbed many of these approaches to education, much of which is summed up in the term "tradition," from the Greek word *paradosis.* While that term can have a negative connotation in the New Testament (see Mark 7:1–13), it can also have a positive one, such as when Paul writes to the Thessalonians to "stand firm and hold to the traditions (*paradoseis*) that you were taught by us, either by our spoken word or by our letter" (2 Thess. 2:15), or when he tells the Corinthians, "Maintain the traditions even as I delivered them to you" (*kathōs paredōka hymin tas paradoseis katechete*) (1 Cor. 11:2). In these passages, *paradosis* refers to a dynamic process of actively *handing over* the faith and an equally active *reception* of it.

There are three aspects of *paradosis*:

1. an evangelical, kerygmatic element, or the proclamation of the gospel;
2. a ritual or liturgical element, especially with reference to baptism and the Eucharist; and
3. an ethical or moral element, or a set of teachings about how to live.[8]

First, the proclamation of the gospel was central to early Christian instruction. Luke records several instances of such kerygmatic sermons in the book of Acts. We also find in the New Testament several instances of creed-like formulas: brief, compact phrases that could be taught easily and learned and memorized. Most of these statements focus on the identity of Jesus—"Jesus is Lord," Jesus as the "Son of God," Jesus as the Messiah, and so on. Second, liturgical traditions are found in the passing on of Christian hymnody (such as Phil. 2:5–11), set times for prayer and worship, and guidance for the eucharistic meal (as, for example, in 1 Cor. 11). Third, there are several traditions of ethical or moral reflection. Paul writes to the Thessalonians: "Now we command you, brothers and sisters, in the name of our Lord Jesus Christ, that you keep away from any brother who is walking in idleness and not in accord with the tradition that you received from us" (2 Thess. 3:6). He also uses proverb-like aphorisms, like "if we have died with Christ, . . . we will also live with him"

8. For helpful introductions to the concept of tradition in the early church, see D. H. Williams, *Retrieving the Tradition and Renewing Evangelicalism: A Primer for Suspicious Protestants* (Grand Rapids: Eerdmans, 1999), and D. H. Williams, *Evangelicals and Tradition: The Formative Influence of the Early Church* (Grand Rapids: Baker Academic, 2005).

(Rom. 6:8), to teach his hearers how to live as Christians. Paul envisioned this kind of teaching as concerned with passing on how Christians lived as much as with what they prayed and thought about Jesus Christ.

Besides the emphasis on *paradosis,* New Testament writings provided a seedbed for catechetical formation in other ways as well. The Gospels themselves have a quasi-catechetical function in the way they provide foundational narratives for those already familiar with the message of Jesus (see Acts 1:1–4). Some have seen 1 Peter, with its call to holiness and baptism, as the equivalent of a New Testament guide for baptismal candidates.[9] Hebrews 6 may also provide a template for catechetical instruction. When the author tells his readers there is no need for him to repeat the "elementary doctrine of Christ" that he has already taught them, he lists six items—repentance, faith, washings, the laying on of hands, the resurrection of the dead, and eternal judgment—as the elementary foundation that Christians build upon as they "go on to maturity."[10]

While it is stretching the evidence to say that there was an established system of catechesis in the New Testament period, there was clearly a deliberate effort to pass on the living faith to new believers in dynamic ways. More importantly, early Christians based the emerging practice of catechesis on the forms of education that appeared in the writings of Scripture and the apostolic tradition. With the proclamation of the gospel came a corresponding need to appropriately prepare Christians for this extraordinary new way of life.

The Emergence of the Catechumenate

While we don't hear much about catechesis in the first two centuries, by the end of the second century, Christians were writing about catechesis as a specific practice aimed at preparing new believers for baptism. In his *First Apology,* perhaps written sometime around the year 150, the apologist Justin Martyr wrote that baptism was permitted to those who had "dedicated themselves to God when they were made new through Christ." He then gives a brief snapshot of the general features of instruction and initiation: "All those who are persuaded and believe that these things that we teach and say are true, and

9. See J. I. Packer and Gary E. Parrett, *Grounded in the Gospel: Building Believers the Old-Fashioned Way* (Grand Rapids: Baker Academic, 2010), chap. 2. Some biblical scholars might find some of these claims more doubtful from a historical-critical perspective.

10. For an example of this approach, see Curtis Freeman, *Pilgrim Letters: Instruction in the Basic Teaching of Christ* (Minneapolis: Fortress, 2021).

who give an undertaking that they are able so to live, are taught to pray and ask with fasting for forgiveness from God for their past sins, and we pray and fast for them."[11]

We don't know how long this process lasted, but some later writings suggest several years.[12] Bringing together classical *paideia* and New Testament *paradosis*, early Christian catechesis involved several notable features: a rigorous examination of life, especially with a view to how catechumens cared for the poor; a philosophical style of doctrinal and biblical instruction; and the exhortation to take on an ascetical lifestyle, usually in the context of a small fellowship of believers gathered around a teacher. In the early days, this was not a highly regulated or systematic process. But across different regions, with different styles and needs, a consistent process of conversion and education evolved into what scholars often now call the catechumenate.

A text called the *Apostolic Tradition*, attributed to a third-century figure named Hippolytus, is one of the earliest accounts of this process.[13] Those who are "newly brought forward to hear the word" gather at the home of a Christian teacher, along with their sponsors, and are asked why they want to join the church. What are they looking for? What do they expect? They are also asked about their family life and occupations. Do they have just one spouse? Do they have children? What do they do for a living? Some occupations, especially those bound up with pagan religion, were forbidden. Candidates had to give them up if they wanted to become catechumens. Other jobs like military service or schoolteaching could be maintained so long as the duties of the job did not require participation in immorality or idolatry. Those in the military were not permitted to kill or comply with orders to do so; schoolteachers could not teach the pagan histories and gods.

11. Justin Martyr, *First Apology* 61.1–2, in *Justin, Philosopher and Martyr*, ed. and trans. Denis Minns and Paul Parvis (Oxford: Oxford University Press, 2009), 236–39.

12. The main source for this theory is a text attributed to Hippolytus called the *Apostolic Tradition*, which I discuss below. As a so-called church order document, its contents were adapted and diffused around the Mediterranean world.

13. For this text, see Alistair Stewart, ed., *Hippolytus: On the Apostolic Tradition*, 2nd ed. (Crestwood, NY: St. Vladimir's Seminary Press, 2014). Scholars have heavily debated whether this text was written by Hippolytus of Rome in the third century, or whether it was another Hippolytus, or whether it was part of a "school" of Christian learning that developed over a long period of time. There are many surviving variations of the text, in many different languages. Nonetheless, the editor of this volume, Alistair Stewart, makes a good case for why the section describing the catechumenate may indeed represent third-century practice.

After this initial review, inquirers became catechumens and were brought under instruction for two to three years. They would meet regularly in the homes of a teacher, usually before the start of the workday. After this time of instruction, catechumens prayed together in groups separated by gender and baptismal status. Baptized men prayed in one area, baptized women in another; male catechumens gathered in one place, female catechumens in another. After this time of prayer, the instructor laid hands on the catechumens and prayed for them.

While the overall time frame for this process was generally two to three years, in certain cases where catechumens showed exceptional progress, that period could be shortened.[14] Catechumens who were martyred during this period could be assured they would still receive the same heavenly reward as those baptized. Their martyrdom gained the same eternal glory, for it was a "baptism in blood."[15]

After two to three years, those seeking baptism would undergo another round of examination. This time, the bishop asked their sponsors how the catechumens lived. Had they honored widows, taken care of the sick? Had they lived the faith in deeds as well as words? If so, catechumens could proceed to a final stage of preparation for baptism. If not, they were to be "put to shame," the text says, because they "have not heard the word in faith."[16] From this time on, catechumens underwent further exorcisms and anointings; they fasted and prayed in preparation for baptism and their first reception of the Eucharist. This was a time not only of learning but also of cleansing and preparation. At last, they were ready for full membership in Christ's body, the church.

While the *Apostolic Tradition* gives a nice account of the structure of the catechesis, it doesn't say much about what was taught. What, then, did early Christians teach during this multiyear process? It's not always clear from our sources, but it seems that most Christians were taught the basic biblical narrative, the key doctrines of the faith, often summarized in the "rule of faith" (*regula fidei*), and the moral life incumbent on the Christian faithful.[17]

The second-century theologian Irenaeus of Lyons states that Christians receive the rule of truth in baptism.[18] In another work, a short treatise called the *Demonstration of the Apostolic Preaching*, he explains in more detail what the

14. Hippolytus, *Apostolic Tradition* 17.2.

15. Hippolytus, *Apostolic Tradition* 19.2.

16. Hippolytus, *Apostolic Tradition* 20.3.

17. For a good summary of the rule of faith in early Christianity, see Everett Ferguson, *The Rule of Faith: A Guide* (Eugene, OR: Wipf & Stock, 2015).

18. Irenaeus, *Against Heresies* 1.9.4 (ACW 55:48).

rule of faith entails and how it aligns with the biblical story.[19] Addressed to a Christian named Marcianus, perhaps himself a catechist, the work is described by Irenaeus as a "summary memorandum" of the apostolic preaching.[20] This summary was meant to provide an entryway into the whole "body" of Christian faith and life. Just as a human being is made up of body and soul, Irenaeus says, so Christian catechesis provides guidance for both what to believe and how to live. Furthermore, he writes that the truth received in the rule of faith is based on what is "really real" in the world. By carefully studying and keeping the rule, Christians "may have a true comprehension of what is."[21]

The rule of faith, in other words, contains spiritual and metaphysical commitments, and in its teaching draws Christians into the true nature of being. It is a call to see creation as it really is—the artistry of a divine creator. After presenting this rationale for the rule of faith, Irenaeus goes on to tell the narrative of salvation history, with an eye toward how the gospel of Christ's birth, death, and resurrection is enfolded in the larger biblical story. He shows Marcianus what it looks like when you read Scripture with Christ at the center.

But again, catechesis included not only doctrinal or biblical instruction but also guidance in the moral life. Catechesis was a time for allowing new believers to become accustomed to Christianity's distinctive ethos. Origen writes to catechumens: "having heard the word of God, root out vice and set right your barbarous habits that, having taken on gentleness and humility, you can receive also the grace of the Holy Spirit."[22] The North African bishop Cyprian of Carthage compiled a three-volume collection of Scripture passages for the purpose of catechetical instruction. The first volume includes twenty-four sections gathering key Scriptures on the topic of salvation history. The second volume comprises thirty topics on Christology, broadly following the outline of the rule of faith. The third volume, meanwhile, contains no fewer than 120 topics on morality, such as church unity, generosity, patience, and faithfulness under difficult circumstances, which were especially relevant to Cyprian's context of martyrdom and church fracturing.

19. For a good study of this text from a catechetical perspective, see Everett Ferguson, "Irenaeus' *Proof of the Apostolic Preaching* and Early Catechetical Instruction," in *The Early Church at Work and Worship*, vol. 2, *Catechesis, Baptism, Eschatology, and Martyrdom* (Eugene, OR: Wipf & Stock, 2014), 1–17.

20. Irenaeus of Lyon, *Demonstration* 1, in *On the Apostolic Preaching*, trans. John Behr, Popular Patristics Series 17 (Crestwood, NY: St. Vladimir's Seminary Press, 1997), 39.

21. Irenaeus, *Demonstration* 3 (Behr, 41).

22. Origen, *Homilies on Leviticus* 6.3 (FC 83:118–19; translation slightly altered).

This twin emphasis on faith and practice, or doctrine and morals, comes together in the way early Christians thought of preparation for baptism as a kind of education for martyrdom. The martyrs were the supreme example of Christian faithfulness in the early church ("martyr," after all, simply means "witness" in Greek). And by exalting the martyrs, early Christians wanted ordinary Christians to identify with them and, through them, with Christ. When Christians read about the Scillitan martyrs confronting their executioners with the phrase "I am a Christian," they heard an echo of every Christian's identification with Christ in the watery death of baptism.[23] The martyrs were witnesses in word and deed. They willingly gave their lives for the claim that Christ was the Son of God, the one true God who created and ruled the world, and they were unwilling to participate in pagan worship and immorality. Given the close links between martyrdom and baptism as two kinds of "dying with Christ" (Rom. 6:1–11), Christians in the second century came to see catechesis as a preparation for sharing the death of Christ. Early Christian martyrdom and, by implication, the catechetical preparation for baptism were two ways of powerfully reflecting the image of God in Christ.

The catechumenate emerged at a critical moment in the church's life. Amid missional expansion, persecution, and engagements with various philosophical traditions, catechesis developed into a robust process of conversion and education. And yet, despite a relatively high bar for entry, the young church grew rapidly. Many scholars have explored the various reasons for this, one of the main reasons being the extraordinary claims of the gospel, that Jesus Christ is the Son of God, the Lord of creation in human flesh. But as a social minority, and often under threat of persecution, Christians did not have the means to proclaim this message widely or openly. Many non-Christians were attracted to the beautiful lives they saw Christians living. Christians cared for the poor and the sick, they provided homes for orphans, and they willingly embraced martyrdom for the sake of the gospel. As the third-century apologist Minucius Felix put it, "As for the daily increase in our numbers, that is no proof of error, but evidence of merit; for beauty of life (*pulchro genere vivendi*) encourages its followers to persevere, and strangers to join our ranks."[24] The beauty of life

23. For this text, see *Acta Martyrum Scillitanorum: A Literary Commentary*, ed. Vincent Hunink (Turnhout: Brepols, 2021), 29–37.

24. Minucius Felix, *Octavius* 31.7 (LCL 250:411–13). I owe this reference to my friend Michael Distefano, who has written on the role of beauty in early Christian apologetic writing in his "Embodied Theology in the Greek Apologetic Writings of the Second Century" (Master's thesis, Baylor University, 2023).

among early Christians, instilled during the catechumenate, played a critical role in drawing outsiders to the faith.

Catechesis in the Fourth Century

The fourth century was a critical period in the history of Christianity. Brilliant minds debated how best the church should understand the meaning of Christ's divine nature; Christianity became legalized and eventually the dominant religious expression of the Roman Empire; and missionaries took the gospel all over the known world.

Amid this turbulent period, catechesis carried on in a relatively stable manner.[25] It continued to provide a robust moral, biblical, and theological formation. It presented Christianity as a radical transition out of the kingdom of "the world, the flesh, and the devil" and into the kingdom of God. Doctrinal, ritual, and moral formation were all part of the process of entering the mystery of Christ—what one scholar calls "a dramatic journey into God's dazzling light."[26] There are, to be sure, many more sources about catechesis in the fourth century, and we will touch on many of them in the following chapters.[27] In this section, I want to give a brief overview of catechesis in what's been called the "golden age" of patristic catechesis.[28]

25. As I see it, the fourth century sees more of a logical development of pre-Constantinian catechesis than a failed departure. For the alternative view that catechesis underwent a dramatic alteration (for the worse) as a result of the Constantinian settlement, see Alan Kreider, *The Change of Conversion and the Origin of Christendom* (reprint, Eugene, OR: Wipf & Stock, 2006), and Everett Ferguson, "Catechesis and Initiation," in *The Early Church at Work and Worship*, 2:18–51.

26. Gregory Jones, "A Dramatic Journey into God's Dazzling Light: Baptismal Catechesis and the Shaping of Christian Practical Wisdom," in *Knowing the Triune God: The Work of the Spirit in the Practices of the Church*, ed. James J. Buckley and David S. Yeago (Grand Rapids: Eerdmans, 2001), 147–77.

27. Among many other sources, some of the most relevant are Cyril of Jerusalem's *Catechetical Lectures* and *Lectures on the Sacraments*, Gregory of Nyssa's *Catechetical Discourse*, Gregory of Nazianzus's *Orations* 38–40, John Chrysostom's *Baptismal Homilies*, Theodore of Mopsuestia's *Sermons on the Creed, the Lord's Prayer, and the Sacraments*, Ambrose's *On the Mysteries* and *On the Sacraments*, and Augustine's *On Catechizing the Uninstructed*, the *Enchiridion*, along with several sermons on the Lord's Prayer (sermons 53–56) and the baptismal creed (sermons 212–216 and 398).

28. Jean Daniélou, "Catechesis in the Patristic Tradition," trans. Alex Fogleman, *Communio: International Catholic Review* 47, no. 3 (2020): 617–33.

In the fourth century, a person could be a catechumen from an early age, even infancy, yet not baptized until many years later. For adults who joined, the catechist would make an initial inquiry about their life and why they wanted to become Christian. In North Africa, there was a designated ritual for initiating catechumens. After the initial instruction and inquiry, a priest would make the sign of the cross and rub salt on their foreheads, signaling that they were to be "the salt of the earth" (Matt. 5:13). Catechumens occupied a status between non-Christian and Christian. Augustine referred to them as servants of the kingdom who were not yet sons (a reference to Gal. 4:1–11).[29]

Catechumens could attend church services to hear the preaching of the Word, but they could not participate in the sacraments. Early Christians viewed the sacred mysteries of baptism and Eucharist as holy rituals that only the baptized could participate in. This practice is often referred to as the *disciplina arcani*, or the "discipline of secrecy." It began as a way to protect Christian communities from suspicious outsiders who might report their neighbors to the authorities. But it also reflected a sense of the holiness of the church's central mysteries. Knowledge of God was a divine gift and a participation in holy fellowship. Such participation required preparation—one could not cast pearls before swine (Matt. 7:6). The Eucharist and other rites, such as the Lord's Prayer or the kiss of peace, were reserved for the faithful alone. Even the Lord's Prayer was restricted to the baptized, for addressing God as "our Father" implied that one was a son or daughter of God through baptism. Catechumens thus left the service after the preaching of the Word while the baptized remained for the Eucharist.

When catechumens made the decision to receive baptism, which would occur at the Great Vigil of Easter, they submitted their names for enrollment in an intensified period of preparation during Lent. They received a new name and status for this period: in Jerusalem, they were called "the enlightened" (*phōtizomenoi*); in the West, the "elect" (*electi*) or "copetitioners" (*competentes*). This time involved various ascetic practices like fasting and sexual abstinence; it also entailed a series of exorcisms and prayers for the catechumens. Some places also developed a ritual called "the scrutiny," which was something like a spiritual examination before baptism. Lenten catechesis involved regular instruction in the Bible and Christian doctrine. One reference states that catechumens in Jerusalem met with the bishop for three hours a day for the seven weeks leading up to Easter![30] Instruction varied from place to place but

29. Augustine, *Homilies on the Gospel of John* 11.4 (WSA III/12:214).

30. This comes from the tremendous eyewitness account of the process of catechesis and baptism in perhaps the 380s by the Spanish pilgrim Egeria in a text called *The Pilgrim-*

generally included the biblical narrative, the necessity of moral formation, and the meaning of the creed. Several churches developed a ritual of "handing over" (*traditio*) and "returning" (*redditio*) the baptismal creed and the Lord's Prayer in the weeks before baptism. The bishop would hand over these texts by teaching them to catechumens and encouraging them to study and memorize them. Then the catechumens would "return" the creed by professing them to the bishop at their baptisms. Bishops spoke of this as entrusting the catechumens with the sacred deposit of the teaching of Jesus handed down by the apostles. They were to safeguard it like the pearl of great price.

But catechetical teaching went far beyond just lecturing. Fourth-century Christians recognized the importance of personal examples in teaching, for "guidance by example is clearer than instruction in words," as Gregory of Nyssa put it. The difference between one who teaches only in words and one who teaches by both words and deeds is like the difference between a "lifeless icon" and a human being who is "truly alive and outstandingly beautiful and effective in his movements."[31] Ambrose of Milan thought similarly. But rather than holding up Odysseus or Aeneas as paragons of virtue, like many non-Christian educators of his day did, Ambrose taught catechumens to see the Old Testament patriarchs like Abraham, Isaac, Jacob, and Joseph as moral examples worthy of imitation.[32]

Along with instruction in moral virtue, fourth-century catechists approached teaching as mystical encounter with God. Gregory of Nazianzus viewed teaching the creed in baptismal instruction as the divine law being written in the catechumens with the very finger of God (a reference to Deut. 9:10). Augustine thought of it as the fulfillment of Jeremiah's prophecy that the new covenant would be written on our hearts (Jer. 31:33).[33] In addition, many Christian leaders used music and hymnody for catechetical purposes. Ephrem the Syrian and Ambrose were innovative in the writing of hymns and poems to "enchant" catechumens with the beauty of truth.[34] They did not want catechumens merely to know God in an abstract way but to be enraptured by his glory.

age of Egeria, sections 45–47. For a good recent edition of this text, see Anne McGowan and Paul F. Bradshaw, trans., *The Pilgrimage of Egeria: A New Translation of the Itinerarium Egeriae with Introduction and Commentary* (Collegeville, MN: Liturgical Press, 2018).

31. Gregory of Nyssa, *On Virginity* 23.1 (FC 58:68–69).

32. Many of these can be found in *Ambrose of Milan: Seven Exegetical Works*, ed. Michael McHugh, FC 65 (Washington, DC: Catholic University of America Press, 1972).

33. Gregory of Nazianzus, *Oration* 40.44–45; Augustine, *Sermon* 212.2.

34. The significance of "enchantment" here is well articulated in Brian Dunkle,

This enrapturing education occurred in baptism itself. In the fourth century, baptisms mostly happened at Easter, as the culmination of the Lenten season of repentance. Baptisms were dramatic public rituals: the "Christian spectacles" (*spectacula Christiana*) that countered the popular pagan spectacles of the gladiator games and the amphitheater.[35] Augustine reflected on the powerful effect of these rites. The power, mercy, and nature of God "are being handed down quite secretly and firmly through the sacred realities by which we are being initiated and in which the life of the good is most easily purified, not by the runarounds of disputations but by the authority of the mysteries."[36] Gregory of Nazianzus likewise expounded the extraordinary gifts conveyed in the rite of baptism, which he referred to as the illumination of the Holy Spirit: "This illumination is renunciation of the flesh, following of the Spirit, communion in the Word, setting right of the creature, a flood overwhelming sin, participation in light, dissolution of darkness."[37]

Just before the baptism, catechumens faced west and publicly renounced Satan and "all his pomp," and then they turned east and confessed their allegiance to the triune God. Stripped naked, they were led down into the baptismal font, which in some cases was a large, eight-sided font that symbolized their entrance into the time of resurrection, the "Eighth Day." Arising from the tomb of their watery graves, the newly baptized were anointed with oil, adorned with white robes, and given a taste of milk and honey. These rites symbolized their entrance into the life of the Holy Spirit, being "clothed" with Christ, and entering the promised land. They were at this point permitted to exchange the kiss of peace and join the faithful in celebrating the Eucharist for the first time. They were now welcomed into full membership in the church.

The week following Easter, the newly baptized were finally taught the meaning of the sacraments. Having not received instruction on the meaning of the sacraments before baptism, they now learned it in what is often called "mystagogical" preaching. Mystagogy simply means "leading into the myster-

---

Enchantment and Creed in the Hymns of Ambrose of Milan (Oxford: Oxford University Press, 2016).

35. On the following, see Thomas Finn, *From Death to Rebirth: Ritual and Conversion in Antiquity* (New York: Paulist, 1997).

36. Augustine, *On Order* 2.9.27, in *St. Augustine: On Order*, trans. Michael Foley (New Haven: Yale University Press, 2020), 75.

37. Gregory Nazianzus, *Oration* 40.3, in *Saint Gregory of Nazianzus: Festal Orations*, trans. Nonna Verna Harrison (Crestwood, NY: St. Vladimir's Seminary Press, 2008), 100.

ies," and the term "mystery" was roughly equivalent to the term "sacrament."[38] The bishop would teach the newly baptized about prayer, worship, and the sacraments, which were now available to them through the anointing of the Holy Spirit.[39] With Spirit-opened eyes, they could now begin to comprehend the awesome power of the mysteries of faith.

In the early centuries of the church's life, catechesis emerged as a converting education. Instruction was bound up with spiritual and social transformation in which catechumens learned new ways of believing, living, and loving. Catechesis was a pedagogy of enchantment and an education of desire—a time when believers were formed in heart and mind, building knowledge and love of God on the one foundation of Jesus Christ.

38. It's possible that Cyril of Jerusalem's *Mystagogical Catechesis* is the first instance of this term applied to this kind of teaching. Ambrose's *On the Sacraments* and *On the Mysteries* are also examples of this genre. For an excellent study of "mystagogy," see Hanna Lucas, *Sensing the Sacred: Recovering a Mystagogical Vision of Knowledge and Salvation* (Eugene, OR: Wipf & Stock, 2023).

39. For neophyte, which means "new growth," as a term referring to new believers, see 1 Timothy 3:6.

Katēcheō in the New Testament and Early Christian Writing

The Greek word *katēcheō* does not appear in the Septuagint (the Greek version of the Old Testament), but it does occur eight times in the New Testament and in the early Christian text known as 2 Clement. Below are these passages with the Greek text included in parentheses and the corresponding English text underlined. Some of these references have hardly anything to do with teaching or instructing (Acts 21), while others seem to gesture toward the later use of catechesis to designate basic instruction in the faith.

- **1 Cor. 14:19**: "In church I would rather speak five words with my mind in order to instruct others (*allous katēchēsō*), than ten thousand words in a tongue."
- **Gal. 6:6**: "One who is taught the word (*katēchoumenos ton logon*) must share all good things with the one who teaches (*katēchounti*)."
- **Luke 1:3–4**: "It seemed good to me also, having followed all things closely for some time past, to write an orderly account for you, most excellent Theophilus, that you may have certainty concerning the things you have been taught (*peri hōn katēchēthēs logōn*)."
- **Acts 18:24–25**: "Now a Jew named Apollos, a native of Alexandria, came to Ephesus. He was an eloquent man, competent in the Scriptures. He had been instructed in the way of the Lord (*katēchēmenos tēn hodon tou kyriou*). And being fervent in spirit, he spoke and taught accurately the things concerning Jesus, though he knew only the baptism of John."
- **Acts 21:21, 24**: James and the apostles addressing Paul: "And they have been told (*katēchēthēsan*) about you that you teach all the Jews who are among the Gentiles to forsake Moses, telling them not to circumcise their children or walk according to our customs. . . . Take these men and purify yourself along with them and pay their expenses, so that they may shave their heads. Thus all will know that there is nothing in what they have been told about you (*hōn katēchēntai peri sou*), but that you yourself also live in observance of the law."
- **2 Clem. 17.1**: "Let us repent, therefore, with our whole heart, lest any of us should perish needlessly. For if we have orders that we should make it our business to tear men away from idols and to instruct them (*katēchein*), how much more wrong is it a soul that already knows God should perish?"[1]

1. *The Apostolic Fathers*, ed. and trans. Michael W. Holmes, 3rd ed. (Grand Rapids: Baker Academic, 2007), 161.

3

A Brief History of Catechesis from the Middle Ages to the Present

Because of the exceptional energy surrounding catechesis in the early church, it can be tempting to think that catechesis simply disappeared over the following centuries. That's the way some Protestant Reformers told the story, and not a few modern historians followed suit. As the story often goes, when Christianity became the dominant religious expression of the Roman Empire and infant baptism became the new normal, there was no longer any need for a rigorous practice of catechesis.[1]

In this chapter, though, I'm going to tell a different story, one of dynamism and change rather than decline and fall. Wherever the Spirit is at work in bringing the gospel to new cultures, we often find catechesis closely behind. Its forms and styles may adapt depending on needs and contexts. Christians may deploy different texts or practices. But catechesis in some form or another has been nearly ubiquitous throughout Christian history. The following is not the whole story by any means, but it will hopefully provide enough to help us expand our historical imaginations for the recovery of catechesis today.

1. This historiography draws from an influential German history of the catechumenate from the late nineteenth century: Peter Göbl's *Geschichte der Katechese im Abendlande vom Verfalle des Katechumenats bis zum Ende des Mittelalters* (1880). The title translates roughly: "The History of Catechesis in the West from the Downfall of the Catechumenate to the End of the Middle Ages." For a more recent rendition of this thesis, see Milton McC. Gatch, "The Medieval Church: Basic Christian Education from the Decline of Catechesis to the Rise of the Catechisms," in *A Faithful Church: Issues in the History of Catechesis*, ed. John H. Westerhoff III and O. C. Edwards Jr. (Wilton, CT: Morehouse-Barlow, 1981), 79–108.

The Early Middle Ages (500–1000)

Christianity was a missionary endeavor from the beginning. From Jerusalem, it soon spread across Europe, Africa, and Asia. By the third century, Christians had reached Arabia and India. Before Constantine adopted the Christian faith, it had already been adopted by the kingdoms of Armenia and Georgia. By the fifth century, Christianity was expanding not only northward to England and Ireland but also eastward to Asia Minor, Syria, and Mesopotamia and southward into the African regions of Nubia and Ethiopia. Well before the great medieval cathedrals and universities of Oxford and Paris, Syria boasted robust centers of Christian faith and learning, such as the renowned School of Nisibis. Meanwhile, merchant missionaries brought Christianity to China along the Silk Road, engaging with Buddhist and Indian thought as they sought to make the faith intelligible to these new communities. In many ways, western European Christianity, which we so often identify simply as mainstream Christianity, was only one of several strands of Christian activity.[2]

To meet the missional needs of the faith, Christians adopted different forms of catechesis. In Syria, for example, a unique kind of catechetical practice appeared among the Sons and Daughters of the Covenant (*Bnay Qyāmā, Bnāt Qyāmā*). These were groups of Syriac Christians devoted to study, fasting, and prayer, but especially hymnody. The fourth-century theologian Ephrem of Nisibis wrote some four hundred hymns, or *madrāšê*, most of which were for use in small quasi-monastic learning communities that Jeffrey Wickes calls "a blurred space between liturgy and classroom."[3] Neither purely monastic nor purely academic, the Sons and Daughters of the Covenant were communities of catechesis where learning and hymnody converged to create a rich "doxological pedagogy."[4]

2. The retelling of the story of Christianity as a missionary endeavor owes much to the work of scholars of world Christianity such as Andrew Walls, Lamin Sanneh, Kwame Bediako, Philip Jenkins, and others. For a good introduction, see Philip Jenkins, *The Lost History of Christianity: The Thousand-Year Age of the Church in the Middle East, Africa, and Asia—and How It Died* (New York: HarperCollins, 2008). And for a good account of the global spread of Christianity in the early Christian period, see Edward L. Smither, *Mission in the Early Church: Themes and Reflections* (Eugene, OR: Cascade, 2014), and Vince Bantu, *A Multitude of All Peoples: Engaging Ancient Christianity's Global Identity* (Downers Grove, IL: IVP Academic, 2020).

3. See Jeffrey Wickes, "Between Liturgy and School: Reassessing the Performative Context of Ephrem's Madrāšê," *Journal of Early Christian Studies* 26, no. 1 (2018): 25–51.

4. Wickes, "Between Liturgy and School," 49. For a collection of hymns that espe-

Another example occurs in the seventh-century mission to China. When Syriac Christians brought the gospel along the Silk Road, they also brought a practice of catechesis and initiation. We read in the famous Xian monument (discussed in chapter 5) about the process of baptism and how they envisioned the new life of believers. In the following centuries, new texts appeared in Chinese, like the so-called *Sutras of Jesus the Messiah*. Some aspects of the *Sutras* are apologetic, attempting to defend the faith against false accusations. Others were more directly catechetical, presenting the core elements of the Christian faith in a language and in literary forms their Chinese hearers could understand.[5]

Missional catechesis can also be seen in the writings of a little-known sect called the Paulicians, who flourished in Armenia in the eighth and ninth centuries. This group held an adoptionist theology, meaning that they believed Jesus was an ordinary man who only became divine at his baptism. Perhaps because of the focus on Jesus's baptism, they stressed that repentance and instruction should precede baptism for all Christian believers, and they argued vehemently against those "who baptize the unbelieving, the reasonless, and the unrepentant." In other words, they resisted the tradition of baptizing either infants or those who did not understand the core tenets of the faith. An Armenian text discovered in the eighteenth century, called the *Key of Truth*, is a possible witness to this, and it shows the need for instruction and guidance in baptismal rituals and catechesis that were related to their theological convictions about Christ.[6]

Many histories of Christianization in Europe during the Middle Ages tell of masses of barbarian conversions where a rigorous catechumenate seems absent. We should interpret such stories cautiously, however, as many of the sources for those stories were meant to convey the miraculous power of God in bringing the faith to new nations, not to present a documentary history of

---

cially focuses on the right pursuit of the study of God, see Ephrem the Syrian, *Hymns on Faith* (FC 130). And for their role in catechesis, see Jung Kim, "Catechesis and Mystagogy in St. Ephrem the Syrian: The Liturgy of Baptism and the *Madrashe*" (ThD diss., Boston University, 2013).

5. On this history, see Glen Thompson, *Jingjiao: The Earliest Christian Church in China* (Grand Rapids: Eerdmans, 2024).

6. This text can be found in F. C. Conybeare, *The Key of Truth: A Manual of the Paulician Church of Armenia* (Oxford: Clarendon, 1898), citation from p. 75. Scholars, however, debate whether this text accurately transmits the beliefs of the medieval Paulicians; because the manuscript is from the eighteenth century, it may incorporate later developments.

teaching practices. When we look more closely, we see consistent appeals for missionaries to take the calling of catechesis seriously. Figures like Gregory the Great and Boniface V provided detailed guidelines for missionaries to England, especially focused on worship, idolatry, and other matters that dominate in early Christian emphases on the rule of faith. In Spain, Martin of Braga closely followed Augustine's *On Catechizing the Uninstructed* by presenting an overview of salvation history.[7]

From the fifth to the ninth century, hundreds of baptismal sermons on the creed and the Lord's Prayer were written. In 740, the archbishop of York declared that "every priest [should] with great exactness instill the Lord's Prayer and the Creed into the people committed to him, and show them to endeavor after the knowledge of the whole of religion, and the practice of Christianity."[8] In the ninth century, the Carolingian renaissance ushered in a new era of educational reform, which had a profound impact on baptismal catechesis. Leading lights such as Alcuin of York (d. 804) and Rabanus Maurus (d. 856) are good examples. Alcuin wrote to Charlemagne about the conversion of the Avar tribes from eastern Europe, stating his intent to use Augustine's writing on catechesis.[9] Rabanus, meanwhile, wrote about catechesis using key gospel passages.[10] In his book *On the Institution of Clerics*, he used the account of Jesus healing the blind man in John 9 as a picture of catechesis and baptism. Because Jesus first washed the blind man's eyes with a mixture of saliva and mud before instructing him to go wash in the waters of Siloam (John 9:6–7), this signifies, Rabanus argued, that the catechumen should first be taught faith in Christ's incarnation, and then admitted to baptism, "so that he may come

7. Martin of Braga, *Reforming the Rustics* (FC 62:71–85). For a good overview of European missionary catechesis, see M. E. Jegen, "Catechesis (II), Medieval," in vol. 3 of *New Catholic Encyclopedia*, 2nd ed. (Detroit: Gale, 2003), 228–32.

8. For baptismal creeds and texts, see Liuwe Westra, *The Apostles' Creed: Origin, History, and Some Early Commentaries* (Turnhout: Brepols, 2002); Wolfram Kinzig, ed., *Faith in Formulae: A Collection of Early Christian Creeds and Creed-Related Texts*, 4 vols. (New York: Oxford University Press, 2017). The Egbert quotation comes from John Hartin, with Jonathan Knight, "Catechisms," in *The Study of Anglicanism*, ed. Stephen Sykes, John Booty, and Jonathan Knight, rev. ed. (London: SPCK, 1998), 168.

9. On the Carolingian renaissance and baptismal education, see Susan A. Keefe, *Water and the Word: Baptism and the Education of the Clergy in the Carolingian Empire*, 2 vols. (Notre Dame: University of Notre Dame Press, 2002); Owen M. Phelan, "Catechising the Wild: The Continuity and Innovation of Missionary Catechesis under the Carolingians," *Journal of Ecclesiastical History* 61, no. 3 (2010): 455–74.

10. Rabanus Maurus, *On the Institution of Clerics* 1.25 (PL 107:310).

to know that grace in which he is a partaker, and to which now a debtor he may be following."[11]

Catechesis also became enmeshed in Christian liturgies and ritual practices. As one scholar describes it, early medieval Christian identity was shaped at the "nexus between rite and preaching, a performance through which Europeans learned what it meant to be Christian."[12] In some cases, this involved new rites for helping believers become accustomed to Christian life. In others, it meant teaching new texts to catechumens. In still other cases, we see how new rites developed that became linked with traditional catechetical topics.

One interesting example is the emergence of a rite called "Pascha Annotinum," a ritual celebrating the one-year anniversary of baptism at Easter. Most evidence for this rite comes from tenth-century liturgical texts like the Gregorian Sacramentary, but its earliest appearance can be found in the writing of fifth-century theologian Peter Chrysologus, who was bishop of the North Italian city of Ravenna. In one sermon, he describes the "weaning" of neophyte Christians in the time after baptism when they are no longer newborn babes, yet not yet mature believers. Between the pure milk of babes and the mature meat of the aged, they need food adequate for their stage of growth in the Christian life.

We also see the use of new texts in catechesis alongside the baptismal creed and the Lord's Prayer, such as Psalm 23. This psalm had already been closely tied with baptism. When the church fathers read of the still waters, bountiful table, and flowing oil, they couldn't help but hear echoes of baptism, Eucharist, and chrismation.[13] In a few regions, though, the psalm itself was taught and memorized in catechesis. In a sermon attributed to Saint Augustine, the preacher addresses those "hastening toward the baptism of Christ" by declaring: "We are handing over this psalm in the name of the Lord to be learned by heart, and so we must explain its inner meaning with divine grace to enlighten us." The preacher gives instruction about the psalm's "inner meaning," drawing out the images of the psalm to illuminate the catechumens' own experience. The green pastures signify the desire for sound doctrine, the still waters rep-

11. Rabanus Maurus, *On the Institution of Clerics* 1.25 (PL 107:310).

12. Nathan J. Ristuccia, *Christianization and Commonwealth in Early Medieval Europe: A Ritual Interpretation* (Oxford: Oxford University Press, 2018), 178.

13. See Jean Daniélou, *The Bible and the Liturgy* (Notre Dame: University of Notre Dame Press, 1956), 177–90, and Matthieu Pignot, *The Catechumenate in Late Antique Africa (4th–6th Centuries): Augustine of Hippo, His Contemporaries and Early Reception* (Leiden: Brill, 2020), 278–86.

resent their upcoming baptism. "Unless your pastures . . . are irrigated by this water," he writes, "it will be impossible for you to be nurtured, because the commandment of God can neither germinate without the baptism of Christ, nor be eaten so as to satisfy the soul."[14]

In other cases, core catechetical texts were integrated with feasts of the church year. The Lord's Prayer, for example, became closely linked with the celebration of Rogation Days, or Rogationtide, in several regions.[15] During this annual liturgical ritual, leading up to the Feast of the Ascension, Christian preachers took the opportunity to recatechize the faithful on the importance of the Lord's Prayer in the Christian life.

In the early Middle Ages, catechesis took on new forms as Christianity expanded into new regions and was adapted into new contexts. The needs of mission required creative ways to bring the beliefs, prayers, and ethical teachings of the faith to new cultures. And these cultures, in turn, provided new opportunities to lay deep foundations for Christian discipleship.

The Late Middle Ages (1000–1500)

Throughout the Middle Ages, Christianity continued to adapt and change from a global perspective. The rise of Islam saw the shrinking presence of Christians in many parts of Asia and North Africa, and we do not know much about Christianity in the Far East during this period. But in areas where we do have more evidence, we again see how catechesis follows missional expansion. We have good evidence that the catechetical outlines in the *Apostolic Tradition* of Hippolytus were translated in many different languages in the Middle Ages. An Ethiopian translation dates from around the sixth century, Coptic translations from the eleventh century, and Arabic translations from the thirteenth century, in addition to a variety of Latin and Syriac translations.[16]

The spread of Christianity in Ethiopia, in particular, is an interesting example of missionary catechesis outside of Europe. Christianity here remained largely independent of western European traditions, but nevertheless had access to its own traditions of catechesis. *The Book of Light*, written by the

14. Ps.-Augustine, *Sermon* 366.1, 3 (WSA III/10:288, 290).

15. For Rogationtide as a time for teaching catechetical standards, see Ristuccia, *Christianization and Commonwealth*, 178–209; Gatch, "The Medieval Church," 95–99.

16. See Alistair Stewart, ed., *Hippolytus: On the Apostolic Tradition*, 2nd ed. (Crestwood, NY: St. Vladimir's Seminary Press, 2015), 55–57.

Ethiopian emperor Zär'a Ya'eqob (ca. 1399–1468), is a good case in point.[17] Zär'a Ya'eqob was a scholar and religious reformer of the Ethiopian Orthodox Church in the fifteenth century. In this treatise, he addressed the ritual of baptism and requirements for instruction for both the baptized and the unbaptized, especially with a view toward the conversion of Jews and Muslims. He drew on early Christian church-order texts like the *Didascalia*, a third-century Syrian writing that addresses the organization of worship and church structure, to exhort priests, deacons, and monks to pursue the task of instruction with zeal and devotion.

Meanwhile, medieval European Christianity was marked by its own series of reforms. Many reforms targeted the papacy, with appeals for church leaders to model their lives on the simplicity and purity of the earliest apostles. Other reforms targeted monastic life, with charters for new orders to embrace more radical ideals of holiness and devotion. In addition, we also see an increasing focus on lay education. The eleventh and twelfth centuries saw a notable rise in lay devotion, including the formation of new spiritual communities who gathered together for prayer, instruction, and mutual encouragement.

A major marker for reform came after the Fourth Lateran Council in 1215. Among several important regulations—most famously, the requirements for papal celibacy and annual confession and eucharistic participation—the council instituted new programs for clerical and lay education. The abundant production of manuals for lay instruction has led historians to describe this period as a "revolution in pastoral care," which occurred alongside the creation of new religious orders like the Franciscans and Dominicans who were tasked with teaching. Not coincidentally, medieval universities appeared at this time, growing out of the monastic and cathedral schools of the early medieval period. The scholastic modes of theology emerging from these schools generated new possibilities for theological education but also aroused suspicion from their monastic counterparts.[18]

The writings of Saint Thomas Aquinas (1225–1274) are one example from this period. One of the most brilliant thinkers of his age, Thomas devoted the final years of his life to catechesis. He began a *Compendium of Theology* to summarize his life's work, basing it on the threefold pattern of faith, hope, and

17. For this text, see Getatchew Haile, ed., *The Homily of Zär'a Ya'eqob's Mäṣḥafä Ḇerhan on the Rite of Baptism and Religious Instruction* (Leuven: Peeters, 2013). My thanks to Anna Wells for directing me to this fascinating source.

18. Jean Leclercq, *The Love of Learning and the Desire for God: A Study of Monastic Culture*, trans. Catharine Misrahi, 3rd ed. (New York: Fordham University Press, 1982).

love—signifying, respectively, knowledge of the truth, the proper goal of life, and the right ordering of affections. (Unfortunately, this work was not completed before his death.) Around the same time, Thomas preached a series of catechetical sermons on the Apostles' Creed, the Lord's Prayer, the Ten Commandments, and the sacraments, preaching in the vernacular Italian rather than academic Latin.[19] Even in more scholarly writing, Thomas addressed theological issues related to catechesis. In the *Summa Theologiae*, for example, he asks whether catechesis should precede baptism: If baptism is truly regenerative, some might argue, why teach anything beforehand? In response, Thomas drew on his central notion of grace completing, not destroying, nature to think through this issue. Grace, he argues here, "presupposes the life of the rational nature, in which man is capable of receiving instruction."[20]

Besides Thomas, there were many other enthusiasts for catechesis. In 1281, the archbishop of Canterbury, John Peckham, issued a constitution "On the Ignorance of Priests" (*Ignorantia Sacerdotum*), which was designed to address the problem of unlearned clergy. It called for priests to teach and preach four times a year on the baptismal creed, the Ten Commandments, and a series of "sevens": the seven works of mercy, seven deadly sins, seven virtues, and seven sacraments. This text became influential for new forms of teaching manuals, such as the so-called *Lay Folks' Catechism*, which appeared in York around 1357 and survives today in twenty-eight manuscripts. Written by a monk named John Gaytrig at the request of Archbishop John Thoresby, the *Lay Folks' Catechism* remained a popular manual over the next century and was sometimes combined with other new instruction manuals, such as *Speculum Vitae* ("Mirror of Life"), a poetic commentary on the Lord's Prayer that originated in France at the end of the thirteenth century. In addition to the use of poetic forms, catechisms from this period also developed image-based approaches. The famous *Biblia Pauperum* ("The Paupers' Bible") and the *Speculum Humanae Salvationis* ("The Mirror of Human Salvation") are good examples. These works were useful for teaching those who could not read, perhaps echoing Gregory the Great's famous maxim that religious images were "books for the illiterate." These works taught the narrative of Scripture typologically: a central image of Jesus's life would be framed by two smaller Old Testament images on either side, with brief explanatory notes at the bottom of the page.

19. These sermons can be found in Thomas Aquinas, *The Aquinas Catechism: A Simple Explanation of the Catholic Faith by the Church's Greatest Theologian* (Manchester, NH: Sophia Institute Press, 2000).

20. See Thomas Aquinas, *Summa Theologiae* III, q. 71, art. 1.

In the fifteenth century, the Parisian theologian Jean Gerson (d. 1429) wrote several popular catechisms. One of the most prominent was called the *The ABC of Simple Folk*, which included a list of items that lay Christians should know: along with the creed, the Lord's Prayer, and the various sevens, other items included the five bodily senses, the four counsels of Christ, the joys of heaven, and the pains of hell. Gerson also wrote books for instructing children, such as *De parvulis trahendis ad Christum* ("Drawing the Little Ones to Christ"). Another work that proved highly influential was his *Opusculum tripertitum* (ca. 1395), one of the first works printed in the New World when Jesuit missionaries brought it to Mexico in the 1540s. Another popular catechism was *The Mirror of a Christian Man*, published by the Franciscan Dietrich Kolde in 1470 and republished nineteen times over the next five decades. In this text, Kolde highlights the uncertainty of death, its timing, and ultimately where it will take a person. The purpose of the catechism is to provide the Christian "a beautiful mirror" that contains "everything necessary for the well-being and salvation of the soul."[21] For users of Kolde's *Mirror*, catechesis was not simply about general education but belonged within the larger sacramental system of the late medieval church and the spiritual and theological concerns of his age.

The Reformation (1500–1600)

While Protestants did not rediscover catechesis after its alleged disappearance in the Middle Ages, the sixteenth century did see a remarkable outpouring of energy for educating believers in the fundament doctrines and prayers of the faith. Luther's *Small Catechism* and *Large Catechism*, both published in 1529, initiated what historian Carlos Eire has called a "craze" for catechisms in the sixteenth century.[22] Over the following two centuries, Protestants and Catholics alike published thousands of catechisms in Europe and the known world.

There were, as we have seen, several precedents for Luther's catechisms in the late medieval texts by Gerson, Kolde, and the anonymous *Lay Folks' Catechism*. At least thirty catechisms were published in Europe before Luther's catechisms, including those by John Colet, the dean of St. Paul's Cathedral; the learned humanist Erasmus of Rotterdam; and the Anabaptist Balthasar Hubmaier. After Luther, though, a flurry of catechisms ensued. In England,

21. Quoted in Denis Janz, ed., *Three Reformation Catechisms: Catholic, Anabaptist, Lutheran* (New York: E. Mellen Press, 1982), 31.

22. Carlos M. N. Eire, *Reformations: The Early Modern World, 1450–1650* (New Haven: Yale University Press, 2016), 592.

the first edition of the Book of Common Prayer (1549) contained a short catechism attached to the Rite of Confirmation, which has remained a staple of many prayer-book traditions ever since. In 1572, the English church designated Alexander Nowell's catechism to function as an authoritative "longer catechism" for standard use. In Reformed churches, the *Geneva Catechism* of 1542, coauthored by Calvin, was highly influential, superseded only by the *Heidelberg Catechism* in 1563. In the following century, the *Westminster Shorter Catechism* and the *Westminster Larger Catechism* became standard for many Reformed, Presbyterian, and even Baptist congregations. Hundreds of others soon followed in their wake.[23]

Among Roman Catholics, the renewal of catechesis was sparked not only by reactions to Protestantism but also by missionary efforts. Juan de Ávila relied on catechisms in his extensive missionary work in Spain. Ignatius of Loyola, Francis Xavier, and other Jesuits made similar use of catechisms in missionary ventures to China, Japan, India, Latin America, and elsewhere. Arguably the first text published in North America was a compendium of a Roman Catholic catechism by a missionary in Mexico, Juan de Zumárraga, in 1539. By the end of the century, Catholics could rival Protestants in their production of catechisms. Three in particular, by Peter Canisius, became central in Roman Catholic use: the large *Summa doctrinae christianae* (1555) was written for priests and teachers; the smaller *Catechismus minimus* (1556) was written for children; and the medium-sized *Parvus catechismus catholicorum* (1558) was written for those in between. These catechisms were translated into nearly every European language, and also appeared in African, Asian, and Latin American editions. Cardinal Robert Bellarmine's 1590 *A Brief Christian Doctrine* ran for more than five hundred editions and was translated into fifty-six languages.[24]

One of the main concerns driving catechesis was the reeducation of laypeople. Luther's frustrations are on full display as he recounts the "deplorable

23. On the different traditions of catechesis in this period (Anglican, Reformed, Lutheran, and Catholic, respectively), see Ian Green, *The Christian's ABC: Catechisms and Catechizing in England c. 1530–1740* (Oxford: Oxford University Press, 1996); Thomas F. Torrance, *The School of Faith: Catechisms of the Reformed Church* (1959; reprint, Eugene, OR: Wipf & Stock, 1996); Timothy J. Wengert, *Martin Luther's Catechisms: Forming the Faith* (Minneapolis: Fortress, 2009); Berard Marthaler, *The Catechism Yesterday and Today: The Evolution of a Genre* (Collegeville, MN: Liturgical Press, 1995).

24. For these figures, see Alexandra Walsham, "Wholesome Milk and Strong Meat: Peter Canisius's Catechisms and the Conversion of Protestant Britain," *British Catholic History* 32, no. 3 (2015): 293–314. For a good history of Roman Catholic catechisms, see Marthaler, *Catechism Yesterday and Today*.

conditions" he encountered during his ventures through the rural German parishes in the late 1520s.[25] The people he met were ignorant of basic doctrine, and their pastors were incompetent to teach them. They received the sacraments but could not recite the Apostles' Creed, the Lord's Prayer, or the Ten Commandments. This was a major reason he claimed to be writing a new catechism. But he was also very interested in education movements more broadly. He saw education as critical for the spread of the gospel. "For the gospel is threatened with untold evils," Luther wrote in 1524, "through neglecting this duty."[26]

Catechesis was also instrumental in shaping Christian identity. Luther's catechisms were written to instill a *Lutheran* reading of Scripture—not a Roman or Genevan one. Reformed Christians and Roman Catholics did the same. While it's not hard to perceive the polemical agendas under the surface of these catechisms, their *stated* intentions were simply to teach basic Christianity. As a result, many of these catechisms treat less contentious doctrines like the Trinity briefly, while devoting many questions to contested issues like the meaning of justification or the presence of Christ in the sacraments.

The Reformers were not just interested in creating catechisms, though. They wanted to create cultures where Protestant views could take root. Calvin envisioned Geneva as a model city of Christian learning and piety—a "catechetical polis," as historian Robert Kingdon has called it.[27] He encouraged catechesis in churches and homes and organized learning opportunities around the city: Bible classes, public lectures, psalm-singing sessions, catechism classes, and eventually the founding of a theological university. These institutions were bolstered by a group called the Consistory, a delegation of about a dozen pastors and public officials who ensured that families and teachers were actively involved in forming their children and living out the faith in a genuine way. For Calvin, at least, successful reform could not occur without a broader vision of educational reform.

25. Martin Luther, preface to the *Small Catechism*, cited in *Martin Luther's Basic Theological Writings*, ed. Timothy Lull (Minneapolis: Fortress, 1989), 471.

26. Martin Luther, "Letter to Jacob Strauss" (April 25, 1524), in *The Letters of Martin Luther*, ed. and trans. Margaret Currie (London: Macmillan, 1908), 125. The original letter, written in Latin, can be found in vol. 3 of *D. Martin Luthers Werke: Briefwechsel* (Weimar: Hermann Böhlaus Nachfolger, 1969), 278, where he writes: "Video enim euangelio maximam impendere ruinam neglectu educandae pueritiae."

27. Robert Kingdon, "Catechesis in Calvin's Geneva," in *Educating People of Faith: Exploring the Histories of Jewish and Christian Communities*, ed. John Van Engen (Grand Rapids: Eerdmans, 2004), 294–313.

Catechesis also became enmeshed in a larger vision of political-ecclesial renewal in England.[28] Amid the different visions on hand for the proper organization of church and state, the English focused their efforts for national unity around worship as outlined in the Book of Common Prayer. The prayer book was intended to provide a common pattern of worship as well as a common language. Many Anglicans have understood the prayer book as providing a template for theological and spiritual formation. Catechesis happens not only through teaching the catechism but also through praying the Daily Office, gathering for Sunday worship, and participating in the shared rituals of prayer-book worship that bind a community together.

After the Reformation (1600–1740)

In the centuries following the Reformation, many Christians continued to build on these efforts. Between the dawn of the Reformation in 1517 and the First Great Awakening in 1740, some eight hundred catechisms were published in England alone.[29] Many Christians viewed catechesis along a threefold axis of church, school, and home.

The English Puritan Richard Baxter (1615–1691) was an avid proponent of catechesis. He taught the catechism to parishioners twice a week, on Sundays and Thursday evenings, for about an hour, and regularly visited parishioners in their homes. He also encouraged parents to envision their homes as schools of prayer, hoping to make catechesis a "permanent ingredient in pastoral care for all ages," not just for children.[30] An earlier Puritan, Richard Bernard (1568–1641), likewise gave thoughtful expression to the instruction of youth and families in his book *The Faithfull Shepheard* (1607). Bernard advises pastors to catechize "with a cheerful countenance, familiarly, and lovingly," because, as he puts it, "hardly anyone will learn from those they hate." Bernard wanted catechists to seek the best in students, to look for a willing spirit more than a sharp wit.

A magnificent example of catechesis in pastoral care comes from the poet-priest George Herbert (1593–1633).[31] While mostly known for his poetry, he

28. On English catechesis, in addition to Green, *The Christian's ABC*, see also Drew N. Keane, "'Let Me Heare . . . If Thou Canst Say': The Utility of the Prayer Book Catechism (1549–1604)," *Journal of Technical Writing and Communication* 52, no. 1 (2022): 19–56.

29. Green, *The Christian's ABC*, 50.

30. This is J. I. Packer's summary in his introduction to Richard Baxter, *The Reformed Pastor* (Carlisle, PA: Banner of Truth, 1974), 13.

31. I have outlined more of Herbert's vision for catechesis in Alex Fogleman, "'Build

also wrote a book on pastoral care called *The Country Parson* (1650), in which Herbert emphasized the importance of catechesis for the whole church: adults as well as children, and not least of all, the pastor himself. "In catechizing there is a humbleness very suitable to Christian regeneration," Herbert explained, "which exceedingly delights him as by way of exercise upon himself." Herbert encouraged the memorization of the prayer-book catechism and the use of dialogue to help students penetrate the sense of the words. Herbert compared the use of dialogue in catechesis with the Socratic method of instruction, although he thought teaching Christianity was not the same as teaching philosophy, since Christianity contained teaching "above nature." Scripture itself modeled this pedagogy in its abundant use of homely metaphors from farming and family life. Similarly, the simple words of the catechism could become symbols of "divine lights" into heavenly wisdom.[32]

In the next century, the Anglican priest and missionary Thomas Bray (d. 1730) took the idea of building catechetical cultures to a new level. Bray was one of the original founders of the Society for the Propagation of Christian Knowledge (SPCK), which helped establish dozens of libraries in England and the Americas. Recognizing that many pastors in poorer regions could not afford books, Bray called on wealthy Christians to invest in church-based libraries. But not just any libraries: Bray had in mind libraries organized around the topics of the catechism. A 1699 pamphlet entitled *Bibliotheca catechetica* suggested some 230 titles on the Bible and sacred history, the articles of the creed, the petitions of the Lord's Prayer, and the outline of holy living found in the Ten Commandments.[33] Bray's text is a fascinating example of how the catechism could shape the very organization of knowledge.

The Puritans brought many of these ideas to the New World.[34] While rejecting certain aspects of English piety and polity, the Puritans maintained a high estimation of catechesis. They used the catechism in public schools and

Up This Knowledge to a Spiritual Temple': George Herbert's Catechetical Poetics," *Crux* 59, no. 2 (2023): 16–27.

32. George Herbert, *The Country Parson*, chap. 21. For an accessible account of this work, see George Herbert, *The Complete English Works*, ed. Ann Pasternak Slater (New York: Knopf, 1995).

33. Thomas Bray, *Bibliotecha catechetica; or, The country curates library: being an essay towards providing all the parochial cures of England, endow'd with not above ten pounds per annum, with a study of usefull books of like value, to enable the ministers thereof to catechise the youth, and to instruct the people in all things necessary to salvation* (London, 1699).

34. For an excellent historical analysis of Puritan catechisms, see Agnes Rose Howard, "'The Blessed Echoes of Truth': Catechisms and Confirmation in Puritan New England" (PhD diss., University of Virginia, 1999).

even codified catechetical instruction in law.[35] A 1642 Massachusetts General Court law mandated that household leaders equip children and servants with the ability to "read and understand the principles of religion and the capital laws of this country." A 1648 mandate declared that children should be catechized at least once a week. A 1660 ordinance in Salem specified that John Cotton's *Milk for Babes Drawn Out of the Breasts of Both Testaments* was to be taught in homes so that children might be prepared for "public catechizing in the Congregation."[36]

Over the seventeenth century, Puritans wrote dozens of new catechisms and adopted older ones.[37] John Cotton's *Milk for Babes* was extremely popular, first published in 1646 and republished frequently over the next two centuries. Puritans also wrote or translated catechisms in various Native American languages, such as John Eliot's famous Algonquian catechism published in 1654.

Overall, catechesis remained a relatively stable teaching institution from the late sixteenth to the early eighteenth century. But we start to see subtle shifts in this period. If Reformation catechesis was primarily about fostering a denominational identity, Puritan catechesis began to focus more on the process of conversion. Driven by the desire to overcome nominal Christianity, many catechism writers began to use other organizational structures besides the three-pillar model of creed, prayer, and Ten Commandments. Catechisms like those of Westminster used the question-and-answer format to drive nominal Christians to recognize their sinfulness and need for true conversion.[38] This approach was perfectly suited for the coming rise of evangelicalism.

The Rise of Evangelicalism (1740–1900)

Beginning in the 1740s, a host of zealous young men and women began discerning what they called a "surprising work of God." Over the next fifty years, an extraordinary cross-continental, interdenominational spiritual awakening

35. On Puritan education, see John Morgan, *Godly Learning: Puritan Attitudes towards Reason, Learning, and Education, 1560–1640* (Cambridge: Cambridge University Press, 1986).

36. The references from this paragraph come from Howard, "'Blessed Echoes of Truth,'" 129, with light modifications of the language.

37. For a list of many such catechisms, see Wilberforce Eames, *Early New England Catechisms: A Bibliographical Account of Some Catechisms Published before the Year 1800, for Use in New England* (New York: Burt Franklin, 1898).

38. Green, *The Christian's ABC*, 565.

arose that we now call the First Great Awakening. Led by intelligent and passionate young ministers like Jonathan Edwards, John and Charles Wesley, and George Whitefield, early evangelicalism brought together strands of English Puritanism, German pietism, and late medieval spirituality to create a potent recipe for proclaiming the ancient faith in the modern world. Above all, evangelicals emphasized the true conversion of the heart. Amid a prevailing culture of nominal belief, early evangelicals stressed the need for a profound Spirit-filled transformation. It was not enough to attend church services and receive the sacraments. Without a genuine conversion of the heart, such a person was little more than what Wesley called a "half Christian."[39]

Caught between the ancients and the moderns, evangelicals could be of two minds about catechesis. On the one hand, they commended it as a historical, time-honored practice. John Wesley used traditional catechisms and wrote new ones. John Newton, the author of the famous hymn "Amazing Grace," was an enthusiastic catechist who taught the catechism to large groups of young children, even offering small monetary rewards for memorization.[40] But on the other hand, there was a noticeable decline in catechizing during the eighteenth century.[41] Worries about "rote memorization" that had troubled earlier authors became even more acute after the Enlightenment. At the same time, evangelicals experimented with new forms of discipleship. Wesley's "band" meetings were close-knit gatherings where believers sang hymns, studied the Bible, and met for accountability. Wesley saw such groups as reminiscent of the ancient catechumenate.[42]

One of the most important developments in this period is the rise of the Sunday school movement. Many educational reform movements were under way at the time, like those of the evangelical reformer Hannah More. But it was the Sunday school movement, begun by Anglican layman Robert Raikes, that would dominate religious education for the next several centuries. The

39. For good introductions to this complex period, see Mark A. Noll, *The Rise of Evangelicalism: The Age of Edwards, Whitefield, and the Wesleys* (Downers Grove, IL: IVP Academic, 2003); Bruce Hindmarsh, *The Spirit of Early Evangelicalism: True Religion in a Modern World* (Oxford: Oxford University Press, 2018).

40. See the wonderful description in Bruce Hindmarsh, *John Newton and the English Evangelical Tradition* (Oxford: Oxford University Press, 1996).

41. F. C. Mather, "Georgian Churchmanship Reconsidered: Some Variations in Anglican Public Worship 1714–1830," *Journal of Ecclesiastical History* 36 (1985): 279–81.

42. On the connections between the ancient catechumenate and the Methodist bands, see Tory L. Baucum, *Evangelical Hospitality: Evangelical Catechesis in the Early Church and Its Recovery for Today* (Lanham, MD: Scarecrow, 2008).

Sunday school movement arose to teach reading and literacy to children, but mainly to help them read Scripture. Early on, many Sunday school teachers used catechisms in their teaching, but catechisms were gradually eclipsed by the use of Bible stories. Ironically, it seems that the rise of Sunday schools is part of the reason that catechesis went out of fashion.[43]

One of the more deplorable developments in this period was the use of catechisms in the context of American slavery. In the early days of the American settlement, catechesis was a lengthy and rigorous process, yet any slaves or Native Americans who underwent instruction and baptism acquired a surprising level of social equality.[44] As historian Albert Raboteau has put it, baptized slaves in the early colonial period "attained full if not equal communion with their white fellow Christians," resulting in "a kind of stepbrotherhood" among blacks and whites.[45] This changed over time, however, and gradually baptism no longer bestowed social equality. The link between catechesis and literacy made the issue a civic threat.[46] Missionaries to slaves like Francis Le Jau (1665–1717) had to assure their readers that catechizing slaves would not lead to their rejecting the "duty and obedience" owed to masters.[47] But eventually, especially during and after the Great Awakenings of the 1740s and early 1800s, slave conversions rose dramatically, eventually leading to the creation of new denominations like the African Methodist Episcopal Church, founded by

43. For this argument, see J. I. Packer and Gary E. Parrett, *Grounded in the Gospel: Building Believers the Old-Fashioned Way* (Grand Rapids: Baker Academic, 2010), 71–72.

44. The Massachusetts governor John Winthrop recorded the first slave baptism in New England—a woman named "Dorcas ye blackmore" in 1641 at Dorchester First Church—as coming at the end of "divers years of experience" in which she demonstrated "sound knowledge and true godliness." Quoted in Albert J. Raboteau, *Slave Religion: The "Invisible Institution" in the Antebellum South*, updated ed. (Oxford: Oxford University Press, 2004), 109. In 1710, the Anglican missionary Francis Le Jau reported a two-year catechumenate for slaves, in which he taught them to read, expounded the catechism, and entertained questions. See Raboteau, *Slave Religion*, 115.

45. Raboteau, *Slave Religion*, 126, 128.

46. In the 1700s, new legislation was passed forbidding slaves to read. In 1831, a North Carolina law prohibited teaching slaves to read and write because "it has a tendency to excite dissatisfaction in their minds, and to produce insurrection and rebellion, to the manifest injury of the citizens of the State." Quoted in Willie Jennings, *The Christian Imagination: Theology and the Origins of Race* (New Haven: Yale University Press, 2010), 234.

47. Raboteau, *Slave Religion*, 123.

Richard Allen in 1816. Over the course of the seventeenth century, the meaning of baptism changed: no longer creating social equality, baptism reinforced divisions based on race.[48] While conversions became more prolific, they were also less equalizing. The door to "stepbrotherhood" among the baptized was closing.

Worse, the door was opened for the use of catechesis to justify the subjugation of slaves. White Christians wrote new catechisms to instill proslavery readings of the Bible and nullify the potential for faith to lead to social unrest.[49] The Reverend Charles Colcock Jones (1804–1863), for example, wrote in one slave catechism about how slaves were to behave toward their masters:

> QUESTION: When Negroes become religious, how must they behave to their masters?
>
> ANSWER: The Scriptures in many places command them, to be honest, diligent and faithful in all things, and not to give saucy answers; and even when they are whipped for doing well, to take it patiently and look to God for their reward.[50]

While such catechisms were not normative in American Christianity, they were tragically not uncommon. This example goes to show that catechesis is no simple antidote to malformed Christian identity but can be deployed to perpetrate our cultural sins.

Catechesis in the Modern Age (1900–Present)

The missional energy of evangelicalism birthed an extraordinary explosion of Christian expansion around the world. Today, the most vibrant currents of faith flow not through Europe and North America but through Africa, Asia, and Latin America. Once again, this created new opportunities for catechesis. "The mission field," as Lamin Sanneh put it, "demanded that Christians respond to local feedback about the meaning and potential of the gospel."[51] Cate-

48. For this thesis, see Rebecca Anne Goetz, *The Baptism of Early Virginia: How Christianity Created Race* (Baltimore: Johns Hopkins University Press, 2011).

49. Jennings, *The Christian Imagination*, 237.

50. Quoted in Jennings, *The Christian Imagination*, 237–38.

51. Lamin Sanneh, "Global Christianity and the Re-education of the West," *Christian Century*, July 19, 1995, 715–18.

chisms were instrumental in the mission field. Easier to translate and quicker to publish, they were sometimes the first texts written in a new language. Church structure was affected, too. Especially in churches with a more hierarchical leadership structure, where ordained leaders were harder to procure, lay catechists played a key role in bringing the gospel to new areas.[52]

Several Roman Catholic mission organizations established a multistage catechumenate.[53] The French bishop Louis-Simon Faurie (1824–1871) noted that a three-stage catechumenate was used in some parts of China. In Latin America, provincial councils in Peru and Mexico required a forty-day period of instruction before baptism. In the East Indies, a twenty-day rule was the minimal standard. One of the most robust recoveries of the catechumenate was in Africa under the leadership of Charles Lavigerie (1825–1892). A former professor of early church history, Lavigerie saw the African mission as a renewal movement, not a novel one, and he encouraged a "great affection for the Fathers of the Church of Africa." His missionaries wrote dozens of catechisms in local languages and developed a three-stage catechumenate, which could last up to four years.

In Europe, however, catechesis was undergoing pressure from critics of its seemingly outmoded didactic methods.[54] Especially in Germany, advocates of the so-called Munich Method looked to modern psychology to reform Catholic education. They emphasized embodied and noncognitive approaches to learning rather than doctrinal instruction. The "kerygmatic" movement, however, helped reform rather than reject catechesis. The Austrian Jesuit Josef Jungmann (1889–1975) was a major voice in this movement. His groundbreaking work, *Die Frohbotschaft und unsere Glaubensverkündigung* (1936), pub-

52. Already in the early nineteenth century, Anglican missionary John Venn appealed to the early church to advocate for the recovery of lay catechists as an ecclesial status, intended to help spread the gospel where it was difficult to send ordained clergy. See Andrew Walls, *The Missionary Movement in Christian History: Studies in the Transmission of Faith* (Maryknoll, NY: Orbis, 1996), 164–65.

53. On the examples in this paragraph, see Paul Turner, *Hallelujah Highway: A History of the Catechumenate* (Chicago: Liturgy Training Publications, 2000).

54. The following paragraphs follow the summary in Brian Pedraza, *Catechesis for the New Evangelization: Vatican II, John Paul II, and the Unity of Revelation and Experience* (Washington, DC: Catholic University of America Press, 2020), chap. 2: "The History of Modern Catechetics." Pedraza in turn draws from Berard Marthaler, "The Modern Catechetical Movement in Roman Catholicism: Issues and Personalities," in *Sourcebook for Modern Catechetics*, ed. Michael Warren (Winona, MN: Saint Mary's Press, 1983), 275–89.

lished in English as *The Good News Yesterday and Today* in 1959, gained traction especially through the efforts of one of his students, Johannes Hofinger (1905–1984), who organized a series of global "Study Weeks" on catechesis in the 1950s and '60s.[55] Some among the following generation, however, such as Gabriel Moran (1935–2021), critiqued the kerygmatic movement of Jungmann and Hofinger, claiming that it remained still too intellectualist, merely replacing the older emphasis on propositional content with an emphasis on story and narrative. Catechists needed to connect doctrine with an account of how people actually experienced the transforming message of Christ.

Vatican II was a key moment for Roman Catholic catechesis. The 1963 *Constitution on the Sacred Liturgy* (*Sacrosanctum Concilium*) made a bold declaration for the recovery of the patristic catechumenate: "The catechumenate for adults, comprising several distinct steps, is to be restored and to be taken into use at the discretion of the local ordinary."[56] The Vatican bishops envisioned a new era of catechesis focused on the Christian's encounter with the Christ in the Scriptures and the liturgy. Several new proposals soon went into effect. The *General Catechetical Directory,* which gave recommendations for catechetical practice, was approved in 1971. The Rite of Christian Initiation of Adults (RCIA) was approved in the United States in 1974. John Paul II's 1979 apostolic exhortation *Catechesi Tradendae* presented a robust christological vision of catechesis and laid the groundwork for understanding catechesis as part of the "pedagogy of God."[57] Popes Benedict and Francis encouraged the ministry of catechesis, with the latter issuing a document called *Antiquum Ministerium* to make the lay catechist an official order in the church in 2021.[58]

By far the most important text to emerge was the *Catechism of the Catholic Church* in 1993, the first universally authoritative catechism to appear since the Council of Trent in 1570. While many Catholics in the early twentieth century

55. Pedraza, *Catechesis for the New Evangelization,* 102.

56. *Sacrosanctum Concilium* 64. Available online at www.vatican.va. For a good study of the developments leading up to the council, see Edward Yarnold, "'The Catechumenate for Adults Is to Be Restored': Patristic Adaptation in the Rite for the Christian Initiation of Adults," *Studies in Church History* 35 (1999): 478–97.

57. See John Paul II, *Catechesi Tradendae: On Catechesis in Our Time* (Manchester, NH: Sophia Institute, 2014). For an analysis, see Pedraza, *Catechesis for the New Evangelization,* 241–85.

58. See, for example, Joseph Cardinal Ratzinger, *Handing on the Faith in an Age of Disbelief* (San Francisco: Ignatius, 2006), and Pope Francis's *Evangelii Gaudium* ("Joy of the Gospel").

had opposed the use of catechisms, its publication was met with remarkable favor. It offered catechists and lay Christians a source of authoritative doctrine and a substantive guide for biblical, spiritual, moral, and social reflection. Over the thirty years since its publication, the catechism has opened new pathways for catechetical renewal in evangelization and mission.[59]

But catechesis has not been the exclusive domain of Roman Catholics in the twentieth century. A quiet but steady stream of Protestants and evangelical voices has advocated for the renewal of catechesis. Lutheran and Reformed traditions have continued to use their historic catechisms in teaching the faithful.[60] Even Baptists, whom many today associate with anticreedalism, have a rich legacy of catechisms, such as "Keach's Catechism," which was especially popular in the 1800s. Today, new efforts are under way to help Baptists recover catechesis as an integral part of their identity and mission.[61] Another less well-known example is a work by the Dutch Reformed theologian K. H. Miskotte called the *Biblical ABCs* published in 1941.[62] In a Barthian vein, Miskotte saw the work of catechesis as essential to Nazi resistance. He described his project as a spiritual grammar for enabling Christians to remain faithful to biblical truths against the false gospel of Hitler.

In Anglican and Episcopalian traditions, a short catechism linked with the Rite of Confirmation has been a part of most prayer books since the first Book of Common Prayer in 1549.[63] But as the confirmation rite came under suspi-

59. In addition to the works already cited, see also Joseph Cardinal Ratzinger, *Gospel, Catechesis, Catechism: Sidelights on the "Catechism of the Catholic Church"* (San Francisco: Ignatius, 1997); Petroc Willey and Scott Sollom, eds., *Speaking the Truth in Love: The Catechism and the New Evangelization* (Steubenville, OH: Emmaus, 2019).

60. See, for example, Timothy Wengert, *Martin Luther's Catechisms: Forming the Faith* (Minneapolis: Fortress, 2009).

61. See especially Curtis Freeman, *Pilgrim Letters: Instruction in the Basic Teaching of Christ* (Minneapolis: Fortress, 2021); and Freeman, *Pilgrim Journey: Instruction in the Mystery of the Gospel* (Minneapolis: Fortress, 2023).

62. Kornelis Heiko Miskotte, *Biblical ABCs: The Basics of Christian Resistance*, trans. Eleonora Hof and Collin Cornell (Lanham, MD: Lexington Books, 2022). Another catechetical text in this line of thought was Heinrich Vogel, *The Iron Ration of a Christian*, trans. W. A. Whitehouse (London: SCM, 1941).

63. In the United States today, the main prayer book for use in the Episcopal Church, the 1979 prayer book, contains a longer catechism called "An Outline of Faith." The 2019 prayer book, used in many Anglican Church in North America congregations, does not include a catechism, instead using a supplemental catechism called *To Be a Christian: An Anglican Catechism* (Wheaton: Crossway, 2020).

cion in many parts of the Anglican world in the twentieth century, it has often been neglected. Nevertheless, there have been several advocates of catechesis among high- and low-church Anglicans: Edward Pusey's *The Rule of Faith, As Maintained by the Fathers, and the Church of England* (1851) is a good example of Tractarian catechesis.[64] Others include W. C. E. Newbolt's *The Church Catechism* (1903) and Ashton Oldham's *The Catechism Today* (1929). More recently, the Episcopalian scholar John Westerhoff III (1933–2022) sought to recover patristic catechesis with his popular book *Will Our Children Have Faith?*, published in three editions (1976, 2000, and 2012) and translated into six languages.[65] Among evangelicals, few have been more devoted to the renewal of catechesis than J. I. Packer. A self-described "latter-day catechist," Packer saw the fractious divides in the Anglican-Episcopal Church as stemming from decades of catechetical amnesia. Packer showed evangelicals that catechesis was both biblical and traditional, especially among his beloved Puritans.[66] Packer also gave oversight for the writing of a new Anglican catechism, eventually published in 2020 as *To Be a Christian: An Anglican Catechism.*

One final notable mention is the late Presbyterian pastor Tim Keller. Keller helped produce the *New City Catechism,* published in 2014. Inspired by the great Reformation catechisms, this catechism comprises fifty-two questions and can be adapted for use with adults or children. While Keller acknowledged the important role of older catechisms, he thought that Christians today needed a new approach to catechesis that was suited for a post-Christian, secular age. While Reformation catechisms were designed to produce confessional identities (Catholic versus Protestant), Christians now need a form of catechesis that can counteract the secular narratives prevalent today.[67]

The history of catechesis is a multifaceted and vibrant one. While certain moments stand out, we find traces of catechesis wherever the Spirit has led

64. My thanks to Clinton Collister for this reference.

65. On Westerhoff's approach to catechesis, see Alex Fogleman, "Ecclesial Enculturation: John Westerhoff's Appeal to Catechesis in Contemporary Theological Education," *Journal of Anglican Studies,* 2023, https://tinyurl.com/52byk957.

66. See especially Packer and Parrett, *Grounded in the Gospel.* For Packer's significance to the recovery of Anglican evangelical catechesis, see Joel Scandrett, "'To Be a Christian': J. I. Packer and the Renewal of Evangelical Catechesis," *Crux* 52, no. 1 (2016): 4–12.

67. See especially Timothy Keller, *How to Reach the West Again: Six Essential Elements of a Missionary Encounter* (New York: Redeemer City to City, 2020).

Christians in mission and wherever the church has sought to form the faithful in the essentials of the faith. Much more could be said, but hopefully we've glimpsed something of the rich heritage of catechesis that belongs to us. This is the exciting story of God's salvation in history, and it is still going on today. What role will we have in it?

4

Catechesis and Worship

Sometime in the late fifth century, a violent earthquake shook the city of Vienne, France, days before the Feast of the Ascension (April 25). Many Christians feared the worst, perhaps thinking the end of the world had come. When it did not, it was seen as nothing less than a miracle, a dramatic divine intervention. In response, the bishop of Vienne, a man named Mamertus, introduced a new celebration and corresponding liturgical rites to commemorate this event. Rogation days, or Rogationtide, occurred on the three days before Ascension and was modeled on the three-day repentance of the city of Nineveh in the book of Jonah. Also corresponding with the annual springtime harvest, it became a time of repentance, gratitude, and prayers for the blessing of crops and agriculture. The whole community processed around the parish, "beating the bounds" to ward off demonic forces and pray for the flourishing of the land. One of the main Scripture passages preached on was Luke 11:5–13, the parable of the friend seeking bread at midnight.

By the eighth century, Rogationtide also became an annual time when clergy instructed the faithful in core aspects of catechesis, especially the Lord's Prayer.[1] The Venerable Bede in the 740s was one of the first preachers who taught on the Lord's Prayer during Rogationtide, and many others followed suit. In the tenth century, Aelfric of Eynsham and Rabanus Maurus published a series of sermons for clergy to use during this festival. These preachers drew further connections between the ritual of Rogationtide and the meaning of the Lord's Prayer, weaving together liturgy and catechesis. Given the associations of Rogationtide with agriculture, for example, Rogation preachers taught the

1. For Rogationtide as a time for teaching catechetical standards, see Nathan J. Ristuccia, *Christianization and Commonwealth in Early Medieval Europe: A Ritual Interpretation* (Oxford: Oxford University Press, 2018), 178–209.

Lord's Prayer in ways that accented the themes of repentance, community, and dependence on God. Several preachers connected the lectionary text of Luke 11:5–13 with the Lord's Prayer, which immediately precedes this passage in Luke 11:1–4. In Rogationtide sermons, clergy found a fitting season for re-catechizing the Christian faithful.

This example introduces an important concept for our account of catechesis: namely, the relationship between catechesis and worship, or liturgy. Worship is the aim of catechesis; it is the end to which catechesis is directed. In the next chapter, we will look at the relationship between catechesis and *mission*, the outward pull of evangelism and proclamation. There, we'll focus on the catechesis and conversion of adult converts to the faith. But I want to start by putting the end in view first: What is catechesis pointing to? Where is it headed? In this chapter, we'll first look at liturgical catechesis more generally, then at the specific contexts of children's and family catechesis and the catechesis of lifelong believers. While distinct, missional and liturgical catechesis aim at the same goal of building foundations for mature Christian discipleship.[2]

Liturgical Catechesis

Worship is at the heart of Christian existence. The church can be involved in many noble deeds in the world, but "worship is what distinguishes the church as the church."[3] The worshiping church is where we learn who God is, who we are, and what's really going on. The church doesn't exist just to proclaim the kingdom but to be a foretaste of the kingdom here and now. Liturgical *catechesis* is not worship. It is how we are taught *by* and *for* worship. We can think of it as a two-way dynamic movement in which (a) we enter more deeply into

2. In my own Anglican tradition, we call these two approaches catechesis "from the front porch" and catechesis "from the font"—that is, the baptismal font. The former is about preparing adults for entrance into the church from the "front porch" of the church; the latter is about building faith from infancy. This approach is outlined in a report from the Anglican Church in North America's Catechesis Task Force entitled "Toward an Anglican Catechumenate: Guiding Principles for the Catechesis Task Force, Anglican Church in North America," published in 2010. The use of "front porch" to describe catechesis originally comes from Tory Baucum, *Evangelical Hospitality: Catechetical Evangelism in the Early Church and Its Recovery for Today* (Lanham, MD: Scarecrow, 2008).

3. Simon Chan, *Liturgical Theology: The Church as Worshipping Community* (Downers Grove, IL: InterVarsity Press, 2005), 42.

the triune life with God and (b) our everyday lives are ordered by the rhythms and practices of worship.

First, though, what is liturgical worship? By liturgy, I mean a church's structured patterns of organization for worship. We refer to some churches as "liturgical" and others as "nonliturgical," but really all churches have set patterns and practices for worship. What is important is how these liturgies both express and shape our relationship with God and other people. By liturgy, I would include the standard rituals of Sunday morning worship, which include things like the call to worship, the public reading of Scripture, the sermon, prayers of the people, tithes and offerings, confession of sin, Eucharist, and dismissal. But we would also want to include the seasons of the Christian year, such as Advent, Epiphany, Lent, Easter, Pentecost, and Ordinary Time, as well as the celebration of certain holy days. Liturgies may also include regular patterns of daily prayer, as well as other major rituals that occur at specific moments in a person's life: baptism, confirmation, marriage, and so forth.

A proper theology of liturgical worship does not begin with *our* actions but with God's actions. Liturgy begins with the mutual self-giving love of Father, Son, and Holy Spirit. This love enters into human life through Christ's incarnation, which in turn generates a return to the Father in which we are caught up in the Spirit's sanctification through being incorporated into the Son.[4] Worship, in other words, is not telling us something about God's redemption. Worship enacts it. As the late Robert Webber used to say, "worship *does* God's story."[5] Worship is the actual lived experience of our ongoing redemption.[6]

Worship is what the church does when it is most fully alive. It is not just a means to an end but the end itself. As a result, worship is a powerful site for theological and spiritual formation. Liturgies direct our most basic desires, habits, and intuitions. More than just changing what we think, worship changes what we love. But this doesn't happen automatically. We all know Christians who regularly participate in Christian worship but who lead lives

4. Liturgical theologian David Fagerberg describes Christian liturgy, in a dense but theologically rich formula, as "the Trinity's perichoresis kenotically extended to invite our synergistic ascent into deification." David Fagerberg, *On Liturgical Asceticism* (Washington, DC: Catholic University of America Press, 2013), 9.

5. See, for example, Robert Webber, *Ancient-Future Worship: Proclaiming and Enacting God's Narrative* (Grand Rapids: Baker Books, 2008).

6. For this argument, see Khaled Anatolios, *Deification through the Cross: An Eastern Christian Theology of Salvation* (Grand Rapids: Eerdmans, 2020).

of abject moral turpitude. Many massive failures of the church happen right alongside frequent participation in liturgical worship.[7] We should never imagine our projects of spiritual formation as being untouched by the Fall.

At the same time, we can approach liturgical catechesis in better or worse ways. It is not just an exercise in the history or theory of ritual. We want to facilitate participation in the church's liturgy so that Christians can perceive all of reality anew—to have their eyes, ears, mouths, and hearts shaped by beholding images of Christ and the saints, by hearing the Word, by tasting the Eucharist.[8] Liturgical catechesis is about unlocking the spiritual senses and learning to see all reality anew.[9]

What, then, does liturgical catechesis entail? First, most basically, *liturgical catechesis involves a symbiotic, back-and-forth relationship between instruction and liturgy*, that is, a back-and-forth interchange between teaching about worship and the actual experience of worship. In worship, we *do* the liturgy. And this activity generates new questions. Why do we stand at this point? Why do we kneel here? Why does the reading of Scripture happen in this way? In liturgical catechesis, we allow these questions to surface, not simply to explain them away but to help others reenter worship the next time with a heightened awareness of what's at stake. Experience and instruction go hand in hand.

Second, *liturgical catechesis orders daily life in accordance with Sunday worship*. If worship exemplifies in the present age the fullness of divine-human communion that will one day characterize all of life, then liturgical catechesis brings that reality into effect. The rites of Christian worship have a "spilling over" effect. What we experience in worship affects the way we live day by day—what Tish Harrison Warren calls the "liturgy of the ordinary."[10] Take the practice of confession and the passing of the peace. Each Sunday, Christians get down on bended knee, admit their failures and need for healing, hear the

7. Willie Jennings, *The Christian Imagination: Theology and the Origins of Race* (New Haven: Yale University Press, 2010); Lauren Winner, *The Dangers of Christian Practice: On Wayward Gifts, Characteristic Damage, and Sin* (New Haven: Yale University Press, 2018). For a response to this critique, what he calls "the Godfather problem," see James K. A. Smith, *Awaiting the King: Reforming Public Theology* (Grand Rapids: Baker Academic, 2017), 165–208.

8. See here Timothy O'Malley, *Divine Blessing: Liturgical Formation in the RCIA* (Collegeville, MN: Liturgical Press, 2019).

9. We'll develop this idea in more detail in chapter 7, where we look at the role of Scripture and the sacraments in catechesis.

10. See Tish Harrison Warren, *Liturgy of the Ordinary: Sacred Practices in Ordinary Life* (Downers Grove, IL: InterVarsity Press, 2016).

word of forgiveness proclaimed over them, and then stand and exchange a greeting of peace with their fellow believers. By the weekly performance of this rite, our bodies and hearts are "learning" several abstract truths: that we are forgiven sinners, that Christ has broken down barriers of our own making, that we have peace with one another through Christ. And yet by Monday afternoon, how often are we holding a grudge against our spouse and refusing to give and receive forgiveness? Liturgical catechesis offers an opportunity to expand the logic of the liturgy into everyday life—to make explicit the implicit modes of living inherent in Christian liturgy.

Third, *liturgical catechesis fosters deeper engagement in worship*. This means that liturgical catechesis holds a place for the role of experience in Christian worship. For some, "experience" is taboo, signaling a touchy-feely faith disconnected from belief, a fuzzy spirituality without any substance. That's a legitimate concern in many corners of American evangelicalism. However, the proper response isn't rejecting experience but articulating experience theologically. We cannot avoid experience, but we can ground it in Scripture and the life-giving teaching of the church.

One practical point is worth noting here. It can be tempting for clergy to teach laypeople about the liturgy from *their* experience of gathered worship. That is, after all, what clergy know best. But that is not the experience of most people in the pews. Most laypeople don't think about whether the musicians are in place, whether the candles are lit, whether the readers remember what to read. They have different concerns: squirmy children, wandering attentions, sniffling neighbors. Helping Christians enter more deeply into worship through catechesis begins by taking their perspective and confronting the obstacles that they face in worship.

Like the focus on the Lord's Prayer in Rogationtide, we can approach liturgical catechesis in many ways. My friend Joe Gasbarre, when he was pastoring a church in Savannah, Georgia, developed a unique style of liturgical catechesis tied to the church calendar. During the season of Advent, he would teach his congregation the Lord's Prayer, which went along with the themes of hope and desire characteristic of that season. During Epiphany, when the church celebrates the light of Christ to the nations, Joe taught the creed to align with the theme of the announcement of the good news of the gospel. During Lent, the church went through the Ten Commandments, with a focus on repentance and confession. Finally, at Easter, he taught the meaning of the sacraments and worship, again drawing on the corresponding themes of joy and light incumbent on the season. Year after year, the rhythms of catechesis and the liturgical calendar seeped into the natural reflexes of the church's life together.

Another example of liturgical catechesis comes from Paul Gutacker, who directs a program called Brazos Fellows in Waco, Texas. Brazos Fellows is a residential program where young adults, usually in their twenties and thirties, take on a common rule of life for about nine months. For this season, they commit to a quasi-monastic discipline of daily prayer, weekly worship and rest, spiritual direction, common meals, and theological study. Twice a week they meet for several hours to discuss great books from the Christian tradition. But these studies are not framed by the usual academic rhythms of essays, tests, and grades. They are framed by prayer and a shared life together, which becomes a powerful context for the Spirit to transform lives and build lasting habits of holiness together. The goal of the program isn't to help young people get fancy jobs or get connected to important civic leaders in the community. The goal is to help these emerging adults develop true friendships and habits of prayer and study that will help them grow into mature Christian faith.[11]

These are two very different examples of liturgical catechesis. You might consider other approaches like this, or something completely different. The point is to ask how catechesis can come alongside and enhance the liturgies and practices already in place. What are the rhythms of your church's life that naturally accommodate this kind of catechesis? How is the liturgy of your church already doing the work of catechesis, and how could you accentuate those features to help people engage them more deeply?

Liturgical catechesis teaches what the liturgy means and how it constitutes a formative effect in our lives. It involves a dialogue between worship and teaching, and above all, it connects liturgy with life, showing what it means for all of creation to become a means of abiding with God.

Children's and Family Catechesis

Children have a more natural capacity for mystery, for sensing the sacred. Liturgy speaks the child's native language of imagination, symbol, and play.[12] In fact, many liturgical theologians have compared worship with children at play, since both worship and play gesture toward an experience of life unburdened from the constant demands of productivity and efficiency. Like the child at play, worship offers an "oasis of freedom, where for a moment we can let life flow freely."[13]

11. You can learn more about Brazos Fellows at www.brazosfellows.com.

12. See here Sofia Cavalletti, *The Religious Potential of the Child: Experiencing Scripture and Liturgy with Young Children* (Chicago: Liturgy Training Publications, 1992).

13. Joseph Cardinal Ratzinger, *The Spirit of the Liturgy*, trans. John Saward (San Francisco: Ignatius, 2000), 13.

We saw in the last chapter that the catechesis of families became especially pronounced in the Reformation and in the following centuries. From Luther and Calvin to Herbert and Baxter, Christian leaders encouraged parents to view their role as spiritual teachers and guides. They wanted to empower parents to see the catechizing of children as a central duty.

Luther's method of catechizing his children was simple and is easily adoptable today. First, he taught children to memorize the words of the catechism, especially the Apostles' Creed, the Lord's Prayer, and the Ten Commandments. Whatever catechism parents decided to use, Luther encouraged them to stick to a fixed form so that children would not be confused by switching to different wordings. Second, after memorizing it, children were taught the meaning of the different articles and asked to explain in their own words what each phrase meant. Third, they then studied Luther's *Large Catechism*, going deeper into each of the commands, petitions, and articles of faith. Catechists who saw particular weaknesses or temptations in their students could focus on certain areas more than others. Craftsmen and merchants might need to focus on the commandment "Do not steal," while children might need more time with "Honor your father and mother." The catechist needs discernment here.

Luther could also be quite demanding. While he generally resisted the idea that faith could be compelled by force, he was not opposed to using strict discipline with children unwilling to learn the catechism. He encouraged pastors to withhold the sacrament of communion from them and parents to threaten to kick them out of the house![14] To more mature Christians, he was no less strict. In his *Large Catechism*, he warned against the "shameful vice and secret infection of security and satiety." Older Christians should guard against the indolence of those who "regard the Catechism as a poor, mean teaching, which they can read through at one time, and then immediately know it, throw the book into a corner, and be ashamed . . . to read it again." For children or adults, the catechism should be a mainstay of daily, weekly examination.[15]

I also love the way the Puritan pastor Cotton Mather (1663–1728) writes about catechizing children and families. When children are old enough, the pastor invites them to church and examines them carefully concerning their "improvement in knowledge, conversion to God, resolutions for a life of piety, and inclinations to the remembering and renewing of their baptismal covenant." Those who provide satisfactory answers could submit their names for

14. Luther, preface to the *Small Catechism*, in *Martin Luther's Basic Theological Writings*, ed. Timothy Lull (Minneapolis: Fortress, 1989), 472–73.

15. Martin Luther, preface to the *Large Catechism*, in *The Annotated Luther*, vol. 2, *Word and Faith*, trans. Kirsi Stjerna (Minneapolis: Fortress, 2015), 279.

confirmation, which came with the full privileges of adult membership in the community. Those who did not pass such examinations would have "suitable admonitions bestowed upon them."[16]

While Mather was emphatic about the necessity of catechesis, he was more flexible about the method. Pastors could have children answer questions about the catechism on Sundays before the sermon, or they could meet with parishioners during the week or have parishioners visit their home. Other pastors, Mather writes, could catechize "the Pauline way," meaning that they visit each parishioner's home during the week. By visiting in the home, the pastor could assess not only the child's learning but also what he called the family's "everlasting interests." He could offer any supplemental instruction here and provide families with advice on how to apply the teachings of the catechism in their lives. Mather saw this practice in alignment with the patristic models of Cyprian, Chrysostom, Augustine, and Prosper of Aquitaine. These great pastors of old, for Mather, modeled an understanding of ministry in which the teaching of the gospel was both a public and a private duty.[17]

Recent sociological research confirms the vital role that parents play in the transmission of faith to their children. More than pastors or youth ministers, it is parents living out their faith and talking openly with their children about it who have the most impact on children's faith formation.[18] But too often, children's catechesis is marked by a strange paradox. On the one hand, we think catechesis is for the "professionals"—ordained pastors, Sunday school teachers, youth ministers—while parents remain on the sidelines, disempowered and disengaged. But on the other hand, parents can often feel like the entire weight of their child's eternal future depends on them. Overwhelmed by the pressure to "train up a child in the way he should go" (Prov. 22:6), parents are riddled with anxiety and confusion about how to disciple their children.

Liturgical worship charts a pathway forward. This approach frames family discipleship as a process of helping children encounter God on their own through the rhythms and practices of the liturgy. It is responsive to the ev-

16. Cotton Mather, *Ratio Disciplinae Fratrum Nov-Anglorum: A Faithful Account of the Discipline Professed and Practiced; in the Churches of New-England with Interspersed and Instructive Reflections on the Discipline of the Primitive Churches* (Boston, 1726), 103, 104.

17. Mather, *Ratio Disciplinae*, 105–6.

18. For a good study, see Christian Smith and Amy Adamczyk, *Handing Down the Faith: How Parents Pass Their Religion on to the Next Generation* (Oxford: Oxford University Press, 2021).

eryday situations that arise around the dinner table and at school, and it is intentionally proactive in facilitating encounters for children to think, pray, and live out the faith.[19] Christ speaking through the Holy Spirit is the true catechist, not the parent. Parents and pastors are active and engaged; they're off the sidelines and in the game. But their labors are rooted not in their own strength but in the trust that God is at work in children's lives to seek after them and nurture them into a deeper relationship with their true Father. Liturgical catechesis is the Lord's work.

Catechesis doesn't just happen on Sundays. It's about how the family lives the rhythms of the church each day. The home, as Saint John Chrysostom put it, is a "little church," a space where Sunday worship sets the rhythms for the habits of the household.[20] What might this look like? It might look like memorizing Scripture or discussing catechism questions together. It might include family devotions, guided practices of prayer and spiritual conversations, or family service projects.[21] At mealtimes, the family can do what Sarah Cowan Johnson calls a "God hunt"—that is, when members of the family reflect on their day and look where God was at work, perhaps in ways they didn't realize.[22] There are many good resources to help parents celebrate the seasons of the church year.[23] One church I know developed a three-year cycle of daily prayers that families can pray together, which incorporates a question from

19. For an excellent resource with many practical examples, see Sarah Cowan Johnson, *Teach Your Children Well: A Step-by-Step Guide to Family Discipleship* (Downers Grove, IL: InterVarsity Press, 2022).

20. For a good practical book on how liturgical habits can shape everyday family life, especially with young children, see Justin Whitmel Earley, *Habits of the Household: Practicing the Story of God in Everyday Family Rhythms* (Grand Rapids: Zondervan, 2021). For the home as a "little church," see John Chrysostom, "Homily 20 on the Ephesians," in *St. John Chrysostom: On Marriage and Family Life*, trans. Catherine Roth (Crestwood, NY: St. Vladimir's Seminary Press, 1986), 57.

21. For two excellent approaches to family catechesis focused on spiritual practices, see Johnson, *Teach Your Children Well*, and Jared Patrick Boyd, *Imaginative Prayer: A Yearlong Guide for Your Children's Spiritual Formation* (Downers Grove, IL: InterVarsity Press, 2017).

22. Johnson, *Teach Your Children Well.*

23. Some of my personal favorites include the resources from Allysa Case, director of Little Way Chapel (www.littlewaychapel.com), and Danielle Hitchen of Catechesis Books (www.catechesisbooks.com). See especially the latter's *Sacred Seasons: A Family Guide to Center Your Year around Jesus* (Eugene, OR: Harvest House, 2023).

the church's catechism each day. This is a wonderful way to bring together the liturgy of daily prayer and regular study of the faith.

In family catechesis, we want the rhythms and patterns of the home to echo the liturgies of the church. James K. A. Smith says that every household has an unspoken "vibe," the "constant background noise generated by our routines and rhythms."[24] What are the routines and rhythms of our homes? Are they a frenzy of hurry and busyness in which we're constantly rushing from one thing to the next? Or is there a sense of connection, delight, and attention? What is the vibe and hum of your family's "little church"?

To be clear: I'm not talking about a façade of peace and quiet. My wife and I have four boys at home, ages ten and under, and things at the Fogleman house are anything but quiet! We often feel very much out of sync with the church's rhythms and routines. And it seems like we're constantly fighting the temptation to compare ourselves with those picture-perfect families we see on social media—the kind with nonfighting children who wear matching pastels and effortless smiles while adorning a spotless white couch. That's not what family catechesis is about. It's not one more thing for already tired and worn-down parents. It's about inviting our children to live in the world as God's creatures. It's about listening for the Holy Spirit at work in our children's lives.

In Deuteronomy 6, we see a beautiful picture of God's heart for family catechesis. About the commandments of the law, God tells Moses: "You shall teach them diligently to your children, and shall talk of them when you sit in your house, and when you walk by the way, and when you lie down, and when you rise" (Deut. 6:7). Liturgical catechesis happens at home, around the table, in the car, in the yard, on the way to school, and many other places. It happens through questions and conversations, through silence and prayer. It happens in visits with your lonely neighbor, at the checkout line at the grocery store. It happens in the slow passing of seasons. It happens amid conflict and healing, in slow times and hard times. Liturgical catechesis is, simply, life as a family in the kingdom of God. A great responsibility, it is also an extraordinary gift.

A Four-Stage Model of Children's Catechesis

Catechesis for children is not dumbed down, but it is age appropriate. It begins from the church's liturgy and adapts these rhythms to a tempo and cadence suitable to the child's stage of development. There are many different theories out there about childhood development, but one model I've found

24. James K. A. Smith, *You Are What You Love* (Grand Rapids: Brazos, 2016), 127.

helpful is the four-stage model developed by John Westerhoff in his book *Will Our Children Have Faith?*[25] The stages are: experience, affiliation, searching, and ownership.

1. *Experience.* In preschool and early childhood (roughly ages zero to six), faith is often encountered through experience. In this stage, children encounter the faith affectively, through their intuitions, emotions, and imaginations. Catechesis for this stage will especially highlight the deep love of God for children, and parents often become the primary point of reference for what "love" is. Programs like Catechesis of the Good Shepherd are especially good at understanding this. The Montessori style of learning behind Sofia Cavalletti's approach to catechesis is focused on providing tactile, embodied forms of learning that connect children's experience of the world with the worship of God in the liturgy. In this stage, parents can begin learning and memorizing the words of the Lord's Prayer or the Apostles' Creed together. Parents can experiment with imaginative prayer, where they ask their kids to imagine having a conversation with Jesus, inviting them to listen to what Jesus might be saying to them. Experience, rituals, habits, and practices that help children embody the love of God are especially helpful for this stage.
2. *Affiliation.* For older children and adolescents (roughly ages seven to eleven), community and friendships begin to play a much larger role in faith formation. During this stage, children learn more through belonging to the church community. Their identity is formed in relationships in the context of the believing community. In many societies, this is the age in which boys and girls undergo some kind of rite of initiation to enter adulthood, and it is no coincidence that many church traditions baptized or confirmed children during this period. With the loss of such cultural rituals, is it surprising that many young people never "grow up" into the faith? In this stage, we can foster friendships for our kids with others in the church, or explore family camps and other occasions for kids to learn to follow Christ from other believers. This is also a great stage for building memory. Kids in this stage can easily memorize the staples of the catechism, as well as other Scripture verses, songs, and poems. This is also a great time to introduce kids to the stories of Christian saints and other "heroes of the faith." We can help our kids see that belonging to God's family means more than just

25. John Westerhoff III, *Will Our Children Have Faith?* 3rd ed. (New York: Morehouse, 2012).

being a part of our local church. We belong to our brothers and sisters in Christ throughout time and history.

3. *Searching.* In the searching stage, preteens and teens (ages twelve to eighteen) test and examine the faith in more depth. They wrestle with the difficult challenges of faith and life, and question whether their faith is up to the task. This can be a scary phase for parents, but it is necessary for moving to the final stage of owned faith. Without it, children remain dependent on their parents' faith; it is borrowed faith, and it won't hold up to the difficult questions they will face. In this stage, our children have a much greater capacity for wrestling with challenging aspects of the faith, engaging deep theological questions, and confronting hypocrisy and sin in the church. At the same time, they also have a deeper capacity for growing in prayer and works of service. Connecting teens to other adults in the church is especially helpful, as is offering opportunities to serve the poor and suffering.
4. *Owned.* In the owned stage (eighteen to midtwenties—or longer!), faith becomes our own, as it were, no longer something borrowed from our parents. Faith at the owned stage is a powerful agent of identification and authority. It guides and shapes their lives in a deeply rooted and foundational way. This is not so much a stage of family catechesis, as children will (hopefully) be out of the house. But it can be a time of continued struggle as adult children seek and wander from the faith beyond their parents' direct oversight. If we as parents have been helping our children follow the Lord for themselves, facilitating encounter rather than mediating it for them, when we are no longer around, our absence will not mean the absence of God.

During each of these stages, catechesis will look different, but the point is that parents and catechists can adapt the foundational elements of catechesis—doctrine, prayer, and ethics—in ways appropriate for each stage. Some children are more cerebral and gravitate toward learning the faith by study and thinking and questioning. Others are more experiential and gravitate to God through prayer and contemplation. The more action-oriented will lean toward experiencing God through service and mission. Whatever the precise shape it takes at different stages, catechetical formation is a process that takes time.

Lifelong Catechesis

The Scriptures encourage us to be childlike but not childish. We can't enter the kingdom of heaven unless we "become like children" (Matt. 18:3). But at the same time, we're to put away "childish ways" and not be "children in [our] thinking" (1 Cor. 13:11; 14:20).

Catechesis helps us grow up by growing childlike. It is sheer hubris to think we can outgrow the catechism or to imagine we are too mature for the childish doctrines of the creed, prayer, and commandments. Recall what Luther said about people who "regard the catechism as a simple, trifling thing, which they can absorb and master at one reading and then toss the book into a corner as if they are ashamed to read it again." But he wanted ever to remain a "child and pupil of the catechism."

> But this I say for myself: I am also a doctor and a preacher, just as learned and experienced as all of them who are so high and mighty. Nevertheless, each morning, and whenever else I have time, I do as a child who is being taught the catechism and I read and recite word for word the Lord's Prayer, the Ten Commandments, the Creed, the Psalms, etc. I must still read and study the catechism daily, and yet I cannot master it as I wish, but must remain a child and pupil of the catechism—and I also do so gladly.[26]

Catechesis is a lifelong endeavor. The Letter to the Hebrews reminds us that we should not go back and rebuild the foundations of the faith (Heb. 6:1). But that does not mean that we ever "graduate" from catechesis.

Catechesis is a form of Christian learning applicable to all ages and stages of the Christian life because it understands Christian formation in a way that is patterned on the life of Christ: We ascend upward to God by descending with Christ to the cross (Phil. 2:5–11). The way up is down, not linear but spiral. Catechesis draws Christians into deeper communion with God not by moving *beyond* the basic elements of doctrine, prayer, and moral formation but by entering them more deeply. We can recall that many of the greatest works of theology—from Origen's *On First Principles* to Calvin's *Institutes*—are often little more than deep reflections on the church's basic rule of faith. As we grow in the faith, we return to the start, seeing it anew as if for the first time. Like Luther, we run from pride and seek to remain children of the catechism.

Encouraging catechesis for the whole church, not just children, has many benefits. George Herbert lists four reasons why all members of a parish should participate in catechesis. First, doing so recognizes the "authority of the work," meaning that the presence of everyone at catechesis signifies the high esteem that the community places on catechesis. When the whole church shows up for

26. Martin Luther, preface to *The Large Catechism*, 290–91.

catechesis, it signals that something important is happening. Second, all should attend so that parents and caretakers can oversee the catechesis of their children during the week. With parents present at catechesis, they will be able to provide a bridge between the catechesis at church on Sundays and the catechesis at home the remaining days of the week. Third, it gives an opportunity for adults in the congregation who are not well grounded in the faith to learn the catechism in a way that does not publicly embarrass them. As Herbert puts it: that "by an honorable way [they may] take occasion to be better instructed." Finally, having everyone present at catechesis enables all the faithful to "renew their vows" and "enlarge their meditations." Like recollecting one's wedding vows, renewing our baptismal vows is not a simple reminder of a historical event but a formative practice that enables us to grow deeper in our love for Christ—to "enlarge our meditations" on God's goodness and faithfulness over the years.

Lifelong catechesis, then, is not mere repetition. It involves an ongoing education and spiritual formation tethered to the fundamentals of the faith as presented in ways suitable to the capacities of the hearer. The core elements of the catechism contain an infinite surplus of meaning in simple words and phrases. They warrant a lifetime of learning.

What might this look like in our contexts today? In some cases, it may involve offering guided instruction on the catechism for various levels of learning. Like Luther, we might begin by memorizing a small catechism and then proceed to studying a larger one. It need not, though, involve lessons strictly on the catechism. It may look like a Bible study or small-group gathering to read Scripture, read a great book, or discuss a movie or piece of art. My friend Jonathan is a pastor at a large suburban church in Texas. Over the last several years he has gathered a group of men and women in the church who have gone through a course on the catechism and developed a curriculum that reads through many of the "great books" of Christian history. Each semester, they will read three to four books, from early Christian theologians like Justin Martyr and Tertullian to recent spiritual masters like G. K. Chesterton and C. S. Lewis. But the key is: Jonathan organizes the overall theme based on the core categories of the catechism. The catechetical standards of the creed, the Lord's Prayer, and the Ten Commandments serve as a framework for understanding further stages of the Christian life.

Other churches are starting to develop rigorous programs for lay theological education. For most people, there is nowhere to go between Sunday school and seminary. But Christians are still hungry for rich theological education and spiritual formation. They often do not need the kind of professional education of those training for ministry. They need more opportunities for learning the Bible, Christian doctrine, the spiritual life, and Christian ethics. Candler Seminary in Atlanta began a program called the "Foundry," which is designed to offer graduate-level theological education but primarily for laypeople. They offer an array of courses on the Bible and theology, but they are designed for everyday working people seeking to grow deeper in their faith. In our time, when many seminaries are struggling to maintain financial stability, what new opportunities might emerge for churches and seminaries to work together to create opportunities for ongoing, lifelong catechesis?[27]

Lifelong catechesis is not necessarily didactic in character. What would it look like for your church to pray through the catechism, or to develop spiritual exercises like *lectio divina* or those of Ignatius of Loyola that are organized around the core topics of the catechism? What might it look like for catechesis to run in step with spiritual direction and prayer?

The big question for lifelong catechesis is how our churches can become catechetical cultures. What does mature Christian discipleship look like, and how can we cultivate habits to foster this kind of formation?

Liturgical catechesis is a way of coordinating our efforts of education and formation with regular participation in liturgical worship to guide Christians in a lifetime of seeking and savoring the Lord, enjoying God and worshiping him forever.

What Does Mature Christian Discipleship Look Like?

The prophet Jeremiah envisioned a future day when learning would come to an end. With God's law written on our hearts and our sins forgiven, we won't need to teach each other. I won't need to say to you, "Know the Lord," because you and everyone else, from the greatest to the least, will know God directly (Jer. 31:33–34). How does this "end" of teaching help shape our approach to catechesis today? I've been using the phrase "mature Christian discipleship" as shorthand for the goal of catechesis. But how do we know if we're on track? What does the well-catechized soul look like? How do we recognize discipleship built on the solid foundation of Christ?

Paul's letter to the Ephesians provides one of the best pictures of mature Christian discipleship. He writes that the apostles, prophets, and teachers have been given "to equip the saints for the work of ministry, for building up the body of Christ, until we all attain to the unity of the faith and of the knowledge

27. I learned about this ministry from Ted Smith's provocative and challenging book *The End of Theological Education* (Grand Rapids: Eerdmans, 2023).

of the Son of God" (Eph. 4:11–13). This is biblical maturity: "the measure of the stature of the fullness of Christ." This is where we're no longer like children tossed in the wind, chasing after flashy new ideas. This is where we won't be taken in by crafty schemes and cunning tricks. "Rather, speaking the truth in love, we are to grow up in every way into him who is the head, into Christ, from whom the whole body, joined and held together by every joint with which it is equipped, when each part is working properly, makes the body grow so that it builds itself up in love" (Eph. 4:15–16).

This passage contains several important insights about spiritual maturity. First, it is clear that doctrine matters for spiritual health and Christian flourishing. Poor doctrine stunts our growth. Without sound doctrine, we become anemic, susceptible to whatever clever and crafty ideas happen to be floating around. But the purpose of sound doctrine is not for the sake of having more knowledge that puffs us up (1 Cor. 8:1). Rather it is knowledge *for* the sake of love—"speaking the truth in love." Many have followed Saint Augustine in making a distinction between knowledge and wisdom—*scientia* and *sapientia*—to describe the telos of theological doctrine.[28] If *scientia*, or knowledge, is about acquiring new ideas about things, *sapientia*, or wisdom, is knowledge that entails love of God and neighbor. It is knowledge as love and holiness.

Second, Christian maturity is ecclesial. Catechesis is not just about my individual growth in holiness but is also about the fullness of the body of Christ. Paul claims that Christ has become "our peace," breaking down the dividing wall between Jews and gentiles so that "he might create in himself one new man in place of the two" (Eph. 2:14–18). Christian maturity pertains to the whole body of Christ. It's a picture where enemies are reconciled, where wounds are healed. The Christian vision is one that Paul calls a "new humanity" formed into one body, the body of Christ.

Third, Christian maturity is cosmological. As Paul puts it at the beginning of Ephesians, God has set forth a plan in Christ "to unite all things in him, things in heaven and things on earth" (Eph. 1:9–10). The scope of salvation is as wide as heaven and earth. Christ comes not simply to change our hearts but to bring about a "new heaven and a new earth" (Rev. 21:1)

Finally, and most importantly, this view of Christian maturity has in view Christlikeness, growing into the full stature of Christ. We do not have in view some vague, general notion of maturity. We have a very specific one—Christ.

28. This distinction comes from Augustine's *On the Trinity* 15.21. For a recent account of this idea, see Kevin J. Vanhoozer, *The Drama of Doctrine: A Canonical Linguistic Approach to Doctrine* (Louisville: Westminster John Knox, 2005), 13.

Christ, the image of God, is the perfect picture of what human life is supposed to look like: perfect in power, love, humility, justice, and mercy. Christ is the telos of human life. And this is a lifelong task, a never-ending journey from glory to glory. This is why Gregory of Nyssa claimed that we are never wholly satisfied with seeing the face of God, for to see God is to desire him more and more. To have our thirst quenched on the Truth is to thirst for it more deeply.

Mature Christian discipleship is a lifelong venture in the company of Christ followers. Conversion is not the end but the beginning—a "long obedience in the same direction," as Eugene Peterson well put it.[29] As we grow up in Christ, we become the kind of people who will, in the fullness of time, see God face-to-face, and teaching and learning will fall away. We do not know what will be then, but we know that we will be like Christ, for we will see him as he is (1 John 3:2). This is what it means to grow up in Christ.

In worship we taste and see that the Lord is good. We practice for the kingdom; we learn to inhabit the land of the living. Worship forms us into the kinds of people who know and love God. So this is the most immediate aim of catechesis: becoming acquainted with the ways of God in the school of prayer.

But if worship is the end, and so takes a certain priority in vision for catechesis, we also want to position catechesis in relation to mission—the other pole of the church's life. That's the task of the next chapter.

29. Eugene Peterson, *A Long Obedience in the Same Direction: Discipleship in an Instant Society* (Downers Grove, IL: InterVarsity Press, 2000).

5

Catechesis and Mission

In the seventh century, a Persian Christian named Alopen became the first recorded missionary to arrive in China, reaching the Tang empire's capital city of Xian around the year 635. The famous Xian monument, composed in 781 and discovered in 1624, recounts Alopen's difficult journey along the Silk Road and his warm reception. He impressed the learned emperor, Taizong (629–649), who soon began building Christian churches and cataloguing sacred texts. The monument also records, fascinatingly for us, the process of initiation. It reads: "By the rule of admission, it is the custom to apply the water of baptism; to wash away all superficial show and to cleanse and purify the neophytes," and then goes on to describe the almost monastic quality of the life that new Christians are to lead: they hold the cross as a seal signifying the unity and universality of the faith; they fast, pray, and cut their hair a certain way; they commit to sharing a common bank account and agree that no one will hold slaves. The Xian monument also draws out the connections between sacred teaching and holy exemplars. Without holy examples, there is no one to expound sacred teaching, but without doctrine, there is nothing to enlighten humankind. "But with holy men and right principles, united as the two parts of a signet, the world becomes civilized and enlightened."[1]

Where there is mission, there is catechesis. As the first Christians brought the gospel to the "ends of the earth," the catechumenate emerged to meet an important need: to make the strange message of Jesus intelligible to those with no background in the Jewish Scriptures or way of life. The early church maintained a deep commitment to evangelism, but they did not dilute the startling

1. See Glen Thompson, *Jingjiao: The Earliest Christian Church in China* (Grand Rapids: Eerdmans, 2024).

message of the gospel to make it fit neatly in the paradigms of the neighboring cultural worldviews. Catechesis emerged to bridge the gap between the world and the church.

The need for catechesis in mission began at least by the second century. Irenaeus of Lyons thought that Paul's labors in catechizing the gentiles were the reason why he "labored more than the rest" of the disciples" (see 1 Cor. 15:10). Philip, for example, could baptize the Ethiopian eunuch shortly after explaining the meaning of Isaiah to him (Acts 8:26–40), but this was because he was already well versed in the Jewish Scriptures and moral life. Irenaeus says that Paul needed to first "catechize" the gentiles on certain fundamental issues: the need to put away idols and worship the one God who created heaven and earth through his Son, the Word, who was made man for our sake, died, rose, and will come again.[2] These are in essence the core features of the rule of faith, the main curriculum of Irenaeus's catechesis.

Our situation today will sometimes be like Philip's, but more often like Paul's. To introduce new people to the faith, we'll need to "labor more than the rest" by patiently taking the time to introduce new Christians to the building blocks of catechesis. And to do this well, we first need a clear grasp of conversion and the church. What is the church and how does becoming part of it shape the way we approach catechesis?

Catechesis, Conversion, and the Church

The church is God's family, the body and bride of Christ, and the temple of the Holy Spirit. It is a holy fellowship bound in Christ by the Holy Spirit through waters of baptism and the life-giving body and blood of Jesus. The church has its own culture, though it's not a culture of this world (John 17:16).[3] The church is a counter city that can rightly be accused of turning "the world upside down" (Acts 17:6), but it's not one among other kinds of cities. The lordship of Christ may be a threat to the Caesars of the world, but that's not because Jesus wants Caesar's throne.[4]

The Letter of First Peter offers a robust ecclesiology founded on Christ as the rejected cornerstone: "As you come to him, a living stone rejected by men

2. Irenaeus, *Against Heresies* 4.23.2–4.24.1 (ANF 1:495, translation altered).

3. For the idea of the church having its own "culture," see Robert Louis Wilken, "The Church as Culture," *First Things* 142 (April 2004): 31.

4. This phrasing draws from C. Kavin Rowe, *World Upside Down: Reading Acts in the Graeco-Roman Age* (New York: Oxford University Press, 2009), 140.

but in the sight of God chosen and precious, you yourselves like living stones are being built up as a spiritual house, to be a holy priesthood, to offer spiritual sacrifices acceptable to God through Jesus Christ" (1 Pet. 2:4–5). First Peter quotes Isaiah 28:16,

> "Behold, I am laying in Zion a stone,
> a cornerstone chosen and precious,"

to emphasize both the centrality and alterity of Christ. If Christ is the stone the builders rejected, how much more will his followers be rejected? As a result, Peter encourages Christians to think of themselves as a "chosen race," a "royal priesthood," and a "holy nation." They are God's people, and their identity as such calls them as "sojourners and exiles to abstain from the passions of the flesh, which wage war against your soul" (1 Pet. 2:9–11).

A second-century text known as the Letter to Diognetus develops this ecclesiology further. Christianity is a "third way" among the Jews and the Greeks, not distinguished by "country, speech, or customs" but by Christians' divinely inspired teachings and morals. Christians "reside in their respective countries, but only as aliens. They take part in everything as citizens and put up with everything as foreigners. Every foreign land is their home, and every home a foreign land." They stand out, but not in the usual ways that cultures are distinguished from one another. Christians obey public laws yet rise above them, especially in terms of their sexual codes and care for the poor. "They share everything except their wives," the letter declares. When they suffer abuse, Christians respond with patience, mercy, and love.[5]

This view of the church warrants a corresponding account of conversion. We shouldn't think of conversion to Christianity in the ancient world as, say, like switching from the Baptists to the Methodists today. By and large, the ancients had two kinds of conversion: the religious and the philosophical. If you converted to a religious cult like the Cult of Isis or Mithras, this wasn't so much a radical transformation of being. You would adopt new rituals, sacrifices, or prayers to help you acquire whatever benefits these gods offered. Philosophical conversion, by contrast, was more involved. If you became a student of Stoic or Epicurean philosophy, you would learn and discuss their teachings about cosmology, logic, epistemology, and ethics. In some cases, you would give up family ties and other kinship networks. Epicureans, in particular, were one of the more socially despised philosophies in the ancient world, derided as "atheists"

5. Letter to Diognetus 5 (ACW 6:138–39, translation altered).

because they rejected the view that the gods were actively involved in the affairs of this world. Because of the high demands for joining, one scholar calls conversion into Epicureanism a "resocialization into an alternative community."[6]

Conversion to Christianity involved elements of both the religious and the philosophical. On the one hand, Christian conversion involved learning new rites and religious rituals: prayers, exorcisms, and the rites of baptism and the Eucharist, for example. But on the other hand, it involved a robust doctrinal, ethical, and social formation. This was because, as David Bentley Hart puts it, baptism was understood as nothing less than "a total transformation of the person who submitted to it."[7] It entailed the renunciation of an entire spiritual and social world and the embrace of an all-encompassing allegiance to Christ. We see this view of conversion already in the writings of the New Testament, where becoming Christian involves both physical trials and persecutions and also a dramatic transferal from "the domain of darkness" to the "kingdom of his beloved Son" (Col. 1:13). First Peter and Hebrews encourage their first audiences to endure persecution as an expression of Christian discipleship. And Saint Paul taught the Philippians to "count everything as loss because of the surpassing worth of knowing Christ Jesus my Lord" (Phil. 3:8).

The catechumenate emerged to facilitate this dramatic transferal. Because the church was not just another philosophy or religious cult, it required a formidable process to acclimate new believers to its distinctive beliefs and ethos. As Gerald Sittser has put it, "Christian belief was so new . . . that it required Christians to develop a process of formation in the Third Way to move new believers from conversion to discipleship, from outsider to insider, from observer to full-fledged member."[8] Christian catechesis arose in tandem with the early church's unique beliefs about Jesus, the nature of the church, and what it meant to cross over from the world to the church.

Conversion and Transformation

As heirs of the eighteenth- and nineteenth-century Great Awakenings, we don't often think of conversion this way. We more often view conversion as

6. Wayne Meeks, *The Origins of Christian Morality: The First Two Centuries* (New Haven: Yale University Press, 1993), 26.

7. David Bentley Hart, *Atheist Delusions: The Christian Revolution and Its Fashionable Enemies* (New Haven: Yale University Press, 2009), 111.

8. Gerald Sittser, *Resilient Faith: How the Early Christian "Third Way" Changed the World* (Grand Rapids: Brazos, 2019), 17.

a onetime experience rather than a process of transformation.[9] I will refer to these as punctiliar conversions and transforming conversions, respectively.

We can see a shift toward punctiliar conversions in the more practical bent of Puritan theology. Puritans emphasized a "doctrine of godliness," or "living unto God," and taught "doctrine of a godly life" focused on faith and obedience.[10] While at the height of Puritanism we see a balance of the theological and practical, as questions about salvation and conversion became more pressing, especially after the Calvinist-Arminianism debates about election, catechisms began to shift toward fostering punctiliar conversions.

We can see this in one of the most popular catechisms of this time, John Cotton's *Milk for Babes*. The catechism begins with a series of questions that locate the encounter with God in the relationship of sin and debt. The first question, "What hath God done for you?" is soon followed by questions about the nature of sin and the Ten Commandments, concluding this section with the question, "Whether have you kept all these Commandments?" and the supplied answer: "No, I and all men are sinners." The catechumen is then asked:

> Q: What are the ways of sin?
> A: Death and damnation.
> Q: How look you then to be saved?
> A: Only by Jesus Christ.

Next come ten questions on the saving power of Christ, and how the law and the "ministry of the gospel" bring sinners to salvation. There is only one question on prayer, and no references to the Lord's Prayer. Questions about the church and the resurrection are included, but not as they relate to the creed. They appear as they relate to the order of salvation.

While the emphasis on punctiliar conversion highlights the personal and dramatic character of God's action in our lives, it can also shift the focus of cat-

9. The theologian Gordon Smith has made a strong plea for evangelicals to recover a robust understanding of conversion as lifelong transformation. See Gordon T. Smith, *Transforming Conversion: Rethinking the Language and Contours of Christian Initiation* (Grand Rapids: Baker Academic, 2010).

10. E. Brooks Holifield, *Theology in America: Christian Thought from the Age of the Puritans to the Civil War* (New Haven: Yale University Press, 2003), 62. For this reason, as historian Agnes Howard describes it: "The work of redemption lay at the heart of New England catechisms." Agnes Rose Howard, "'The Blessed Echoes of Truth': Catechisms and Confirmation in Puritan New England" (PhD diss., University of Virginia, 1999), 190.

echesis away from forming deep foundations and toward procuring a certain experience of conversion. Evangelical theologian Gordon Smith lists twelve negative effects of the revivalist view of conversion:[11]

1. a confusion between salvation and conversion (to be saved is to be converted)
2. a heavy emphasis on human volition (and an emphasis on decisions)
3. thinking of conversion as only a onetime event
4. a tendency toward anti-intellectualism (if I'm converted, what does the life of the mind matter?)
5. understanding conversion in transactional terms
6. an ambivalence toward the sacraments (again, what's the point if you're already converted?)
7. a conversion that does not cost anything
8. the reduction of evangelism to "technique"
9. a failure to grapple with "second-generation" Christians (how to pass on the faith)
10. no meaningful connection between conversion, baptism, and the Holy Spirit
11. a reduction of mission to obtaining conversions
12. a focus on the afterlife with minimal reference to this world

This list resonates with my own experience of contemporary Christianity, but I don't think we need to reject the evangelical emphasis on authentic conversion to develop a robust vision of transforming conversion. I want instead to situate conversion within the larger scope of Christian theology and practice we've been tracing. Again, Smith offers a helpful set of parameters. Transforming conversion, he writes, is:

1. *Anthropological.* Conversion must account for the range and depth of "the human predicament." Understandings of conversion depend on what we're being converted *from* and what we're being converted *to*. Conversion thus needs to account for the "intellectual, affective, penitential, and volitional dimension" of human being, the bodily as well as spiritual dimensions, the corporate as well as individual.
2. *Personal.* Conversion is an experience of *Jesus*. It's not about an encounter with ideas, principles, or laws. Conversion is the result of an experience with a person.
3. *Cosmological.* We need a way of talking about conversion that stresses its

11. Smith, *Transforming Conversion*, 3–16.

cosmological dimensions. Conversion is about more than what happens "in our hearts." It has to do with God, life, the universe, and everything else. Smith wants to think about this in kingdom language: "Our understanding of conversion needs to be located in the light of the in-breaking of the reign of Christ."

4. *Corporate.* Conversion needs to take on a distinctly corporate character. It's personal but not individualistic. Conversion is conversion into *this* way of life, a way of life that actually exists in real space and time, a way of life that exists in a lived community of those who make up the church.
5. *Transformational.* Conversion needs to be logically related to sanctification, or Christian maturity. We need to follow the Bible's way of talking about conversion, which sees conversions as the "beginning of a life in which one ultimately experiences the sanctifying and transforming grace of God." Conversion must be organically connected with spiritual maturity. "It is a good beginning."[12]

To summarize: we need a theology of conversion that has a robust conception of sin and salvation, is rooted in Christ, has cosmic implications, is located in the church, and results in holiness and sanctification. Accounting for conversion within these parameters will help guide a rich practice of catechesis.

Missional Catechesis

With this outline of ecclesiology and conversion in mind, we can now focus more directly on missional catechesis. Missional catechesis mainly has in view teenagers, young adults, and older adults who have either not grown up in Christian settings or whose church affiliation played only a marginal role in their lives. Often, missional catechesis serves as a preparation for baptism, though it may also look forward to confirmation or an equivalent rite of formal church membership. However your tradition understands the relationship between baptism, catechesis, and membership, which is not an insignificant question,[13] the key issue is that missional catechesis presents a Christian framework in a context where there are few, if any, shared assumptions about what orthodox Christianity is and how it is lived.

12. Smith, *Transforming Conversion,* 41.

13. For a clear account of the different implications of structuring baptism, catechesis, and entrance to the church, see Jonathan Watson, *In the Name of Our Lord: Four Models of the Relationship between Baptism, Catechesis, and Communion* (Bellingham, WA: Lexham, 2021).

Missional catechesis provides a bridge from the culture of the world to the culture of the church, and the bigger the gap, the bigger the bridge.[14] When the culture of the world is more amenable to the faith, catechesis can connect the dots that already exist. But when the culture is far removed from the faith and life of the church, we need a more intentional form of catechesis to help people make the difficult transition to the faith. We can't connect the dots because there aren't any dots to begin with.[15]

In the introduction to his instructional guide for catechists, *Catechetical Discourse*, Gregory of Nyssa notes the importance of adapting one's manner of teaching to the audience. "The same manner of teaching will not be suitable for all who approach the word," he writes. "Catechesis must be made to suit the differences of religions, looking to the same aim (*scopos*) of the discourse, but not using proofs in the same manner for each."[16] Those coming from Judaism bring one set of assumptions and beliefs; Greeks bring another. The end goal, or scope, is the same, but the means and methods vary. Like a skilled doctor, the missional catechist needs the right diagnosis for the right illness.

Missional catechesis requires a studied perception of the cultural milieu. It is attuned to the dominant narratives and visions of life that shape the predominant culture, including those deeply involved in church. This does not mean the catechist has to be "into" whatever the kids are into these days. (After age thirty, let's face it, you just can't keep up.) Nor does it mean the catechist is a belligerent cultural warrior, constantly lambasting the deviance and decadence of our society. Rather, the missional catechist studies the culture's core beliefs and assumptions, digging beneath the surface-level discussions to discover the beliefs, habits, and intuitions that animate the way people encounter the faith today.

Tim Keller, following J. I. Packer, calls this "counter catechesis." Jesus addressed those at the Sermon on the Mount with this bold claim: "You have heard it said . . . but I say unto you" (Matt. 5:21–44). He challenged conventional culture and religion at its very core. Today's catechist strikes a similar note in confronting the core narratives of our secular, post-Christian society. Keller puts it this way: "Secular narratives are beliefs about reality that most cultural institutions inculcate as inarguable, obvious truths. They come to us

14. For the bridge metaphor, see Sittser, *Resilient Faith*, 157.

15. The dots metaphor comes from Tim Keller, *How to Reach the West Again: Six Essential Elements of a Missionary Encounter* (New York: Redeemer City to City, 2020), 7.

16. Gregory of Nyssa, prologue to *Catechetical Discourse*, trans. Ignatius Green (Crestwood, NY: St. Vladimir's Seminary Press, 2019), 60, lightly altered.

now dozens of times a day—or even an hour—in ads, tweets, music, stories, opinion pieces, etc."[17] Some of these might include:

- *Identity*: "You have to be true to yourself."
- *Freedom*: "You should be free to live as you choose, as long as you don't hurt anyone."
- *Happiness*: "You must do what makes you happiest. You can't sacrifice that for anyone."
- *Science*: "The only way to solve our problems is through objective science and facts."
- *Morality*: "Everyone has the right to decide what is right and wrong themselves."
- *Justice*: "We are obligated to work for the freedom, rights, and good of everyone in the world."
- *History*: "History is bending toward social progress and away from religion."[18]

One of the main tasks of missional catechesis is understanding these tenets as belonging to a secular worldview at odds with the Christian worldview—although, because our society is largely premised on Christian ideas, many of these views have a seed of truth to them. In missional catechesis, we will have the opportunity to unearth the ways that these beliefs are baked into many of our day-to-day experiences. We can inspect them in the light of the gospel and show how the true faith presents a more compelling and more radiant alternative.

- You have heard it said, "You have to be true to yourself," but I say to you, "Your identity is found in Christ."
- You have heard it said, "You should be free to live as you choose, as long as you don't hurt anyone," but I say unto you, "True freedom is found in the obedience of the cross."
- You have heard it said, "You must do what makes you happiest. You can't sacrifice that for anyone," but I say unto you, "Blessed are you who are persecuted for the sake of Christ, for yours is the kingdom of heaven."

17. These examples come from Keller, *How to Reach the West Again*, 39–40. A similar idea is found in J. I. Packer and Gary Parrett, *Grounded in the Gospel: Building Believers the Old-Fashioned Way* (Grand Rapids: Baker Academic, 2010), 162–64.

18. Keller, *How to Reach the West Again*, 39–40. For a similar approach, see Rebecca McLaughlin, *The Secular Creed: Engaging Five Contemporary Claims* (Austin, TX: Gospel Coalition, 2021).

And so on. Missional catechesis engages counternarratives with grace and articulates a more compelling and comprehensive framework that the gospel invites us to embrace. It moves beyond polarizing hot takes and addresses fundamental issues—Jesus Christ and his love for humanity.

A similar challenge in missional catechesis is confronting what Ross Douthat calls "bad religion."[19] In this framework, the catechist does not encounter explicitly anti-Christian claims but rather sub-Christian ones. As Douthat tells the story, American Christianity over the last fifty years has been transformed from a largely healthy spiritual moral vision in America to a variety of religious expressions loosely categorized as Christian but which have hardly any real connection with traditional or orthodox Christianity. Versions of this would include Prosperity Gospel Christianity, which views the faith as a means of securing material wealth and physical well-being. Another version pictures Christianity as a private psychological therapy—a way of becoming a better version of yourself (think Oprah Winfrey or *Eat, Pray, Love*). Still another version of this includes various forms of politicized Christianity, whether on the right or the left, which weaves Christian identity inextricably into a particular political vision of life.

One of the most pervasive forms of "bad religion" is what sociologist Christian Smith dubs "moral therapeutic deism" (MTD). In the 2005 book *Soul Searching*, Smith summarizes MTD as a five-point creed:

1. A God exists who created and orders the world and watches over human life on earth.
2. God wants people to be good, nice, and fair to each other, as taught in the Bible and by most world religions.
3. The central goal of life is to be happy and to feel good about oneself.
4. God does not need to be particularly involved in one's life except when God is needed to resolve a problem.
5. Good people go to heaven when they die.[20]

Even more than Douthat's catalogue of contemporary heresies, MTD forms the basic substructure for how many ordinary Christians understand

19. Ross Douthat, *Bad Religion: How We Became a Nation of Heretics* (New York: Free Press, 2012).

20. Christian Smith, with Melinda Lundquist Denton, *Soul Searching: The Religious and Spiritual Lives of American Teenagers* (New York: Oxford University Press, 2005), 162–63.

Christianity, including those who would demur from a prosperity gospel or Oprah Winfrey faith. If the catechist were to present this list, many might be left wondering: What's wrong with that?

Most obviously, of course, Jesus is suspiciously absent. Nothing in MTD requires belief that Jesus is God incarnate, that he lived a fully human though sinless life, that he died and rose from the dead. Moreover, it has no need for the doctrine of the Trinity, the forgiveness of sins, the indwelling of the Holy Spirit, or the final judgment. It believes in a unitary "god" who providentially arranges human affairs (like helping you find a parking spot at a crowded grocery store), helps you negotiate difficult circumstances in your life, and prompts you to live an upstanding "moral" life.

Confronting bad religion is not as simple as dismissing certain ideas as unorthodox. We again need to focus on foundations. What underlying beliefs about God, creation, and human nature are at work? What's the implicit vision of the good life? What are the hidden assumptions about how we ought to live? This is where catechesis hits home. Why is it, in fact, wrong to understand God as a distant God who wants you to be happy? Why might it be problematic to construe human nature as an infinitely malleable set of desires untethered from the body? Missional catechesis means digging beneath the surface of bad religion and exposing the narratives that shape the way many people, Christians and non-Christians alike, approach the faith.

Ultimately, missional catechesis doesn't depend on clever arguments or eloquent defenses. Missional catechesis appeals to goodness, truth, beauty, and belonging.[21] It appeals to the logic and integrity of truth, presenting a coherent vision of the world that offers compelling answers to life's biggest questions. It appeals also to goodness, presenting Christianity as a way of living in the world that echoes the love of God, especially in the lives of the saints and in the care for "the least of these." To cite the apologist Minucius Felix again, it is the "beauty of our lives" that encourages Christians to endure and newcomers to join our ranks.[22] Finally, the Christian community—belonging to the body of Christ—is its own persuasive appeal. Especially in a time when loneliness and isolation have reached the level of a public health crisis in the United States, catechesis presents a pathway into belonging to the family of God.

Missional catechesis, in all these ways, lays the groundwork for a comprehensive vision of the Christian faith. It enables us, in Saint Paul's great phrase,

21. For a winsome approach to spiritual formation along these lines, see Alex Sosler, *A Short Guide to Spiritual Formation: Finding Life in Truth, Goodness, Beauty, and Community* (Grand Rapids: Baker Academic, 2024).

22. Minucius Felix, *Octavius* 31.7 (LCL 250:411–13).

not only to be "rooted and grounded in love," but also "to comprehend with all the saints what is the breadth and length and height and depth, and to know the love of Christ that surpasses knowledge, that [we] may be filled with all the fullness of God" (Eph. 3:17–20).

Stages of the Catechumenate

To be intentional about forming disciples in a missional context, we need to think about the *process* of becoming Christian. How do Christians actually become part of the church? How do they become part of *your* church? Every church has a process, but it's often unstated or confusing, and confusion breeds haphazard and unintentional formation. To put missional catechesis into practice, we need a clear vision of the stages of the catechumenate.

Inspired by the early church, we can set this out in four stages. This is not a step-by-step program or formula. As always, churches will need to adapt this process to something usable and organic to the life of the church. The number and names can vary. What is important is being intentional about the goals of formation and the process for getting there. Recalling our sketch of mature Christian discipleship in the last chapter, we can ask now: What are the things we can put in place to help people get there?

Keeping with our building analogy, I will refer to four main stages. In the precatechumenate stage, we gather the materials. In the catechumenate proper, we lay the foundation. In the prebaptismal stage of preparation, we test our structure. And finally, in the postbaptismal stage of mystagogy, we move into the house.[23]

1. *Precatechumenate: Gathering Materials.* The first stage, the precatechumenate, could also be called evangelization or inquiry. This is the stage when a person encounters the gospel and seeks to learn more. It is a time for forming relationships and dialogue with believers.

Augustine's treatise *On Catechizing the Uninstructed* is an excellent example of how a catechist should approach this stage.[24] There is certain information

23. Several other books have also advocated a similar four-stage catechumenate. See, for example, Robert Webber, *Ancient-Future Faith: Rethinking Evangelicalism for a Postmodern World* (Grand Rapids: Baker Books, 1999); Simon Chan, *Liturgical Theology: The Church as Worshiping Community* (Downers Grove, IL: IVP Academic, 2006); Gordon Smith, *Transforming Conversion*.

24. Augustine, *Instructing Beginners in the Faith*, trans. Raymond Canning (Hyde Park, NY: New City, 2006). For a more detailed account of how this text aligns with contemporary pedagogy theory, see Christopher J. Richmann and Alex Fogleman,

you want to give new people at this stage. You want to present a clear vision of the gospel grounded in the salvation narrative of the Bible and Christian history. But you don't need to tell them everything about the faith. More importantly, you want to get to know them. Where are they coming from? What kind of work do they do? What kind of families do they come from? Augustine even asks them what they have read about the faith and what kind of schools they went to. Some misconceptions may need to be corrected, but others will change over time. It's God's work ultimately. Most of all, we want newcomers to see the extraordinary love of God in the incarnation of Jesus Christ as the central thread running through salvation history.

The evangelization stage could be short or long, several months or several years. Some churches employ a more formal approach, such as the popular Alpha courses.[25] Or it may be a more informal setting in homes, workplaces, coffee shops, or other public meeting places. Simple gatherings for conversation and fellowship are all that is needed. By presenting the gospel, forming relationships, and creating space for dialogue, we begin to embody what Saint Paul describes when he writes to the Galatians, "Let the one who is catechized in the word share all good things with the one who catechizes" (Gal. 6:6, altered).

2. *Catechumenate: Laying the Foundations.* The next stage is the catechumenate proper. It is a time of laying the key foundations of doctrine and spiritual practices through formal instruction and through solidifying relationships with other catechumens and believers. If the precatechumenate is about hearing the good news for the first time, the catechumenate is about laying down the doctrinal, spiritual, and moral foundations of the faith so that catechumens can be "rooted and grounded in love." The kind of teaching will vary. It is often an ideal setting in which to teach the main topics of the catechism—the Apostles' Creed, the Lord's Prayer, and the Ten Commandments (discussed more in the next chapter). Regardless of what is specifically taught, the key issue is that, in this stage, catechumens receive a comprehensive but basic introduction into the faith. It expands the key elements of the gospel into a wider, more all-encompassing framework that includes doctrine and belief, prayer and spiritual practice, and moral and ethical formation. It acclimates believers not only into the key doctrines of the faith but also into the church's moral and social way of life. They get a taste of what it means to live as a Christian from an insider's perspective.

"Augustine's *De Catechizandis Rudibus* and the Scholarship of Teaching and Learning," *Teaching in Higher Education* 28, no. 7 (2023): 1640–55.

25. Learn more at www.alphausa.org.

In some parts of the early church, a ritual was used to initiate people into this stage, and some contemporary churches have retrieved similar practices.[26] Such a rite marks a new transition in conversion. No longer inquirers, catechumens are hearers, learners, and seekers. They are resolved to move forward toward the goal of Christian initiation, and this stage provides space for making the way there.

The length of time for this stage varies. It could last several months or several years. There is no need, unless someone is on the brink of death, to rush baptism. We obviously want people to be baptized and make a firm commitment to Jesus. But our motives should be guided by the Holy Spirit and a commitment to caring well for new Christians rather than insecurities about annual church membership rosters. This is a good opportunity to resist the technocratic impulse for efficiency and expediency in all things.

The reason for a lengthier catechumenate is simple: it takes time to transition from the kingdom of darkness to the kingdom of light—to put off the "old man" and put on the new (Col. 1:13; Eph. 4:22). Conversion involves more than acquiring a new set of ideas. It is a transfer in our "cosmic station," as David Bentley Hart puts it.[27] And this transfer entails both objective and subjective elements. Objectively, it is a change in status granted by Christ. But subjectively, it involves the slow, often difficult process of changing what we love. This is why Augustine could ask: "What is all that time for, when they hold the status and title of catechumen, if it is not for them to hear what a Christian should believe and what kind of life a Christian should lead, so that, when they have proved themselves, they may then eat from the Lord's table and drink from his cup?"[28]

This second phase of the catechumenate, then, is a time for learning not only the doctrines of the faith but also the habits of the heart. Learning doctrine is essential, especially in a culture that has forgotten the metaphysical foundations that make truthful speech possible. However, a concern for truth is also balanced by attention to the formation of the heart. The role of the community is especially important here. We cannot learn to live true, good, and beautiful lives apart from living within a community shaped by what is

26. For a contemporary example, see J. I. Packer and Joel Scandrett, eds., *To Be a Christian: An Anglican Catechism*, approved ed. (Wheaton, IL: Crossway, 2020), 123–25.

27. David Bentley Hart, "Baptism and Cosmic Allegiance: A Brief Observation," *Journal of Early Christian Studies* 20, no. 3 (2012): 457–65 (at 458).

28. Augustine of Hippo, *On Faith and Works* 6.9 (WSA I/8:232).

true, good, and beautiful.[29] In addition, we learn the habits of faith through engagement with the arts—through imagination and beauty. Finally, we learn the faith through spiritual practices, such as prayer, fasting, study, and service.

Each of these aspects belongs to this crucial stage of the catechumenate. In this stage, catechumens learn to live the Christian life through belonging to a community whose life only makes sense in light of the gospel of Jesus Christ. Learning comes by living.

3. *Preparation: Testing the Work.* Once the materials have been gathered and the foundations laid, the work needs to be tested. Not long ago, I built a treehouse in the backyard for our kids to play on. After days and weeks of sawing wood and hammering nails, the treehouse was complete. The kids were excited and ready to play, but guess who my wife voted to be first up the ladder?

The third stage of the missional catechumenate is the preparation stage, or baptismal candidacy. This is the time for preparing for baptism. Usually this takes place in the weeks leading up to Easter, in the season of Lent, though it could be adapted to other times of the year. This stage, too, may also include distinct rites of passage associated with formally enrolling for baptism. Recall that in the early church, catechumens received a new name at this stage—*competentes* ("coseekers") or *photizomenoi* ("the enlightened"). The use of a rite of passage or new designation signifies that the intermediary phase has passed, and the time of baptism is at hand. Augustine reflects on the etymology of the name *competentes* to highlight the significant feature of this stage of catechesis: "Your very name—*competentes*—signifies that you are longing for the kingdom and aiming at it with all the energy of your minds. What else, after all, are *competentes* but people asking together? . . . And what is this one thing that you are asking and longing for? . . . 'One thing have I asked from the Lord, this will I seek; to dwell in the house of the Lord all the days of my life . . . to contemplate the delight of the Lord, and to be protected by his temple' (Ps. 27:3–4)."[30]

This stage is marked by purification, asceticism, and more focused instruction. It intensifies the transition from the old kingdom to the new and gathers what the catechumens have been learning to help them make these doctrines their own. This stage need not be especially long. Its potency owes to a focused intentionality rather than a lengthy duration of time.

The actual process may look different depending on one's context. Churches may elect to hold special classes during this time to help draw together what

29. On the role of "moral ecologies" in catechetical virtue formation, see Keller, *How to Reach the West*, 41–45.

30. Augustine, *Sermon* 216.1 (WSA III/6:167).

has been learned, helping catechumens distill and instill this knowledge. This is also an opportune season for fasting, confession, and service. A church could host formal or informal retreats in which candidates and sponsors devote special time to prayer and contemplation. There could also be space in the weekly worship service for a ritual of "handing over" the creed, signaling that this sacred text is now entrusted to the candidates, and they are to guard it carefully the rest of their days.

Origen of Alexandria imagined the season of the catechumenate in terms of Israel's wilderness wandering.[31] While many other church fathers saw the crossing of the Red Sea as the paradigmatic type of baptism, Origen proposed that the Red Sea was not baptism but entrance into the catechumenate. It was the crossing of the Jordan into the promised land that best signified baptism. My friend Elizabeth, who is a thoughtful spiritual director, once asked a great question about Origen's image of the catechumenate: What does it do to our experience of the Christian life if we do *not* begin with a catechetical season of wilderness? What do we come to expect of the life of discipleship if we bypass this crucial season of repentance, testing, and prayer?

I love Origen's image for this stage of the catechumenate. It's a time of discipleship and discipline—the *paideia* of the Lord (Heb. 12:4–11). This image captures the importance of purification, testing, and hope fostered in baptismal preparation. It's a time of learning Christian hope through prayer; learning to desire God's name, kingdom, and will; learning to pray for daily bread, mutual forgiveness, and deliverance for temptation. This period of candidacy is a desert season whose heat refines the longings of the heart and readies the candidate for the refreshing waters of baptism.

4. *Mystagogy: Moving In.* Mystagogy is the final stage of the missional catechumenate. After the foundations have been set and tested, we're ready to move in. We're ready to go from guests on the front porch to those who call this house a home.

The word "mystagogy" means "leading into the mysteries." By the fourth century, it became common to refer to instruction immediately following baptism at Easter as mystagogy. This kind of teaching signifies not the *end* of the journey but the beginning. Mystagogy is about celebrating and expanding the Christian's new life in Christ by being drawn deeper into the church's sacramental life.

In the early church, the newly baptized were called neophytes, a term Saint Paul used to refer to new believers (often translated as "new convert";

31. Origen, *Homilies on Joshua* 4.1–2.

see 1 Tim. 3:6). They wore white robes as a sign of their new life in Christ, a life washed clean by the blood of the Lamb. During this phase, bishops gave instruction on the sacraments and rituals of the church, especially baptism, the Eucharist, and the Lord's Prayer.[32] This developed from the custom of the *disciplina arcani* (the "discipline of secrecy"), in which Christians were not allowed to divulge to the nonbaptized the central rituals of the church's life, especially baptism and the Eucharist.[33]

There are key theological and pedagogical insights here. Saint Paul writes in 1 Corinthians 2 about the wisdom of God:

> But we impart a secret and hidden wisdom of God, which God decreed before the ages for our glory. None of the rulers of this age understood this, for if they had, they would not have crucified the Lord of glory. But, as it is written,
>
> "What no eye has seen, nor ear heard,
> nor the heart of man imagined,
> what God has prepared for those who love him"—
>
> these things God has revealed to us through the Spirit. For the Spirit searches everything, even the depths of God. (1 Cor. 2:7–10)

No eye has seen, no ear has heard, no heart has imagined the glorious things of God. And yet God reveals this hidden wisdom to his children through the Spirit. It is okay if catechumens do not grasp everything about the faith before they're ready to take the plunge of baptism. Having a comprehensive knowledge of God is certainly not a requirement; if it were, no one could be baptized. Furthermore, catechists wouldn't want their limited abilities to constrain the pedagogy of the divine Word. Mystagogy embodies the principle that God is beyond our finite capacities to explain who he is or what he has done. We can't keep silent, but we also know our words eventually fall short. Even still, God calls from deep to deep, calling us further up and further in.

What might a corresponding practice of mystagogy look like today, when we have access to a nearly infinite amount of information at our fingertips? We may not want to use the language of mystagogy or secrecy. This may strike some as too elitist, or like we're trying to hide something. I think we can ask

32. For examples of this genre, see Ambrose of Milan's two treatises, *On the Mysteries* and *On the Sacraments*, and Cyril of Jerusalem's *Mystagogical Homilies*.

33. For an early example of this text used in baptismal arguments, see Tertullian, *On Baptism* 18.

instead: How is our teaching aligned with our doctrine of God? Do we implicitly think of God as a subject we can study like other subjects in school? Is God revealed truly in word and image yet not conflated with any man-made idol? How do our processes of teaching reflect this view of God?

What I love about the patristic conception of mystagogy is that it captures the posture of celebration and praise that matches the joy of Easter. Mystagogy is a time of joy, or splendor. It means festivities and merriment, gatherings of friendship and fellowship. Instruction in this time can focus on the meaning of the sacraments and the rites of the church, providing guidance on the rule of life or the lived character of the faith. Above all, it is a time of rejoicing. The neophytes, in this way, embody in this season the dawning of a resurrection life. A new day has begun. A new journey awaits.

Soundings from the Field

To close out this chapter, I want to provide three examples of missional catechesis—three soundings from the field that give concrete expression to the ideas presented in this chapter. Missional catechesis will look different depending on our specific contexts, so take these examples as inspirational rather than prescriptive.

At my home church in Waco, Texas, we take a fairly simple approach. A catechist will gather for about an hour before Sunday morning worship, and over the course of about ten months, we work through the questions of our church's standard catechism (*To Be a Christian*). We begin in late August or September and go until late May or early June. Our church is in a university town, so we begin a few weeks after people return from summer travels (or refuge from the blazing heat of Texas summers). We build in a few weeks before starting catechesis to promote it especially to new people. Everyone new to the church, whether a lifelong believer or brand-new to the faith, goes through a year of catechesis. This way we avoid the kind of false pretentions to Christian maturity that can sneak in when we think we're "beyond" the need for catechesis. By making it more or less mandatory for everyone, catechesis becomes a standard that unifies the church and gives us a common theological vocabulary and experience. When my wife and I joined the church, I had just completed a graduate degree in theology, and we went through a year of catechesis with others who were brand-new to the faith and others who had been teaching Christianity at the university level for forty years. We were all "children and pupils of the catechism."

In the weeks before we get started, we try to meet with any newcomers one on one to learn more about their story and where they're coming from. This becomes important over the course of the year, as so often our backgrounds shape the kinds of questions we ask in catechesis. Once catechesis begins, we gather on Sunday mornings before worship, either in the sanctuary or in a meeting room arranged to resemble a liturgical space. Images of Christ and the saints surround us, reminding us that we are joining a great cloud of witnesses. We begin by standing and singing a hymn or the doxology to engage our hearts and minds in the kind of "doxological pedagogy" we associated with Ephrem the Syrian. Most of the hour is spent reading and discussing questions from the catechism. I read the question aloud and we all read the answers together. I pull out one or two themes from the question, reference one or two relevant biblical passages, and offer one or two examples of how the topic affects our everyday life.

The most interesting part, though, comes through the questions. We encourage asking questions (more on this in chapter 8), not so that I can simply answer them but so that we can pursue the biblical and theological foundations of these questions. This is where the countercatechesis we outlined above really kicks in. Sometimes we spend a week on just two or three questions. Sometimes we move through ten or fifteen in an hour. Our goal isn't to "get through" the material but to bring the living tradition to bear on the real lives of the people in our midst. We close the hour in prayer or some other spiritual practice, such as *lectio divina*, in a way that is linked to the topics we've been discussing.

During Lent, those considering baptism or confirmation meet with church leadership to submit their names for admission to these rites. Then the whole church joins together in prayer, fasting, and service. For us, adults are baptized during the Easter vigil and confirmations usually occur in the weeks thereafter. Much of this is specific to our Anglican tradition, but much applies elsewhere. Every year is a different experience because the people are different. Each person brings his or her own questions and stories, but all aspire in different ways to the same goal of knowing Christ in the power of the Spirit.

This is by no means the only model, though. When my friends Ryan and Elizabeth oversaw catechesis at their church in San Francisco, they experimented with different versions of a cohort model of catechesis they called "the catechumenate." A group of about ten to twenty people within the church participated in the cohort for a designated season, ranging from three to nine months. Along with weekly worship and Sunday morning teaching, they committed to a common rule of life based on study, discernment, fellowship, and prayer. They began the cohort with a two-day retreat outside of the city, which helped them prepare their hearts and devote this season to laying deep foundations. Over the next several months, the group met regularly for teaching and fellowship. They met weekly as a group, often reading through a book together and sharing a common meal. Smaller groups of two or three would also meet regularly during the week, thus allowing more intimate friendships to form. Ryan and Elizabeth also encouraged the cohort to receive spiritual direction and craft a personal or family rule of life. Finally, at the end of the cohort, they closed their time with another retreat, in which they reflected on and celebrated what God was doing in that season.

What I love about this cohort model is the way it gives people a concentrated time to set aside distractions for a season and focus on laying deep foundations. It draws winsomely on the monastic impulse that sees the Christian life as pursuing single-minded devotion to God, and it gives believers, new and old, the space to step away from the all-consuming constraints of consumption and become acclimated to the slow rhythms of grace. Having known several people who have gone through their catechumenate, I can attest to its transformative effects. Years later, cohort members look back to that season as one that set the course of their spiritual journey on a new trajectory.

One final example comes from an Eastern Orthodox priest named John Parker, who developed a twelve-week missional catechesis model that is heavily inspired by the patristic model of a Lenten catechumenate in preparation for Easter.[34] During those twelve weeks, catechumens leave the worship service after the reading of Scripture and the sermon, while the rest of the church remains for the Eucharist. During that time, catechumens participate in a series of studies: the first three weeks they learn the creed; the second three weeks they study the moral teachings of the church; the third three weeks they go through the Sermon on the Mount; and the final three weeks they focus on the prayers and liturgies of the church. Catechumens also study Scripture based on a reading plan that includes the four Gospels, Acts, Genesis, Isaiah, and the Psalms. Additionally, a lay catechist reads aloud one of John Chrysostom's *Twelve Baptismal Instructions*, which is a series of twelve short sermons summoning baptismal candidates to embrace the high calling of life in Christ.

Along with formal teaching, the catechumens also undertake various service projects. Catechumens clean the bathrooms, make coffee, wash dishes, and tend to other practical needs of the building; they are also given Scripture passages to meditate upon as they do so. Through this they are learning that the Christian life is a life of service. As Parker puts it, during the twelve weeks of catechesis, the catechumens "go last" in things both ecclesial and practical, until their bap-

34. John Parker, "Radechesis: A Return to Radical Catechesis," in *Healing Humanity: Confronting Our Moral Crisis*, ed. Alexander F. C. Webster, Alfred K. Siewers, and David C. Ford (Jordanville, NY: Holy Trinity Seminary Press, 2020).

tism at Easter, at which point they "go first" in the community. In this way, the whole church shares in the formation and initiation of new believers.

These examples, again, are not meant to be prescriptive. These are what three different churches have discerned is the best way to do catechesis in their own settings. In your own church, based on the knowledge you have of your community, you can begin to discern what a missional catechumenate might look like for your context. The main question to ask is: How do people here become Christian? What is the process for being initiated into the life of the church? Attending to questions of *why* and *for what* are so tremendously helpful as you seek to address questions about the practical shape of catechesis in your setting.

Over the last two chapters, we have explored catechesis between the two poles of mission and worship. It has become all too common for churches to pit mission and worship against each other or collapse one into the other. Some churches focus on reaching the lost and being agents of justice in the world, but they feel the need to make worship accessible at every level—to turn worship *into* mission. Others pride themselves in beautiful churches and rich liturgies but don't have any practical ways to help newcomers adapt to these rituals, which can often be inaccessible or unintelligible to newcomers.

Why not have both? Why not have broad mission *and* deep liturgy? Part of the problem is that we don't have anything in the middle to link the outward pole of mission and the inward pole of worship. If mission is outward, facing toward the world, and worship is inward, facing toward the church's liturgical life, catechesis belongs in the middle as a bridge between mission and worship. Catechesis explains the faith to Christians in a way that meets the challenges of mission while also serving as an on-ramp to deep worship. It allows worship to be what it is—the undiluted, self-forgetful praise of God—without having to make worship relevant in light of the standards of contemporary architecture and aesthetics.

In the Great Commission, mission, worship, and catechesis belong together: mission, in bringing the good news to all the world; worship, in baptizing disciples in the name of the Father, Son, and Holy Spirit; and catechesis, in teaching Christians to obey all that Jesus has commanded. With a coherent practice of catechesis, a church doesn't need to sacrifice liturgy for mission, or vice versa. Worship, catechesis, and mission belong together as the bedrock for a flourishing church.

6

The Rule of Faith, Hope, and Love

In the ancient world, mosaics were one of the most revered forms of art, dating back to the third millennium before Christ. Many ornate mosaics from ancient Syria, Greece, North Africa, Italy, and elsewhere still survive in churches and museums today. What's unique about them is that, rather than applying color to blank material, like paint on canvas, a mosaic artist assembles potentially thousands of small pieces of colored glass, stone, or other material, and arranges them to form a distinctive image. Some could be small, but others could cover an entire floor or wall. The interior of St. Mark's Basilica in Venice, built in the Middle Ages, contains over eight thousand mosaic tiles covering some 45,000 square feet.

In the second century, Irenaeus of Lyons compared the Scriptures to a beautiful mosaic. Rightly arranged, the tiles of Scripture formed the image of a noble king. But what heresies do, he said, is rearrange the tiles to form a picture of a fox or a dog—a subhuman image rather than one of beauty and nobility. Christians, and especially new Christians who had not yet read the entirety of Scripture, needed a correct visual of the mosaic to know how the tiles are supposed to be arranged. I think of it like the picture on the front cover of a puzzle box. If I have an image of what the finished puzzle is supposed to look like, I can know how individual pieces come together. (If you're one of those people who refuse to look at the puzzle box, good for you. Just go with it . . .)

This is how Irenaeus described the rule of faith. The term "rule" comes from the Latin word *regula,* which, like the related Greek word *canon,* comes from the world of carpentry. A *regula* is a measuring device: it helps you measure your work against a straight edge. It helps you see rightly. The rule of faith is a mosaic that reveals the image of Christ the king rather than Christ the fox. In stating the essential orthodox beliefs about God in a clear but succinct way, the rule of faith offered Christians a way of taking in the whole of Scripture in a way that provided a true image of Christ.

In this chapter, I want to expand on this idea by proposing that the catechism is a "rule" of faith, hope, and love. The Apostles' Creed, the Lord's Prayer, and the Ten Commandments serve as a *regula* for keeping our vision of Christ straight. They provide clear images of Christian belief, spirituality, and ethics—the life of the mind, the life of prayer, and the life of virtue. The creed signifies the rule of faith, or the doctrinal, intellectual commitments of the faith. The Lord's Prayer guides the affective and spiritual dynamics of the Christian life, expressing the theological virtue of hope. The Ten Commandments represent the moral life, which is our sharing in Christ's own virtue. Together, these three "rules" provide a sound measurement for building solid foundations in Christ.

To reiterate something we said in chapter 4, we never outgrow these basic building blocks. We never outgrow faith, hope, and love; we only grow deeper into them. In this way, the catechism is less like a stepping stool we kick away once we've climbed and more like a poem that moves and delights us more with each reading.

Before looking at each of these rules individually, I first want to make a case for how they hold together according to the doctrine of salvation. The three pillars of the catechism, I suggest, align with the three main models of the atonement: ontological models, relational models, and moral models. Like the pillars of the catechism, these three, though distinct, belong together in a comprehensive picture of Christ's work of healing and reconciliation. They come together to form a breathtaking mosaic of salvation.[1]

The Mosaic of Salvation

The Christian view of salvation is vast and wide-ranging.[2] In this section, I'm going to sketch some of the most common images of salvation in Christian theology to show how they paint a rich mosaic of salvation that can guide our approach to catechesis as a comprehensive integration of faith, hope, and love.

1. I am not original in proposing this structure. It is present implicitly in Augustine's *Enchiridion* and explicitly in Thomas Aquinas's *Compendium of Theology*.

2. For good recent work done on atonement theology that seeks to articulate both the models and the need to integrate them, see Adam Johnson, *Atonement: A Guide for the Perplexed* (London: T&T Clark, 2015); Joshua McNall, *The Mosaic of Atonement: An Integrated Approach to Christ's Work* (Grand Rapids: Zondervan, 2019); Khaled Anatolios, *Deification through the Cross: An Eastern Christian Theology of Salvation* (Grand Rapids: Eerdmans, 2020); Joel Scandrett and William Witt, *Mapping Atonement* (Grand Rapids: Baker Academic, 2022).

Amid the many theories of salvation, we can identify three main models:

1. *Ontological models* focus on the objective reality of salvation, with an emphasis on Christ's incarnation and the healing of fallen humanity.
2. *Relational models* highlight the restoration of our relationship with God, whether through the images of satisfaction, substitution, or justification.
3. *Moral models* focus on the ethical effects that follow from contemplating Christ's life, death, and resurrection.

These three categories belong together in the mosaic of salvation. But each category also aligns with one of the core texts of the catechism. Ontological models pair well with the creed; they focus on the objective realities of salvation in Christ's accomplished work. Relational models correlate nicely with the emphasis on relating to God in prayer. Finally, moral models match with the ethical emphasis of love in the Ten Commandments. By drawing together these three models, we can develop a theology of salvation that undergirds and sustains a comprehensive approach to catechesis.

Ontological models emphasize how salvation occurs through Christ joining together God and humanity and creating a new set of circumstances in the world. This includes the incarnational-recapitulation models associated with patristic theologians like Irenaeus of Lyons and Athanasius of Alexandria, as well as the "Christus Victor" model of Lutheran theologian Gustaf Aulén. In the Word-made-flesh, Christ "sums up" or "recapitulates" human life perfectly, restoring what was lost in the Fall and freeing humanity from captivity to death and demonic forces. Recapitulation (from the Greek word *ana-kephalaiosis,* meaning "to go back to the head") is the word Saint Paul uses to describe the purpose of Christ as summing up, or uniting, all things in heaven and earth (Eph. 1:10). This idea was especially important in early Christianity's battle against heretical forms of dualism that sought to separate God's work of creation and redemption.[3] Biblically, recapitulation expresses the Pauline idea that "as by the one man's disobedience the many were made sinners, so by the one man's obedience the many will be made righteous" (Rom. 5:19).

Another kind of ontological model is the Christus Victor model, which stresses Christ's victory over evil. Popularized by the Lutheran theologian Gustav Aulén, the Christus Victor model looks to patristic sources to highlight Christ's triumphant defeat of death, hell, and the grave. A famous image of this view of salvation comes from Gregory of Nyssa, who pictures Christ's

3. See Irenaeus, *Against Heresies* 3.18.1; 5.21.1.

incarnate flesh as "bait" that Satan devours, only to be destroyed by the unconquerable power of Christ's divine light and life.[4] Ontological models also highlight salvation as deification or *theosis*: the view that God became human so that humanity might become godlike to the extent that is possible.

In ontological models, the emphasis of the good news of the gospel is that "Jesus is Lord." The evangelist who brings the good news of salvation proclaims to Israel, "Your God reigns" (Isa. 52:7). These models place more focus on the person of Christ and his finished work than on what we receive from this work. Jesus is a mighty king, triumphant over his enemies. He is King of kings and Lord of lords.

Relational models, our second category, focus on restoring humanity's broken relationship with God. Attention here is focused on the death of Christ, along with sacrifice, exchange, or justification. We can include the satisfaction models associated with the medieval theologians like Anselm and Aquinas, as well as substitutionary models articulated by Lutheran and Calvinist theologians. In satisfaction models, theologians emphasize that humanity "owes" God certain things—love, praise, holiness, obedience, etc.—yet sin prevents us from adequately making such offerings. Because we cannot, God in his mercy becomes incarnate in Jesus Christ to live a perfect human life, and then, in his death, to make a perfect sacrifice for our sin. He thus allows our sin to be "atoned" and us to be "at-one" with God.

The Reformation, with its heated debates over the nature and operation of justification, highlighted more forensic, or legal, metaphors. Luther, Calvin, and others emphasized salvation as the pardoning of our guilt because of God's pronouncement of the verdict in Christ. God views us as righteous—meaning that we are "in right standing" before the Judge—not because of any activity we have done but because Christ has received the punishment due to us. By God's grace and through the response of faith, we receive the reward due to Christ, while Christ receives the punishment due to us.

Finally, the third main category for understanding salvation focuses on the moral effects of Christ's work. One version, the so-called moral influence theory, often associated with the medieval theologian Peter Abelard, stresses how Christ's love for humanity stirs us to love God and neighbor in gratitude. When we see the great love God shows in Christ, we cannot but be inspired to love God in return. A different take views Christ as a moral example. Here, what we see in Christ's obedient life serves as a model to imitate. By imitating Christ's life, we too can come to share in his salvation.

4. See Gregory of Nyssa, *Catechetical Oration* 24.

These three models of salvation have a rich and complex history, and many more nuances and complexities. But they are not in competition with one another. In Thomas Aquinas's writing about salvation, he lists a series of benefits we receive from Christ: we are delivered from sin; we are stirred to love God; we are given an example of obedience and humility; we merit justifying grace and eternal bliss; we are bound to refrain from sin; and we overcome death and Satan.[5] All of the salvation models are here, arranged in an integrated sequence.

We also see this integration in Scripture itself. In the great prologue of the Letter to the Ephesians, images of recapitulation sit alongside images of adoption, redemption, and forgiveness of trespasses—all with the aim that we might live "to the praise of his glory" (Eph. 1:3–14). In the Letter to the Hebrews, likewise, we see another overlapping of images as the author declares how Christ partook of flesh and blood—becoming like us in every respect except sin—and destroying "the one who has the power of death . . . so that he might become a merciful and faithful high priest in the service of God, to make propitiation for the sins of the people" (Heb. 2:14–18). The Letter to the Romans, similarly, offers a full-orbed image of salvation: recapitulation (Rom. 5:12–21), forgiveness and reconciliation (5:1–11), and the response of love (6:1–12). In the biblical understanding, the overlap of images and metaphors signals the grand scope of God's saving work in Christ. The teaching of theology in catechesis is not unlike the teaching of poetry. We seek to sing the extraordinary gift of God in Christ for us through images, pictures, and symbols that stretch human speech to its limits.

If the competitive approach does not do justice to the comprehensive picture of salvation presented in Scripture, a better starting point would be to understand how these various models hold together as a cohesive set of images. Together, these models create a mosaic of salvation.[6]

A mosaic approach to understanding salvation correlates with one of the chief aims of this book: namely, to articulate a comprehensive and robust theory of catechesis. In particular, I want to suggest that the three main models of salvation can be overlaid with the three main tenets of catechesis: faith, expressed in the Apostles' Creed; hope, expressed in the Lord's Prayer; and love, expressed in the Ten Commandments. Each of these core tenets aligns with one of the main models of salvation.

5. Thomas Aquinas, *Summa Theologiae* III, q. 46, art. 3. This reference comes from Johnson, *Atonement*, 4.

6. The mosaic metaphor comes from McNall, *Mosaic of Atonement*.

We see, first, a congruence between ontological models of salvation and the catechetical focus on faith as articulated in the Apostles' Creed. Here, the primary reference point is the person of Christ over what happens to humanity in the exchange. Martin Luther associated the creed with the gospel, rather than the law, because the creed tells us what is true about God, not about what we need to do to get saved.[7] In the creed, as in ontological models of salvation, we learn first and foremost what is true. God is the creator and redeemer of the world. Through Christ and the Holy Spirit, God's saving action has been manifested on our behalf. Jesus is God's true Son, born of the virgin Mary by the power of the Holy Spirit; he truly died and rose from the dead, and will come again to judge the world. The Holy Spirit forms the church, in which we find remission of sins, the communion of saints, and the hope of resurrection and everlasting life. While implied in the creedal statement are truths about how we benefit from the incarnation, we are directed first to consider and behold Christ—the pioneer and perfector of our faith (Heb. 12:2).

Likewise, there is also a congruence in relational models of salvation and the catechetical emphasis on hope expressed in the Lord's Prayer. In relational models, as we have seen, the focus is on reconciliation between God and humanity in Christ. Whether this is understood in terms of Jesus as a sacrifice for our sins or our justification before God, there is a primary interest in how this process yields a restored relationship: we, who were far off, have been brought near. Or, as Romans 5:10 puts it: "For if while we were enemies, we were reconciled to God by the death of his Son, much more, now that we are reconciled, shall we be saved by his life." The main impetus for teaching the Lord's Prayer in catechesis is similarly about coming to know God in a reconciled relationship.

We do, of course, learn doctrinal truths in the Lord's Prayer: God's kingdom is coming to earth, his name is sacred, etc. We also learn about what it means to live with our neighbors. But the primary aim of learning to pray is learning to be reconciled with God. We are not just interested in learning *about* God. We learn what it means to be a child of God. There is even a natural relationship between relational reconciliation and ontological salvation in the pairing of the Lord's Prayer and the Apostles' Creed. By confessing the triune God in the baptismal creed, we become children and heirs of God, which enables us to pray to God *as Father*. The objective reality named in the creed leads to the subjective relationship expressed through prayer.

7. I owe this point to Phillip Cary, *The Nicene Creed: An Introduction* (Bellingham, WA: Lexham, 2023), 12.

Finally, catechesis is not only about what we believe and how we relate to God. It is also about how we relate to others and to the world around us. In moral models of salvation, the emphasis is less on God's action or the exchange between God and humanity, and more on the human response of love—what we do and how we live in light of the incarnation and our reconciliation with God. This aspect of the Christian life is expressed chiefly in the catechetical emphasis on the Ten Commandments. To be sure, we learn objective truths about God. But the key focus is on how we in turn respond to the God of the gospel. The Decalogue alludes to the third of the Pauline trifecta of faith, hope, and love—bringing to light the way in which our walking in the way of the cross is commensurate with the understanding of salvation we see in Scripture.

In the remainder of the chapter, we will look more specifically at each of the three pillars. I want to distinguish them without separating them. By holding them together, our picture of salvation becomes something truly beautiful, with each piece complementing and reinforcing the others. We do not need to settle for one model any more than we would want to settle for a catechesis that teaches doctrine without prayer or ethics.

The Creed as the Rule of Faith

Christianity is unabashedly dogmatic. In contrast with many other religions, ancient and modern, Christianity places a primacy on orthodoxy—right belief. "It is hopeless," Dorothy Sayers once quipped, "to offer Christianity as a vaguely idealistic aspiration of a simple and consoling kind; it is, on the contrary, a hard, tough, exacting, and complex doctrine, steeped in a drastic and uncompromising realism."[8] Christianity doesn't pronounce some private truth ("my truth" and "your truth"). It doesn't offer opinions as opposed to facts (a modern and largely facetious invention). Christianity makes claims about *reality*—about what is real, about truth. This is because Christianity does not view faith as the opposite of knowledge but as its antecedent. Aquinas describes faith as "a foretaste of the knowledge that will make us blessed in the future."[9]

Why this commitment to truth? Christianity understands doctrine to be good for us—life-giving food for our souls. Salvation comes from the Latin *salus*,

8. Dorothy L. Sayers, "Creed or Chaos?," in *Letters to a Diminished Church: Passionate Arguments for the Relevance of Christian Doctrine* (New York: Nelson, 2004), 46.

9. Thomas Aquinas, *Compendium of Theology* 2, in *Thomas Aquinas: Compendium of Theology*, trans. Richard J. Regen (Oxford: Oxford University Press, 2009), 18.

meaning safety, health, and well-being. Jesus, the Good Physician, offers the medicine of immortality in both his actions and his words. His words are words of *life*; they are "living and active" (Heb. 4:12). False doctrine hurts us. It tears us out of the true order of being, leading to pain and destruction. Theologian Ellen Charry thus says that doctrine is "aretegenic" (the Greek word *aretē* means "virtue"): it is for our growth and health in the Christian life.[10] How we understand doctrine is inseparable from human flourishing and virtuous living.

This commitment to truth is one reason why Christians have often emphasized creeds, confessions, and other summative statements of belief.[11] Creeds serve many functions, but one of their main functions is catechetical instruction. In preparing Christians for baptism, the creed helps new believers learn to know who God is, what God is like, and how God relates to creation. The creed presents us with a condensed statement of who God is and what God has done. The creed gives us the gospel. It provides a pathway to sharing the mind of Christ (1 Cor. 2:16; Phil. 2:5).

Typically, the Apostles' Creed is the main text used in learning what Christians believe. The Apostles' Creed is a shorter and more comprehensive statement than other creeds such as the Nicene Creed or the Athanasian Creed. The Apostles' Creed can be easily memorized, yet it is substantive enough to provide a true account of the creative and redeeming work of God. A version of the Apostles' Creed goes back to the second or third century, when something very similar was used for baptismal initiation and instruction.

What, though, does the creed do in catechesis? Learning the creed in catechesis is like imprinting the new covenant on our hearts. The creed provides a summary of the key elements of Scripture in a way that sinks down in our bones. This makes good sense. Few people can simply pick up a Bible, begin reading from Genesis and go to Revelation, and know what's going on. (Some people do, of course, and that's great!) Most people encounter a bewildering array of stories, commandments, poems, and other kinds of writing, and find themselves wondering: What is going on? A creed is a simple way for people to encounter the overall scope of the Bible so that when they do read the Bible on their own or hear it read aloud in church, they have some idea of what is happening.

The creed condenses and summarizes the entirety of the Bible and packages it in a way that, rather than closing down understanding, opens us up so that we have a greater appreciation of the beauty and depth of the Scriptures. As Trevor Hart puts it, the creed is a "power-packed summary designed precisely

10. Ellen Charry, *By the Renewing of Your Minds: The Pastoral Function of Christian Doctrine* (New York: Oxford University Press, 1997).

11. Frances Young, *The Making of the Creeds* (London: SCM Classics, 1991), 1.

to capture our imagination and, far from shutting it down or rendering it otiose, to send it into paroxysms of visualization, curiosity, and exploration."[12] In addition, and as we will explore in more detail later, the creed is helpful for memory. The creed that has been memorized serves to strengthen the Christian's spiritual life.[13] By having the creed engraved in the heart—in the deep storehouses of memory—it shapes our minds, hearts, and attitudes. The creed becomes the primary framework for how we experience the world.

In his late-in-life catechetical writing on the creed, Thomas Aquinas lists five effects or "goods" that come from the faith acquired in the Apostles' Creed: (1) union with God; (2) a foretaste of eternal life; (3) right orientation to virtue and justice; (4) a guide for overcoming temptation; and (5) an antidote to foolishness.[14] The faith we instill in creedal instruction, in other words, is much more than teaching new Christians the right items to believe about God and the world, as if simply learning these facts will solve our problems. The faith we learn in the creed has objective and subjective aspects. It offers a firm grasp of the objective reality of God and his world. And yet faith is also relational and covenantal. It is *trust* as much as it is *thought*.

Creedal faith binds us to the one who loves us and calls us his own. It is connected to the life of virtue and to living justly in the world. Finally, the faith learned in the creed is a sacramental sign of the blessed life of heaven.[15] What we first touch here in the creed is, in a mysterious sense, nothing less than a small glimpse of God himself, a small sight—veiled yet true—of the beatific vision. In the creed, we encounter God himself.

Teaching the Creed in Catechesis

Two main creeds are commonly used in catechesis: the Apostles' Creed and the Nicene Creed. The Apostles' Creed is shorter and is more traditionally associated with baptism. In some early Christian writings, a version of the bap-

12. Trevor Hart, *Confessing and Believing: The Apostles' Creed as Script for the Christian Life* (Minneapolis: Fortress, 2022), 5.

13. I argue this point in more detail in Alex Fogleman, "*Confitendum et proficiendum*: Augustine on the Rule of Faith and the Christian Life," *Pro Ecclesia* 31, no. 4 (2022): 454–77.

14. Thomas Aquinas, *The Aquinas Catechism: A Simple Explanation of the Catholic Faith by the Church's Greatest Theologian* (Manchester, NH: Sophia Institute Press, 2000), 5–10.

15. For a more developed account of this idea, see Hans Boersma, *Catechized for Beatitude: Theology as Initiation and Discipleship* (Waco, TX: Catechesis Institute, 2023).

tismal creed was said right before or during baptism. Both creeds are based on the threefold name of Father, Son, and Holy Spirit that Jesus commissioned his disciples to baptize with (Matt. 28:19). The Nicene Creed is largely an expansion and clarification of the kind of baptismal creeds that were in common use in the fourth century. Due to the exceptional debates over the meaning of Christ's divinity in the fourth century, the Nicene Creed became the symbol of ecumenical orthodoxy for many churches, and remains so to this day. In the Anglican Book of Common Prayer, the Apostles' Creed is said during Morning and Evening Prayer, while the Nicene Creed is said when the Eucharist is celebrated.

Regardless of which one is more common in your tradition, or what you decide is more suitable for catechesis, the key point is to walk through each article of the creed and allow people to ask their questions about what each article means. The structure of the creed allows people to ask questions about a wide range of items: about God, creation, the birth of Christ, the death and resurrection of Christ, the Spirit, the church. These are questions that people care about and that they are eager to explore. By assuming that "theology" is only for the academic types, we deprive our people of the nourishment that we receive in learning the faith.

There are many good books on the Apostles' and Nicene Creeds.[16] You do not need to be a professional theologian to be able to help people enter the riches of creedal faith.

The Lord's Prayer as the Rule of Hope

"Even the demons believe—and shudder!" (James 2:19). This passage from the book of James is enough to give any catechist pause who would think catechesis is only about learning propositional truths about God without seeking to know God personally through prayer. Catechesis does place a special emphasis on doctrine, but it recognizes that doctrine itself aims at relationship with God. Faith produces *hope*. To put it in Pauline language, we cannot "call upon" the name of the Lord (prayer) without first hearing and believing the Word (the creed) (Rom. 10:13–14). This passage from Romans supplies a logic for teaching the creed and the Lord's Prayer in prebaptismal catechesis. The creed signifies *belief*, while the Lord's Prayer signifies *hope*. The creed is the covenant that makes us children of God. The Lord's Prayer is the script for children to address God *as* father.[17]

16. See some suggestions in appendix 2, "Building a Catechetical Library."

17. Thomas Aquinas put it like this: "Since, in addition to faith, hope is also neces-

The Rule of Hope. The virtue of hope is not merely a rosy optimism for the future. Hope is the desire for ultimate happiness with God in eternity; it is a deep longing for God that shapes our entire existence in the world. We all hope in something, but if we place our hope anywhere short of eternity, we become given to presumption or despair.[18] If we place our hope in this-worldly goods, and think these goods will indeed satisfy our desires, we fall prey to the sin of presumption. We *demand* this-worldly goods to provide eternal happiness, even though they cannot. If, however, we set our hope for temporal goods and realize they cannot satisfy our deepest desires, and we don't have anything else, we become given to despair. Both temptations are but two sides of the same coin of *hopelessness.* Teaching the Lord's Prayer in catechesis is a way of counteracting the deep metaphysical and existential hopelessness of a world that rejects God as its source of beatitude.

The Lord's Prayer trains us to hope rightly in God. It is a pedagogy of desire. Augustine calls the Lord's Prayer the "form of desires," and Aquinas calls it the "interpreter of desire."[19] The Lord's Prayer offers a framework for human longing.

How, though, does the Lord's Prayer train us to desire God? When we pray the Lord's Prayer, we are, in a mysterious way, allowing God himself to pray in us. The Lord's Prayer, we may recall, is not only the prayer Jesus gives to his disciples. It is Jesus's own prayer. It is the prayer he prays to the Father and invites us to pray as well.

In other words, when we pray the Lord's Prayer, Jesus prays to the Father *in us.* And as we are caught up in God's Spirit, we are empowered to pray the audacious words that Jesus gives us to address God. The Spirit encourages us to cry out to God as "Abba"—the intimate name with which the Son addresses the Father (Rom. 8:15). The fundamental reality of prayer, then, is that Jesus prays, and Christian prayer is none other than joining Jesus in prayer. As we pray in the Spirit of Christ, our voice resounds with the words of Christ. Our speech takes on the speech of Christ.

---

sary for our salvation, our Savior, who inaugurated and perfected our faith by instituting the heavenly sacraments, thought it well to carry us on to a living hope by giving us a form of prayer that mightily raises up our hope to God." Aquinas, *Compendium of Theology* 2.3.

18. For a wonderful meditation on hope as an antidote to presumption and despair, see Josef Pieper, "On Hope," in *On Faith, Hope, and Love* (San Francisco: Ignatius, 1997), 89–138.

19. Augustine, *Sermon* 56.4. Aquinas, *Summa Theologiae* II-II, q. 83, art. 9, resp.

As we learn to inhabit the Lord's Prayer, we learn what it means not only for prayer to be "in the name of Christ" but for all of our life to be lived "in the name of Christ." As our voices come to resemble Christ's voice, we learn to relate to God the Father as Christ does—as a beloved child, as one who lacks nothing, as one whose very essence is love. In short, to pray the Lord's Prayer is to have the source and aim of our hope take up residence within us—"Christ in you, the hope of glory" (Col. 1:27).

For many Christians today, the Lord's Prayer is little more than a rote prayer—said routinely and unthinkingly if it is said at all. For many Christians throughout history, though, the Lord's Prayer was understood as a deep wellspring of hope. It contained an infinite depth of meaning that went far beyond its simple wording. The second-century theologian Tertullian called it a "rule of prayer" and a "summary of the whole Gospel"; as much as it is "restricted in words, it is comprehensive in meaning."[20] A generation later, Cyprian of Carthage echoed this idea, saying: "How great . . . are the mysteries of the Lord's Prayer, how many, how magnificent, gathered together in a few words, yet abundant in spiritual power. There is nothing whatever with regard to our pleading and our prayer omitted, nothing not contained in this summary of heavenly doctrine."[21]

And still a millennium later, Saint Teresa of Ávila was finding an unending source of wonder and joy in the Lord's Prayer: "I marvel to see that in so few words everything about contemplation and perfection is included; it seems we need to study no other book than this one."[22] This tradition has a keen perception of the richness in the Lord's Prayer. It is a many-splendored jewel that shines more brightly from each angle, a never-ceasing fountain that springs forth new life.

This is why Christians from Augustine to Bonhoeffer have made the striking claim that we never pray anything except what is in the Lord's Prayer. As Bonhoeffer put it: "At the request of the disciples, Jesus gave them the Lord's Prayer. In it every prayer is contained. Whatever enters into the petitions of the Lord's Prayer is prayed aright; whatever has no place in it, is no prayer at all. All the prayers of the Holy Scriptures are summed up in the Lord's Prayer

20. Tertullian, *On Prayer* 1, in Alistair Stewart-Sykes, *On the Lord's Prayer: Tertullian, Cyprian, and Origen* (Crestwood, NY: St. Vladimir's Seminary Press, 2004), 42.

21. Cyprian, *On the Lord's Prayer* 9, in Stewart-Sykes, *On the Lord's Prayer*, 70.

22. Teresa of Ávila, *The Way of Perfection* 37.1, in *The Collected Words of St. Teresa of Avila*, vol. 2, trans. Kieran Kavanaugh, OCD, and Otilio Rodriguez, OCD (Washington, DC: Institute of Carmelite Studies, 1980), 183.

and are taken up into its immeasurable breadth. They are, therefore, not made superfluous by the Lord's Prayer, but are rather the inexhaustible riches of the Lord's Prayer, just as the Lord's Prayer is their crown and unity."[23]

It is not the case that Christians can only pray the exact words of the Lord's Prayer. It is rather that the Lord's Prayer is contained in every true Christian prayer. Every prayer of the Bible "riffs" on the Lord's Prayer. It is the ultimate melody on which every other prayer improvises, sounding and re-sounding that melody in hundreds of fresh ways.[24]

Teaching the Lord's Prayer. When we teach the Lord's Prayer in catechesis, we offer more than a required prayer. It is powerful prayer that introduces to believers a never-ending wellspring of communion with God. We give language that forms Christ in our hearts and brings the real presence of hope into our lives. In believing, we pray. In calling upon the name of the Lord, we are saved in hope.

There are many effective ways to teach prayer in catechesis. But perhaps the simplest approach is to lead people in different forms of prayer. If you don't feel confident in this area, you can also invite others to join in praying for and with catechumens. But it is not difficult to lead others in different practices of prayer. There are many books on different kinds of prayer, and there are many books specifically on the Lord's Prayer. One of the ways that a catechesis on prayer is unique, perhaps, is that it helps new Christians orient various practices of prayer within the rubric of the Lord's Prayer. You can introduce Ignatian prayer (also known as the examen), along with confession, petition, praise, and contemplation. A simple exercise to do in a group is to pray through Scripture using the practice of *lectio divina*. In each exercise, you can help catechumens see that every prayer has its original form in Christ's own prayer to the Father.

The Ten Commandments as the Rule of Love

Faith and hope abide for now, but love never ends (1 Cor. 13:13). Catechesis thus includes instruction not only on what Christians believe and hope but also on how Christians live. It teaches the theological virtue of love. The Dec-

23. Dietrich Bonhoeffer, *Prayerbook of the Bible*, trans. Daniel Bloesch and James Burtness, Dietrich Bonhoeffer Works 5 (Minneapolis: Fortress, 1996), 157–58. See also Augustine, *Letter* 130.12.

24. I owe the jazz metaphor as applied to the Lord's Prayer to Bruce Hindmarsh.

alogue serves as the primary template for teaching the moral dimension of the Christian life. Here, we learn how to live lives shaped by the love of Christ.

But what is virtue, particularly *Christian* virtue? And how can catechesis train us to live a life of virtue and holiness?

Many have lamented the utter incoherence of moral thinking in our day. Plenty of public figures *talk* about morality and virtue, but mainly as a way to indict those of opposing viewpoints. We live in a time of "the denial of the 'moral' as a category of lived experience," as sociologist James Davison Hunter has put it.[25] What we have is a rather thin version of what it means to live ethically in the world today. In my own teaching in catechesis, I have seen this incoherence play out in numerous ways. For some, Christianity is almost exclusively about morality and ethics. Some people just want clear rules about what to do and not do. For others, however, any kind of attempt at moral formation or virtue is problematic. It is a threat to the pure doctrine of justification by grace alone. If we attempt to teach others how to live morally, we will likely find ourselves on the slippery slope to works righteousness.

When we teach the Ten Commandments in catechesis, we are teaching what it means for our lives to be patterned on Christ. We are showing what it means for believers to be refashioned in the image of Christ—the true image of God. This is because Christ himself is the true meaning of virtue. Any effort to live virtuously is merely our way of allowing Christ to form us into his image. Gregory of Nyssa has a nice way of putting it: he says that if Christ is the true light, then Christian virtue is walking in the rays of the "sun of righteousness" (Mal. 4:2). If Christ is the light of righteousness, as we walk in his light, we lay aside "the works of darkness" (Rom. 13:12) and "walk as children of the light" (Eph. 5:8).[26] This is not Pelagianism or moralism. This is not earning your salvation. This is how we see any human effort toward virtue as a movement of the Holy Spirit in our lives. When I seek to turn away from lying, coveting, and anger, when I seek to honor God's name and put away my idols, I don't see these as my proud achievements. I see these as the work of Christ exercising his own power through the Spirit shed abroad in my heart. Because Christ is virtue, when we teach about the moral life, we simply teach the gospel of Jesus.

Living in Conformity to Christ. Put another way: to say that Christ is virtue is to say that Christ is love. Love is who Christ is, because God is love and Christ is God. The love we see in Jesus Christ is an extension in space and time of the

25. James Davison Hunter, "The Denial of the Moral as Lived Experience," *Hedgehog Review* 26, no. 1 (Spring 2024).

26. Gregory of Nyssa, *On Perfection* (FC 58:103).

perfect, eternal, self-giving love of Father, Son, and Holy Spirit. God is love, as John says, and as a communion of irreducible persons—Father, Son, and Holy Spirit—love is essential to the divine nature. We see the characteristics of this love in the life of Jesus Christ. In Christ, we see a love that is patient, humble, merciful, and just. It forgives rather than holds grudges. It bears wrong rather than lashing out in anger. Most of all, God's love is demonstrated in the giving of his only Son, who died for us while we were still sinners (John 3:16; Rom. 5:8). Love is shaped like a cross.

Why, though, do we teach the Ten Commandments? Why not the Sermon on the Mount or other New Testament teachings on morality? The Decalogue is admittedly a historical latecomer to catechesis. The church fathers did not often use the Ten Commandments as a template for catechesis. The resurgence of the Ten Commandments appears to be a late medieval development, related to their growing use in private confession (the Fourth Lateran Council in 1215 mandated yearly confession).[27] By the time of the Reformation, the Decalogue had become a staple feature of catechetical instruction and has remained in regular use ever since.

The Decalogue is not an outdated set of moral standards, something that can be set aside now that Christ has come. Nor can it be abstracted from the being of God and the history of redemption. The Decalogue provides a concrete pathway for living in conformity to Christ. As John Calvin once put it, it expresses the image of God in our lives.[28] The commandments teach us to have no other gods, to sanctify his name, to keep the Sabbath holy, to honor our parents, and to avoid murder, adultery, slander, theft, and covetousness. They teach us, in short, to love God and our neighbor. If virtue is the life and person of Jesus Christ, as Gregory of Nyssa put it, then the commandments are like the rays of Christ's holy light. As we walk in their glow, our lives shine with the love of Christ.

27. See Lesley Smith, *The Ten Commandments: Interpreting the Bible in the Medieval World* (Leiden: Brill, 2014); Jonathan Willis, *The Reformation of the Decalogue: Religious Identity and the Ten Commandments in England, c. 1485–1625* (Cambridge: Cambridge University Press, 2017).

28. John Calvin, *Institutes of the Christian Religion*, ed. John T. McNeill, trans. Ford Lewis Battles, 2 vols. (Philadelphia: Westminster, 1960), 2.8.51. As Gilbert Meilaender puts it, the commandments are not "an external law imposed upon recalcitrant subjects; rather they give shape to the life directed by the Spirit of Christ." *Thy Will Be Done: The Ten Commandments and the Christian Life* (Grand Rapids: Baker Academic, 2020), 9.

Jesus did not reject the Ten Commandments in the Sermon on the Mount. He fulfilled them. He brought them to fruition. Likewise, Saint Paul states, "The whole law is fulfilled in one word: 'You shall love your neighbor as yourself'" (Gal. 5:14). New Testament moral teaching presupposes and fulfills the Ten Commandments. Especially in catechesis, if we want to focus our efforts on the foundation of Christian teaching, we can do little better than the Ten Commandments.

Teaching the Ten Commandments. How, though, do we teach the Ten Commandments in catechesis? What does this look like? It begins with the recognition that God's own virtue and love are the ground of our own growth in virtue. Because God is love, and because he first loved us, we too can grow in virtue. We love because God first loved us (1 John 4:7).

This response to God's love happens primarily in the community of Christ's body, the church. The church is the social context that images and inculcates the good life. Virtue doesn't make sense apart from a community that maintains a vision of the good life. The community embodies images, stories, narratives, and practices that teach implicitly and explicitly what it means to live well. We learn virtue amid what Hunter calls "moral ecologies," which include our schools, families, workplaces, social organizations, the Internet, media, and other institutions. Virtue formation is never an individual project but always one that takes place in an ecosystem of communities and cultures. Hunter writes: "Character and its formation are inextricably entwined within community and its culture."[29] We learn Christian virtue within the body of Christ, among those called out by God and filled with the Holy Spirit to be conformed to his image.

We learn virtue in at least four ways. First, virtue is learned through examples. We don't live virtuously without seeing virtue lived in real human lives. This was a key theme in many ancient philosophies, and Christians took up the theme, too. "Be imitators of me, as I am of Christ," Paul wrote to the Corinthians (1 Cor. 11:1). As we see virtue modeled in the saints and examples of the church, their actions and habits rub off on us. This is why, in the fourth century, Ambrose of Milan wrote several treatises on the Old Testament patriarchs. He thought that by telling their stories with an eye to how these saints modeled the virtues of Christ, newcomers to the faith would become "accustomed" to the ancient paths that God has laid down for his people.[30] Ambrose told their stories to inspire catechumens to learn from them and to imitate Christ's virtue in them.

29. Hunter, "The Denial of the Moral."

30. See Ambrose, *On the Mysteries* 1.1 (FC 44:5).

Teaching virtue in catechesis, then, begins with highlighting these examples. You might begin to ask: Who are the people in your own life who helped show you how the Christian life was lived? As you look back on your own story, how did you see virtue modeled in the stories you heard or the people you were around? Traditionally, this has been part of the role of godparents or sponsors. These figures serve a crucial role in the catechumen's moral formation. By providing living examples of Christian virtue, they forge bonds of friendship that enmesh the catechumen into the body of Christ.

Of course, we will not want to imitate another's virtue if we don't find something attractive about that person's life. Hence a second feature of learning virtue is the role of the imagination. All communities tell stories that cast a vision of good and evil. Such stories are full of tragedy and peril, triumph and adventure, heroes and villains. Importantly, they shape our perceptions about what and who is *good,* and they make us want to be good as well.

Third, virtue is acquired through moral reflection and accountability. If stories are more formative than principles, that is no reason to avoid clear reflection on how to live well. Saint Paul implores us to set our minds on the good: "Whatever is true, whatever is honorable, whatever is just, whatever is pure, whatever is lovely, whatever is commendable, if there is any excellence, if there is anything worthy of praise, think about these things" (Phil. 4:8). What we think about, what we reflect on, what we meditate upon—these shape the kinds of people we become. As we reflect upon our own life—our decisions and actions—we are able to remember in the future how to act virtuously. In catechesis, it can be especially valuable to introduce catechumens to a spiritual director or some other kind of mentor or spiritual friend. This kind of person helps the catechumen learn to listen to the Holy Spirit and to reflect on Christ's activity in his or her life.

Finally, virtue happens through practice. Saint Paul admonishes Timothy, "Train yourself for godliness" (1 Tim. 4:7). The Greek term behind the English "training" is *askēsis,* and it refers to the way an athlete trains for a competition. But in the spiritual life, as Paul goes on to say, we race not for a temporal but an eternal prize (1 Cor. 9:24–27). While Christian virtue is *unlike* other habits—it requires the infusion of grace from the Holy Spirit—it is like them in the sense that *practicing* virtue makes a difference. Here, a basic competency in the spiritual disciplines can be of great help to catechists.[31] Like practicing the

31. For good introductions, one can still do little better than the classic works by Richard Foster and Dallas Willard. See Richard Foster, *The Celebration of Discipline: The Path to Spiritual Growth* (New York: HarperCollins, 1978), and Dallas Willard,

piano or athletic drills, spiritual disciplines like prayer, fasting, silence, study, Sabbath keeping, and acts of service and mercy can help catechumens "put on Christ" and allow the Spirit to shape them into the kinds of people who begin to naturally live according to the habits of Christ.

Learning virtue is at once supremely ordinary and wholly mysterious. While there are practical steps we can take, it is not a mechanical process. Nor is it a journey of autonomous self-mastery. Growing in virtue means becoming more dependent on Christ, not less. It is an ever-increasing awareness that our lives are the gift of our creator and redeemer. Ultimately, Christian virtue is friendship with Christ. And as we seek this friendship in the church, we come to love and live like the one who first called us his friend.

As we set to work building the foundations of faith, the catechism serves as a trusty tool for measuring faith, hope, and love. The catechism provides a mosaic of Christ the king that guides not only our reading of Scripture but all of our thinking, desiring, and loving in the Christian life. Aquinas says that salvation consists in these three things: knowing the truth, so that the mind is not led astray by falsehoods; intending the right goal, so that we do not fall from true happiness by pursuing the wrong ends; and living justly, so that we are not destroyed by various vices. These three requirements are matched by the three theological virtues of faith, hope, and love: faith brings us to the knowledge of the truth; hope sets our goal on the right end; and love orders our affections.[32]

The catechism is an invaluable tool for helping Christians construct a solid foundation in Christ. In its threefold emphasis on faith, hope, and love, the catechism gives us a straight edge to comprehend with all the saints the height, width, and depth of God's love (Eph. 3:18–19).

The Spirit of the Disciplines: Understanding How God Changes Lives (New York: HarperCollins, 1991).

32. Aquinas, *Compendium of Theology* 1.

7

Inhabiting the World through Scripture and Sacraments

During the season of Lent in the late 370s, Basil of Caesarea, who would later be known simply as "Basil the Great," delivered a weeklong series of homilies on the six days of creation. The *Hexameron,* as it is called, brought together a wide range of biblical, philosophical, and spiritual reflections on the opening chapters of Genesis. He was not the first to do so. Many preachers before and after taught the creation story in the weeks leading up to Easter. But Basil's sermons were unique in their ability to engage the minds of diverse audiences. Merchants and scholars, learned and unlearned, young and old—Basil spoke to each of them in a way that brought them closer to God. Basil's brother Gregory of Nyssa would later say that, "through a gentle persuasion of their souls, Basil led them through the visible world and the beautiful things in it, to a knowledge of him who made everything."[1]

Basil viewed the natural world as a work of art, and he wanted his hearers to see in it the wisdom of the divine Artist. Teeming with beauty and life, the world was radiant with the shining light of the Word, and by displaying such beauty before his hearers, Basil was offering a training ground for the vision of God. Creation, he claimed, "is truly a training place (*paideutērion*) for rational souls and a school (*didaskaleion*) for attaining the knowledge of God."[2] The terms *paidetērion* and *didaskaleion* recall the ancient education system where students were formed in the tradition of Greek culture. For Basil, with Romans 1:20 in mind, the whole world would become a school where one learned to perceive God's invisible attributes in the things that have been made.

1. Gregory of Nyssa, *On the Six Days of Creation* 4, trans. Robin Orton, Fathers of the Church: Shorter Works 1 (Washington, DC: Catholic University of America Press, 2021), 45.

2. Basil of Caesarea, *Hexameron* 1.6, in *Basil of Caesarea: Exegetic Writings,* trans. Agnes Way, FC 46 (Washington, DC: Catholic University of America Press, 1963), 11.

It is no coincidence that Basil preached these sermons during Lent. Basil was preparing catechumens to live in the world as a training ground for seeing God. They were being transformed in their perception of time and the material world. They were learning to inhabit the world Christianly.

This chapter builds on the last by focusing on teaching Scripture and the sacraments in catechesis. Along with faith, hope, and love, Scripture and the sacraments are two important topics for instruction. But why do we teach these things? What are we trying to accomplish? I suggest that teaching the story of the Bible helps Christians live in the world Christianly: we help believers live in time as Christians, learning to see themselves caught up in a larger story about God's salvation. Similarly, teaching the sacraments doesn't just teach catechumens about the peculiar rites we do on Sundays. It helps them see the whole creation in relation to God. Catechizing Christians on the meaning of the sacraments trains them to perceive the invisible powers of God in the visible things that he has made.

But first we need to step back and ask: What is the world, and how does it become a training ground for the vision of God? To bolster our approach to teaching the Scriptures and sacraments, we need a doctrine of creation that understands the world as latent with signs and wonders that can draw us into holy fellowship with the living God.

The School of Creation

Here I want to make two claims: creation is *purposeful*, and creation is *pedagogical*. First, creation is purposeful. "O Lord, how manifold are your works!" the psalmist declares, "in wisdom have you made them all" (Ps. 104:24). God created all things in wisdom, and this does not only refer to *how* God made the world but "in whom." God made the world "in" Christ, the origin and principle of all creation. In saying that creation has an origin or a beginning, then, it means that creation has a providential ordering and is being drawn toward a certain end. The structure of creation is deeply teleological. The world is not created randomly or without purpose but has a logic, order, and direction; it is going somewhere. The deep logic of creation, though, is not always perceptible to ordinary experience. We don't always see creation as radiating the glory of God and as the master artistry of a divine Artist. And this is because creation's logic is not simply identical to Christ the Logos. Each individual thing has unique properties, and yet these properties have their ultimate source in the Word who transcends their individual expressions.

The seventh-century theologian Maximus the Confessor is famous for his idea that Christ and creation relate as Logos to *logoi* (the plural of *logos*)—as divine Word to many "words."[3] Each thing in creation has its own word or principle, its own unique identity. There is a "word" in each thing, and these words are distinct from one another yet bound up in the one Word. There are different *logoi* for the different kinds of angels, heavenly powers, human beings, and animals. There are different *logoi* among plants and rocks and trees. And Maximus argued that if (a) God creates all things out of nothing, and (b) we experience a wide variety of things in the world, then we can conclude that (c) "the one Logos is many *logoi*." Each thing in the world is unique, distinct from all other individual things, yet at the same time, "the many *logoi* are the one Logos to whom all things are related."

Each of the various *logoi* is uniquely related to the Logos, which remains hidden from ordinary sight; the Logos is ineffable and exalted above creation—even "beyond the idea of difference and distinction." This divine Logos is Christ, the Word of God, who exists in the Godhead without confusion. The divine Logos is by nature of the divine essence; he is true God from true God. Yet the world's many *logoi* are "held" in the Logos and continue to exist by sharing in the Word of life. The relation of Logos and *logoi* is one of revelation and recapitulation.[4] The goodness of the divine Logos is revealed in everything, for everything has its origin in God. Yet Christ the Word also recapitulates all things in himself (Eph. 1:10). Through the Logos, the *logoi* are created and have existence. And each thing continues to exist because it participates in God according to its capacity.[5]

This is what it means to say that creation is purposeful: in its vibrant and wondrous diversity, creation finds it origin and end in the God who transcends creation while constantly sustaining life. All created things—whether visible

3. Maximus's writing on this topic belongs to what is often called the Divine Ideas tradition. For good introductions, see Thomas M. Ward, *Divine Ideas* (Cambridge: Cambridge University Press, 2020); Mark McIntosh, *The Divine Ideas Tradition in Christian Mystical Theology* (Oxford: Oxford University Press, 2021).

4. Maximus the Confessor, *Ambiguum* 7.2, in *On the Cosmic Mystery of Jesus Christ: Selected Writings from St. Maximus the Confessor*, trans. Paul M. Blowers and Robert Louis Wilken (Crestwood, NY: St. Vladimir's Seminary Press, 2003), 54.

5. Maximus the Confessor, *Ambiguum* 7.2, in Blowers and Wilken, *On the Cosmic Mystery of Jesus Christ*, 55: Maximus argues that each thing participates in God in proportion to the kind of thing it is, whether by intellect, by reason, by sense perception, by vital motion, or by some habitual fitness.

or invisible, material or spiritual—have their being as *logoi* in the Logos, words in the Word.

And because creation is purposeful, it is also *pedagogical*. Creation serves as a teacher and guide. In Basil's words, it is a "school" and "training ground." Creation teaches first of all through speaking and singing the praise of God. "The heavens *declare* the glory of God," the psalmist announces, "and the sky above proclaims his handiwork" (Ps. 19:1). "The whole sensible world," wrote the medieval theologian Hugh of St. Victor, "is like a book written by the finger of God."[6] As John Calvin described it, creation is a "theater" for displaying the glory of God. Jonathan Edwards wrote about figures and "types" in creation as a kind of language that we learn the way we learn other languages: by "good acquaintance with the language."[7] Creation teaches the glory of God by declaring in symbols and types the "invisible attributes" of God (Rom. 1:20).

In learning about the nature of creation, we learn about the God whose power sustains it and who teaches us about himself through the created order. Creation reveals God to us through its purposefulness. All of creation's *logoi* share in the divine Logos. And because of this logic, creation speaks; it teaches. In the school of creation, we learn to see God as the author of all things.

But we don't normally experience the world as a training for seeing God. More often, creation is a battlefield, appearing to us in horrifying and terrifying ways—concealing more than revealing God. Confronted with natural and moral evils, how are we to retrain ourselves to see the world as a school for the vision of God? In teaching the story of Scripture and the meaning of the sacraments, we help Christians do just that. Teaching Scripture helps believers live in the story of God's salvation in time and history. Teaching the sacraments shows the true meaning of the world as bound up with God's healing and redeeming grace.

The Narrative of Scripture

Midway through J. R. R. Tolkien's epic trilogy *The Lord of the Rings*, faithful Samwise asks, "I wonder what sort of tale we've fallen into?" This is the ques-

6. Hugh of St. Victor, *On the Three Days* 4.3, in *Trinity and Creation*, trans. Hugh Feiss, Victorine Texts in Translation 1 (Hyde Park, NY: New City, 2011), 63.

7. See Jonathan Edwards, "Types," in vol. 11 of *The Works of Jonathan Edwards*, ed. Wallace E. Anderson, Mason Lowance, and David Watters (New Haven: Yale University Press, 1993), 150–51. For a good introduction to this topic in Edwards, see Gerald McDermott, *Everyday Glory: The Revelation of God in All of Reality* (Grand Rapids: Baker Academic, 2018).

tion we all ask. What sort of story are we in? How did it begin and where is it going? Is there some meaning or purpose to it all? This is essential to knowing how to live well. To paraphrase Alasdair MacIntyre, we'll never know how to live unless we know what story we're a part of.[8]

Too often, though, we live in stories of our own making. We live the Enlightenment story that we are self-created and self-directed agents, hindered only by the restraints imposed by tradition and custom. Or we live the technocratic story that says we can solve any problem if we just apply the right method. Or we live the expressive-individualist story that somewhere deep down in us there is an inner core that must be examined and protected at all costs. We can live each of these stories and more.

Catechesis then needs to situate us firmly in God's story. In catechesis, we need our stories renarrated to see how we figure in the story of God's creation and redemption of all things. Holding a common narrative is one thing that binds a people together. It provides a common memory and common identity. As George Stroup puts it, "The community's common narrative is the glue that binds its members together."[9] This was a key feature of patristic catechesis. From Irenaeus to Augustine, many early Christian catechists taught catechumens a narrative summary of Scripture and outline of salvation history. Early catechists recognized that new Christians needed to understand the story to which they belonged before they could know how to live the strange new way of Christ.

Being "biblical" can mean all sorts of things. For some, it can mean having an extensive knowledge of biblical words and phrases, what some people call speaking "Christian-ese." For others, it can mean citing the Bible as a trump card to win the upper hand in an argument. For others still, the Bible can be a kind of magical talisman, as if simply having a high regard for the Bible makes one righteous in the eyes of God. But teaching the biblical narrative in catechesis is different than any of these approaches. Our main purpose is providing a larger narrative framework to help locate our own histories in the history of God. We're learning to live not as authors of own story but as characters in God's story.

8. Alasdair MacIntyre, *After Virtue*, 2nd ed. (Notre Dame: University of Notre Dame Press, 1984), 216.

9. George Stroup, *The Promise of Narrative Theology*, 134, cited in Everett Ferguson, "Irenaeus' *Proof of the Apostolic Preaching* and Early Catechetical Instruction," in *The Early Church at Work and Worship*, vol. 2, *Catechesis, Baptism, Eschatology, and Martyrdom* (Eugene, OR: Wipf & Stock, 2014), 1.

In his massive book *A Secular Age*, Charles Taylor outlines what he calls "secular time." This is when we see time as a series of temporal, sequential events—one thing after another. Events that happened in the past don't have any real connection with things that happen in the future. But for Christians, events that happen in secular time are bound up with a "higher time." Israel's deliverance from slavery in Egypt and the Christian's deliverance from sin are unique historical events that are both caught up in the higher time of Jesus's defeat of death on the cross. By telling the biblical story, we are inviting new believers to live not in secular time but in *participatory* time.[10] In Christian time, the differentiated stories of the world belong within a unified story in which the eternal God is revealing himself and bringing out his good purposes in the world. We come into this understanding of history and time gradually, and it begins with telling the story of the Bible as God's loving redemption and salvation.

Augustine was especially alert to the centrality of love in scriptural history. In his sermons and writing, we see the important ways in which he wove Scripture into his understanding of salvation and the Christian life. For Augustine, the mystery of our salvation is that the humble God takes on human flesh, becoming humiliated in death so that proud-minded people can encounter his transcendent, spiritual glory. Scripture imitates this christological pattern: the humble words of Scripture are like the humble flesh of Christ, able to speak to all Christians, no matter their age, intellect, or depth of sin.[11] It speaks to them in terms they can understand, and then, as understanding increases, Scripture reveals more and more of its infinite depth. In one passage, Augustine writes of the way Scripture is accessible to everyone, yet also never fully comprehensible. "In its easily understood parts it speaks to the heart of the unlearned and learned like a familiar friend who uses no guile, but in those truths it veils in mystery, it does not raise itself aloft with proud speech." Scripture presents clear and concise images to reach even the simplest of hearers: shepherds in search of lost sheep, a father rejoicing over a wayward son. Yet for all its simplicity, Scripture's hidden depths train the lowly mind to ascend toward the infinite heights of Scripture's Author. "The hidden truths arouse longing; longing brings renewal; renewal brings sweet inner knowledge."[12]

10. These terms come from Matthew Levering, *Participatory Biblical Exegesis: A Theology of Biblical Interpretation* (Notre Dame: University of Notre Dame Press, 2008).

11. The relationship between Christology and scriptural interpretation is helpfully laid out in Michael Cameron, *Christ Meets Me Everywhere: Augustine's Early Figurative Exegesis* (Oxford: Oxford University Press, 2012).

12. Augustine, *Letter* 137.5.18, in *Augustine in His Own Words*, ed. William Harmless (Washington, DC: Catholic University of America Press, 2010), 163.

Scripture, like Christ, reaches humans where they are and leads them to fellowship with God. From a person's first moments as a Christian to a lifetime of walking with the Lord, Scripture is milk for babes and meat for the aged (see 1 Cor. 3:2; Heb. 5:12).[13]

In his catechetical treatise *On Catechizing the Uninstructed,* Augustine gives instruction and specific examples of how to do this. The "narration of Scripture is complete," Augustine writes, when each person is instructed in the biblical story, beginning with Genesis 1:1 and continuing "to the present period of the church's history."[14] Depending on the background and education of the catechumen, this can be more or less detailed, but it is important not to overwhelm the catechumen with too much at once. Rather, the catechist ought to provide a "summary sketch" of the narrative, selecting some of the more memorable parts of the story that constitute the critical historical "turning points" (3.5). Details can be woven in here and there, but the first task is to provide a summary sketch that can be committed to memory and serve as a guiding framework for future discussions.

In addition, the catechist tells the story in such a way that the central message of Scripture becomes manifest. "Everything that we read in the Holy Scriptures that was written before the coming of the Lord was written for the sole purpose of drawing attention to his coming and to prefigure the future church" (3.5, altered). This includes all those who lived before and after the coming of Christ in the flesh, and it includes believers all throughout the world. Everything that happened in Scripture points to the central mystery of human history: the love of God made manifest in Christ and the church.

Augustine wanted his catechumens to know this scriptural history so they could know how they themselves belong within God's story of salvation. They become connected with the saints of old as the one body of Christ, united across space and time. Catechumens learn this history so they can learn to see Christ as the turning point upon which all of history turns. Augustine summarizes this approach in a pithy phrase: "in the Old Testament is concealed the New, in the New Testament is revealed the Old" (4.8). Eternity has erupted into time and space and drawn everything—Old and New together—into the all-encompassing time of Christ.

Augustine also emphasizes biblical history in catechesis with the aim of showing catechumens the extraordinary extent of God's love and the impera-

13. Augustine, *Letter* 137.5.18, in Harmless, *Augustine in His Own Words,* 163.

14. Augustine, *On Catechizing the Uninstructed* 3.5, in *Instructing Beginners in the Faith,* trans. Raymond Canning (Hyde Park, NY: New City, 2006), 63. Hereafter, chapter and section numbers from this work will be given in parentheses in the text.

tive to love God and their neighbors in turn.[15] Scripture is not an end in itself but is meant to spur believers on to love. Augustine writes: "Before all else, Christ came so that people might learn how much God loves them, and might learn this so that they would catch fire with love for him who first loved them, and so that they would also love their neighbor as he commanded and showed by his example—he who made himself their neighbor by loving them when they were not close to him but were wandering far from him" (4.8).

The goal of teaching Scripture is to help others see the unfathomable love of God for us and to spur us to love God and neighbor in return. And Augustine wanted to show catechumens this was the case as much as tell them. He wanted to show, as Michael Cameron puts it, "how Christ forms that love in the heart of the reading Christian."[16]

In catechesis, Scripture conveys the truth about time and history and conforms Christians to live according to the image of God in Christ. Telling the story of Scripture reveals the heart of the gospel in God's love for humanity so that Christians will "catch fire" with love for God and neighbor. Scripture, for Augustine, is the chief means by which Christ catechizes us. It is our daily bread until we see God face-to-face (1 Cor. 13:12); it is "the face of God for now."[17]

How to Tell the Old, Old Story

There are many ways to teach the story of Scripture in catechesis. The most important thing is to frame the story within a pattern (a) that can be easily memorized and (b) that focuses on Christ. Again, we're not simply interested in "teaching the Bible" in some vague generic sense but articulating an account of the story of Scripture in a way that is comprehensible and that can provide believers an orienting framework. We want to provide a map that gives people a good sense of the terrain.

Augustine's map was organized into seven historical periods:

1. Adam to Noah
2. Noah to Abraham

15. Love for God and neighbor was central to Augustine's thought. Elsewhere, Augustine compares the person who interprets Scripture "wrongly," but in such a way that it leads to loving God and neighbor, to someone who goes a roundabout way on a journey but ends up in the right destination. See Augustine, *On Christian Teaching* 1.36.41.

16. Cameron, *Christ Meets Me Everywhere*, 241.

17. Augustine, *Sermon* 22.7 (WSA III/2:46, translation mine).

3. Abraham to David
4. David to exile
5. Exile to Christ
6. Christ to the present day
7. The return of Christ and final glory

He stresses these key "turning points" of history so that newcomers won't get bogged down in the details. And he emphasizes the center of the story in Christ and the church. The crux of the biblical narrative is God's *love* for humanity revealed in the incarnation of Christ and the creation of the church.

A contemporary example is biblical scholar N. T. Wright's "five-act play" model.[18] Taking up the metaphor of stage performance, Wright argues that Scripture is a "script" for Christians to enact, as actors learn lines for a play. This play has five acts:

1. Creation
2. Fall
3. Israel
4. Jesus
5. Church

For Wright, Scripture's purpose is to draw human beings into salvation and energize them to become participants in God's new creation. Scripture provides the script, but the magic happens when Christians bring the words to life.

Wright's model of scriptural history is perhaps more linear than Augustine's. For Augustine, Scripture's central motif of Christ and the church is not just one stage in a sequence but something figuratively present in all stages of the story. "The New is in the Old concealed," as he puts it, "while the Old is in the New revealed."[19] Augustine understands history itself as participating in the eternal reality of Christ. For Wright, the emphasis is more on historical time, and telling the story rightly means not being confused about what time we're in. It

18. See N. T. Wright, *The New Testament and the People of God* (Minneapolis: Fortress, 1992), chap. 5. For a simplified account and how it relates to understanding Scripture as authoritative, see Wright, *Scripture and the Authority of God* (San Francisco: HarperCollins, 2011). For a different account of envisioning Scripture in dramatic terms, see Kevin Vanhoozer, *Hearers and Doers: A Pastor's Guide to Making Disciples through Scripture and Doctrine* (Bellingham, WA: Lexham, 2019).

19. Augustine, *On Catechizing the Uninstructed* 4.8.

would be out of place for a character in the fifth act to simply repeat lines from the second act as if the character were still in that time. As Wright puts it, "we must act in the appropriate manner for *this* moment of the story."[20] It will be in continuity with earlier parts of the play. It's still the same play. But we are now in a different stage of the drama. In both approaches, though, we get a clear model for understanding the narrative of Scripture.[21] These frameworks can be adapted to different audiences. For young children, the narrative will proceed differently than if the catechumen is a professor of history. As always, catechists need to adjust the content based on the particular audience.

However we provide it, new Christians need a basic outline of the biblical story to be rooted and grounded in God's time. Teaching the narrative of salvation provides Christians with a sense of the grand scope of salvation history. It helps them live in time in a way shaped by a Christian vision of reality. Most of all, it helps them see how their own stories fit in the one true story of God's healing and redemption of creation. In telling the story of Scripture, we help others see, as Augustine puts it, that "before all else, Christ came so that people might learn how much God loves them."

Sacraments and the Spiritual Senses

If the biblical narrative provides a Christian vision of time, the sacraments provide a Christian vision of matter. In teaching the sacraments, we do much more than merely explain the mechanics of baptism or the historical debates about the Eucharist. That has its place, but the real value of teaching the sacraments in catechesis is introducing Christians to a way of seeing the created order as sharing in God's life.

For this, our guide in this section will be Ambrose of Milan (339–397), who was one of the leading Latin bishops of Italy in the fourth century. A rising figure in Roman politics, he was thrust into church life when he was unexpectedly elected bishop in the early 370s. He learned quickly, however, and would become an astute catechist and spiritual father to many Christians—including Augustine himself, who was baptized by Ambrose in the spring of 387.

In fact, when Augustine tells the story of his catechumenate in Ambrose's church, he recalls how Ambrose taught him how to discern the spiritual sense

20. Wright, *Scripture and the Authority*, 123.

21. There are many others, too. One might think of the videos compiled by *The Bible Project* or, for younger kids, the *Jesus Storybook Bible*, both of which focus on a narrative approach to Scripture.

of Scripture. Ambrose helped him move beyond the "letter" of Scripture and to see the "spirit" that lay hidden beneath. This kind of teaching is what scholars call the "spiritual senses" tradition.[22] Just as we have the five bodily senses of taste, touch, sight, hearing, and smell, so also do we have "inner" or "spiritual" senses that help us encounter God. We hear an echo of this in one of the most famous passages from Augustine's *Confessions*:

> Late have I loved you, beauty so old and so new: late have I loved you. And see, you were within and I was in the external world and sought you there, and in my unlovely state I plunged into those lovely created things which you made. You were with me, and I was not with you. The lovely things kept me far from you, though if they did not have their existence in you, they had no existence at all.
>
> You called and cried out loud and shattered my deafness. You were radiant and resplendent, you put to flight my blindness. You were fragrant, and I drew in my breath and now pant after you. I tasted you, and I feel but hunger and thirst for you. You touched me, and I am set on fire to attain the peace which is yours.[23]

Augustine struggled to find God in the external world. He could not see Christ as the Logos of creation's *logoi*. The world was teeming with lovely things, resplendent with divine beauty. But Augustine was far from God. God needed to shatter his deafness and put his blindness to flight. He was at last able to encounter God because God first awoke his spiritual senses.

Like Augustine, we need spiritual vision to see a spiritual God. We need to have our spiritual senses opened to become receptive to the blinding, deafening, delectable, fragrant, enrapturing encounter with God. But how do we learn to do this? We are fortunate to possess several of Ambrose's catechetical writings, which Augustine himself may have heard. These include Lenten homilies, a homily on the creed, and postbaptismal "mystagogical" sermons.

In the Lenten sermons, Ambrose especially focused on teaching catechumens the moral virtues of the Christian life.[24] Drawing on the book of Prov-

22. For an excellent introduction to this tradition, see Paul L. Gavrilyuk and Sarah Coakley, eds., *The Spiritual Senses: Perceiving God in Western Christianity* (Cambridge: Cambridge University Press, 2012).

23. Augustine, *Confessions* 10.27.38, trans. Henry Chadwick (Oxford: Oxford University Press, 1991), 201.

24. On these sermons, see Marcia Colish, *Ambrose's Patriarchs: Ethics for the Com-*

erbs and the stories of Old Testament patriarchs like Abraham, Isaac, Jacob, and Joseph, Ambrose wanted new Christians to learn these stories so that they might become "accustomed to enter upon the ways of our forefathers and to pursue their road, and to obey the divine commands, whereby renewed by baptism [they] might hold to that manner of life which befit those who are washed."[25] The Christian life of virtue, as we saw in the last chapter, is learned through imitation, by following the footsteps of our spiritual forebearers. Paul's injunction "Be imitators of me, as I am of Christ" (1 Cor. 11:1; see also Phil. 3:17; 4:9) could well apply to Ambrose's Lenten catechesis. His catechesis was a Christ-centered instruction where catechumens learned to hear echoes of Christ in the lives of the saints.

Ambrose's mystagogical sermons emphasized the spiritual senses even more. In texts like *On the Mysteries* and *On the Sacraments,* we see how Ambrose taught newly baptized Christians to perceive the world in faith. The ritual of baptism began with a rite called the *Ephpheta,* or the "sacrament of opening."[26] Based on the gospel accounts of Jesus healing the deaf man at Sidon, this ritual involved the bishop anointing the ears of the catechumens so that they would be able to hear and remember the grace at work in their midst. Afterward, Ambrose went through each of the anointings, interrogations, washings, and exorcisms that were part of initiation, teaching them along the way the difference between physical and spiritual senses. Drawing on texts like 2 Corinthians 4:18 ("We look not to the things that are seen but to the things that are unseen. For the things that are seen are transient, but the things that are unseen are eternal"), Ambrose taught the newly baptized the difference between seeing with the eyes of the body and seeing with the eyes of the heart.[27]

But it was baptism itself where the spiritual senses were most fully unlocked. Before baptism, Ambrose says, we see "corporeal things with corporeal eyes"; we're not able to understand the sacraments because we cannot yet see with the "eyes of the heart."[28] This changes after baptism: "Since you have come

mon Man (Notre Dame: University of Notre Dame Press, 2005); J. Warren Smith, *Christian Grace and Pagan Virtue: The Theological Foundation of Ambrose's Ethics* (New York: Oxford University Press, 2010).

25. Ambrose, *On the Mysteries* 1.1 (FC 44:5).

26. Ambrose, *On the Mysteries* 1.3–4 (FC 44:6); *On the Sacraments* 3.2.12 (FC 44:294). *Ephpheta* is a Latinized form of Jesus's Aramaic command "Be opened" (see Mark 7:34).

27. Ambrose, *On the Mysteries* 3.15 (FC 44:10); *On the Sacraments* 3.2.12 (FC 44:294).

28. Ambrose, *On the Sacraments* 3.2.12 (FC 44:294).

[to the altar], you are able to see what you did not see before. . . . Through the font of the Lord and the preaching of the Lord's passion, your eyes were then opened. You who seemed before to have been blind in heart began to see the light of the sacraments."[29]

Ambrose's catechesis was characterized by a thoroughgoing training in the spiritual senses. And at the heart of this training was the central Christian mystery. If the triune God is the transcendent, immaterial source of all created existence, yet, at the same time, God took on flesh for our redemption, then the orthodox Christian can neither escape to a purely spiritual world nor reduce God to a material idol. Instead, Christians learn to see God in a sacramental way—to see God's invisible powers in the things that are made.

Learning Spiritual Vision

Ambrose's catechesis taught new Christians what it meant to sense God in the world, to live in the new creation while sojourning in the world. The Christian vision of creation is one in which created things are signs that point to God and make God known. Creation shares in the life of God because it is created and continually sustained by God himself, in his own Word and his own Spirit. Though God exceeds matter and time, he has created us to "live and move and have our being" in him (Acts 17:28) because all things "hold together" in Christ, the Logos and *logic* of our being (Heb. 1:3; Col. 1:17).

But we live in a fallen world governed by the false logics of consumption, materialism, and individualism. Liturgical scholar Alexander Schmemann says that "when we see the world as an end in itself, everything becomes itself a value and consequently loses all value, because only in God is found the meaning (value) over everything, and the world is meaningful only when it is the 'sacrament' of God's presence."[30] Seeing the world as sacramental, then, is not intuitive. It takes time. It takes practice. This is why we teach the sacraments.

Teaching new Christians to perceive God in the world takes both spiritual power and human practice. It is both a work of the spirit and also something that requires our disciplined attention. Seeing God is not like looking at a physical object in the world—a chair, a book. Learning to see God entails "purity of heart" (cf. Matt. 5:8) and "having the eyes of your hearts enlightened" (Eph. 1:18). There are both active and passive elements. We *learn* to see God and God *reveals.*

29. Ambrose, *On the Sacraments* 3.2.11 (FC 44:293).

30. Alexander Schmemann, *For the Life of the World,* rev. ed. (Crestwood, NY: St. Vladimir's Seminary Press, 1973), 17.

We see another example of this in a writing on baptism by the second-century North African theologian Tertullian of Carthage. In explaining the difference between pagan and Christian rituals, Tertullian admits that his instruction on baptism seems to have turned into an ode to the element of water. He praises water for its antiquity, authority, and prestige. Before the world was created, God's Spirit hovered over the water. While the other elements remained unformed, there was water—"always perfect, joyous, simple, of its own nature pure, laid down there a worthy carriage for God to move upon."[31] He goes on: "If I go on to tell of all or most of the things I could relate concerning the authority of this element, the greatness of its power or its grace, with all the devices, all the functions, all the equipment with which it supplies the world, I fear I should seem to have composed a panegyric on water instead of a rationale for baptism."[32]

We see here the way Tertullian's treatise on the sacrament of *baptism* has morphed into a way of understanding the world more generally as a sacramental means of God's display of creative and saving action. A teaching on the sacraments proper is at once an introduction to seeing the world through a biblical lens. Tertullian's catechumens learn to see water—an element so basic, so primal—as a fitting vessel for God to bless and heal the world. They are being trained to see the world sacramentally.

I've found this approach to teaching the sacraments to be especially fruitful. Many people will want to know how our church understands the sacraments. What's the Baptist view of baptism? What do the Presbyterians believe about the Eucharist? What about the other sacraments, like marriage, ordination, confirmation, confession, and anointing? Are these sacraments, as the Roman Catholic Church teaches, or something else?

While we need to help people navigate these questions, it's more important to address the fundamental issues of creation underlying these questions. Without this, the polarizing disagreements about the sacraments can be an arbitrary imposition on Scripture. If we don't have some grasp of the importance of water in God's creation, we won't quite understand baptism, and if we don't understand baptism, we won't understand water. But if we can see teaching the sacraments as a window into seeing how all creation shares in the Logos of Christ, we can help catechumens learn to see all of life through the lens of the sacraments. We begin to see other people and the world around us

31. Tertullian, *On Baptism* 3.2, in *Tertullian's Homily on Baptism*, trans. Ernest Evans (London: SPCK, 1964), 8–9.

32. Tertullian, *On Baptism* 3.6, in Evans, *Tertullian's Homily on Baptism*, 8–9.

as icons of divine presence, images reflecting eternal glory. C. S. Lewis once wrote, "you've never met a mere mortal," meaning that despite the often drab and humdrum appearance of those around us, they are in fact bearers of the image of God—creatures that, if we could see them as God sees them, we might be tempted to bow down in worship.

The sacraments help us live more fully alive in creation; they help us see the beauty of a world shimmering with the radiance of God. We don't often see the world this way, but we know by faith and through Scripture that this is true. As we guide catechumens through the sacraments, we put them in touch with the world as it was meant to be.

Having good tools doesn't make one a master craftsman. But good craftsmen know how to use them and what each of them is for. Likewise, a good catechist knows how to wield the "tools" we've been exploring over the last two chapters. In the previous chapter, we looked at the Apostles' Creed, the Lord's Prayer, and the Ten Commandments as expressing the "rule" of faith, hope, and love, respectively. In this chapter, we've touched on teaching the Scriptures and the sacraments as a means of learning to inhabit the world Christianly.

If our goal in catechesis is to provide a basic but comprehensive introduction to the faith, we have here some of the essential tools for this process. But we don't go at this work alone. If it takes a village to raise a child, it takes a church to catechize. That's the topic of the next chapter.

8

The Relational Dimension of Catechesis

Origen of Alexandria (ca. 185–ca. 254) was one of the most gifted theologians of the early church. He taught and wrote in the first half of the third century, first in Alexandria and later in Caesarea, and he was eventually martyred for his faith. Widely recognized as a brilliant scholar, interpreter, and mystical theologian, Origen was also a devoted catechist. For most of his career, he taught at what were called catechetical schools.[1] These were not necessarily institutions for preparing newcomers for baptism but more like quasi-monastic communities gathered around a teacher and a shared way of life. They were communities of friendship and formation.

We are fortunate to possess a delightful account of Origen's teaching from one of his students in Caesarea, a man named Gregory Thaumaturgus ("the wonderworker").[2] As a young man, Gregory came to Caesarea to study under the legendary Origen, with the intention of becoming a public official or lawyer. But he was trepidatious, and for several reasons. Origen had a reputation

1. Tradition credits Saint Mark as the first evangelist to Alexandria, and so, the school there is thought to originate as early as the mid-first century. The main source for this view is Eusebius of Caesarea (d. ca. 339), who refers to a "school" (*didaskaleion*) in Alexandria. In his *Church History*, he records that Mark the evangelist visited Alexandria and preached there (2.16); that there was "of old a school of sacred learning," though he doesn't mention a specific date (5.10); and that there was a succession of heads of the school: "Clement, who succeeded Pantaenus [d. early third century], was head of the catechetical instruction (*didaskaleion*) at Alexandria up to such a time that Origen also was one of his students" (6.6.1).

2. This can be found in Gregory the Wonderworker's *Oration of Thanksgiving* (FC 98). I discuss this passage in more detail in Alex Fogleman, "The Golden Thread of Charity: Love and the Formation of Character in Origen and Augustine," *Journal of Spiritual Formation and Soul Care* 13, no. 2 (2020): 246–61.

for being an exacting teacher, demanding rigorous intellectual dialogue and precise argumentation. Gregory was not sure he could meet the expectations. But he was also not wholly sure about his career. Part of him wanted to become a successful professional, but another part knew that true happiness lay elsewhere. He wavered.

Despite his hesitations, he enrolled in Origen's school, where he learned not only the Christian Scriptures but also grammar, physics, cosmology, music, and other disciplines. Origen taught his students how each of these disciplines belonged within a Christian understanding of the world. He also taught the classical virtues of justice, prudence, temperance, and fortitude, and he stressed that it was not enough to learn *about* them but it was necessary to practice them.[3] Origen modeled this way of education in his own life. He modeled the virtues as he taught students their meaning.[4] As historian Robert Louis Wilken summarizes, Origen's goal was "to form the lives of [his] students in light of the ideal set forth in the Scriptures and imaged in Christ."[5]

All the same, Gregory continued to vacillate until finally, after several months, the budding bonds of friendship eventually won him over. Origen had sunk the "spur of friendship" into him, he says, and this is what allowed him to forgo a life of worldly ambition and wholeheartedly pursue the life of discipleship. In becoming friends with Origen his teacher, Gregory realized he had become friends with the Word himself. "Through Origen, Gregory learned to love the Word 'whose beauty attracts irresistibly,' but he also began to love Origen as well, 'the friend and interpreter of the Word.' Only when 'smitten by this love' was he persuaded to give up 'those objects which stood in the way and to practice the philosophical life.'"[6]

Origen knew that his students needed more than knowing *what* truth was; they needed to see it modeled and mirrored before them. They needed to live in the presence of a truthful life before they could live it themselves.

Relationships are essential to catechesis. In Galatians 6:6, rendered literally, Paul writes that "the one catechized in the word should share all good things with the one who catechizes." For this reason, J. I. Packer has described cat-

3. Gregory, *Oration of Thanksgiving* 11.

4. Gregory, *Oration of Thanksgiving* 9.

5. Robert Louis Wilken, "Alexandria: A School for Training in Virtue," in *Schools of Thought in the Christian Tradition*, ed. Patrick Henry (Philadelphia: Fortress, 1984), 19.

6. Wilken, "Alexandria," 21, quoting Gregory, *Oration of Thanksgiving* 6.

echesis as a "corporate spiritual discipline." If spiritual disciplines like prayer, fasting, silence and solitude, and others are individual spiritual disciplines, catechesis is a communal discipline for the body of Christ to practice together. "Catechizing is a spiritual discipline for both catechist and catechumen—not only a personal discipline for each of them, but also a partnership discipline, one that can only be properly practiced when both parties are properly committed to what is happening."[7]

Catechesis as a Focal Practice

For understanding the importance of relationships in catechesis, I've found it helpful to think of catechesis as a "focal practice." "Focal practice" is a phrase introduced by philosopher of technology Albert Borgmann to describe activities that require attention, effort, and learning, and which afford high levels of meaning and connection.[8] The word "focal" comes from the Latin word *focus*, which literally means a hearth, or fireplace. In an earlier age, the hearth was both the literal and symbolic center of the household—the focal point—and everyone shared in both its labors and its goods. Perhaps Dad would chop the firewood, the kids would tend the fire, and Mom would cook over it. It was a gathering place for warmth and light, a place where the family would share stories, meals, and life. Keeping a hearth obviously requires much more work than turning on a switch and enjoying central heating, but it also gathers the family around a common good and goal. The *focus* of the hearth draws the family to its center.

Borgmann used the phrase "focal practices" for any kind of activity in life that functioned similarly: activities that require attention, patience, and active participation but also more deeply *human* and life-giving experiences. Playing a musical instrument, for example, while requiring more effort than listening to prerecorded music, is more rewarding and also enables its participants to enjoy a greater collective experience. I listen to music now on the radio or on my phone. But these experiences pale in enjoyment and camaraderie to the times that I played music in high school with my friends Pat and Dan. The same goes for cooking. When our family enjoys a salad with fresh tomatoes

7. J. I. Packer with Gary Parrett, "The Return to Catechesis: Lessons from the Great Tradition," in *Renewing the Evangelical Mission*, ed. Richard Lints (Grand Rapids: Eerdmans, 2013), 122.

8. He discusses this concept in Albert Borgmann, *Technology and the Character of Contemporary Life* (Chicago: University of Chicago Press, 1984).

from the garden, the enjoyment and bonds of connection are richer than if we just order pizza.

These other practices occupy what Borgmann calls the "device paradigm." Device paradigm activities reduce the burdens of an activity, but they also reduce human connection and a sense of meaning. In the device paradigm, a tool reduces the hardships of a task, but with hidden costs. Central heating makes it easier to warm the house, but it also makes it possible for family members to go to their own separate rooms. Focal practices are more difficult; they require more of *us*. But they also create a richer nexus of community and meaning. Like the literal hearth, focal practices forge strong connections between those who share in them. Device paradigm practices, meanwhile, reduce burdens but also foster isolation and ennui.

Catechesis is a focal practice. It is not a prepackaged meal, ready-made for the catechist to serve up by heating it in the microwave. Catechesis is not asking new Christians to watch a video or fill out a workbook, or even study a catechism on their own. It is inherently relational. And if we attempt to offload the relational "burdens" of catechesis, we risk losing one of its most central goods: the personal bonds of friendship where the Word of God exerts its irresistibly beautiful appeal.

In the remainder of the chapter, I want to look at the different relationships in catechesis, not only between the catechist and the catechumen but also between the catechumen and the whole church. What does it mean for catechesis to be a corporate spiritual discipline and a focal practice?

The Catechumen: Becoming a Literate Listener

First, let's consider the catechumen. The catechumen's main job, simply, is to listen—to hear the Scriptures, to hear Christian teaching, and ultimately to hear God. Remember that the word "catechumen" literally means one who hears. A catechumen is one in whom the word of Christ "echoes" or "resounds." The name also recalls one of the central Scriptures of the Old Testament, the Shema from Deuteronomy 6:4: "Hear, O Israel: The LORD our God, the LORD is one." The catechumen is first and foremost one who hears.

The Bible is full of admonitions to hear. Along with the Shema, we might think of Jesus's mysterious invocations: "He who has ears to hear, let him hear" (Matt. 11:15). "Blessed . . . are those who hear the word of God and keep it" (Luke 11:28). "Pay attention to what you hear" (Mark 4:24). Paul, too, writes that "faith comes by hearing, and hearing through the word of Christ" (Rom. 10:17), that we did not receive the Spirit by works of the law but by "hearing with faith" (Gal. 3:2). The psalmist proclaims that God does not delight in sacrifice and offering, "but you have given me an open ear"—a phrase that can be rendered literally, "ears you have dug for me" (Ps. 40:6).

Practically, though, listening is hard, especially in an age of mass distraction. I find it immensely difficult to listen. Like many of us today, I'm rarely in a place where I'm simply available and present to listen. More often, I'm surrounded by noise. But it's not just a cultural issue. Listening is also soul work. Cyril of Jerusalem says that before baptism, catechumens hear externally but not yet internally, not yet with understanding.[9] He warns against those who listen to the words of Scripture but "do not hear them, for they have stopped the ears of their heart in order not to hear."[10] We have physical ears, then, but we also have ears of the heart. Hearing is a spiritual matter: a posture and a habit of being. Hearing requires an attentive engagement of our senses, minds, and bodies. It means attending to another, giving of ourselves in small but powerful acts of love.

Theologian Carol Harrison describes the work of teaching catechumens as the cultivation of "literate listeners." Literate listening is like reading literacy but for our ears. We know that reading is more than just decoding scribbles and markings on a page. Likewise, hearing is more than just letting soundwaves reverberate in our eardrums. Once again, it's a matter of one's inner being. "Effective hearing . . . seems to lie, not so much in the acquisition of knowledge as in a right orientation of the will; in opening the 'ears of the heart'; in a willingness to receive what is heard and to allow it to impress itself upon the mind in such a way that it forms or transforms it—a process which could equally well describe how we come to believe."[11]

How do we cultivate "literate listeners"? It starts simply by helping our catechumens practice listening as a kind of spiritual discipline. Are there times when we can simply be silent and still, avoiding the perennial tug to distract ourselves with our phones or devices? Do we have spaces in our day for silence and solitude? When we hear Scripture in church, can we devote our full attention to those moments? What about when in conversation with our

9. See Cyril of Jerusalem, *Procatechesis* 6, in *Lectures on the Christian Sacraments*, trans. Maxwell Johnson (Crestwood, NY: St. Vladimir's Seminary Press, 2017), 70–71.

10. Cyril of Jerusalem, *Catechetical Lectures* 12.13, trans. Leo McCauley and Anthony Stephenson, 2 vols., FC 61 and 64 (Washington, DC: Catholic University of America Press, 1969, 1970), 61:234.

11. Carol Harrison, *The Art of Listening in the Early Church* (Oxford: Oxford University Press, 2013), 90.

friends or coworkers—can we in these moments stop and truly listen? Helping our catechumens develop good habits of listening in ordinary life is one step toward cultivating literate listeners.

One other thing we can do is think of speech in more visual terms. When teaching, what are ways that we can create verbal "pictures" that will stick in the minds of our hearers? This was more ingrained in classical education systems, when public speaking was a more prominent feature of political life. Nevertheless, there are many ways that we can use analogies, metaphors, and other forms of figurative speech to create pictures with our words. In this way, we help catechumens become hearers who both "hear" and "see" what is being taught.

Hearing, then, is closely connected with faith; it involves believing and trusting God with one's whole life. And is this not what catechesis is all about? Catechumens are hearers on the road to becoming *believers*, in the truest sense of the word.

The Catechist: Codisciple in the School of Christ

Catechists are never just distributors of information. Nor are they the center of attention. The catechist's main job is to allow Christ, the Master Catechist, to become the true teacher to the catechumen. This is part of what it means for faith to be grounded in the incarnation. God didn't become a curriculum. He became a person. And he uses people to embody his words and teachings.

This means that the character of the catechist is as important as what is taught. Paul writes to Timothy that "the Lord's servant must not be quarrelsome but kind to everyone, able to teach, patiently enduring evil, correcting his opponents with gentleness" (2 Tim. 2:24–25). "Able to teach," in this framework, is more than just being a fluent communicator. A Christian rhetoric has a moral as a well as technical component. A teacher can know all the pedagogical tricks, but if he or she is quarrelsome, impatient, or unable to correct with gentleness, it is difficult to see how this would amount to a biblical paradigm for teaching. This does not mean that the catechist is wishy-washy, unable to speak the truth clearly and plainly, especially on aspects that are culturally unpopular. But the point is that the catechist's character is just as important as the content and methods of teaching.

Augustine understood well that the role of the teacher was first to be a student in the school of Christ. In many of his sermons, he describes this unique role to his hearers:

> Don't listen to me, but together with me.[12]

> We bishops are called teachers, but in many matters we seek a teacher ourselves, and we certainly don't want to be regarded as masters. . . . We are fellow disciples under one master.[13]

> All of us have one Teacher, and that under him we are fellow disciples, fellow pupils.[14]

> It is Christ who is doing the teaching; he has his chair in heaven, as I said a short while ago. His school is on earth, and his school is his own body.[15]

Catechists, then are first and always students in the school of Christ. They are, with catechumens, codisciples who learn together under the tutelage of the one true teacher: Jesus Christ.

The Church: Becoming Friends with God through God's Friends

Catechesis is not limited to the relationship between catechist and catechumen. It also involves the whole church. Catechesis is about learning to belong to the body of Christ—learning the rites and rhythms of citizenship for the city of God.

When I was about thirteen years old, I began to play guitar in our church's Wednesday night worship gatherings. An older man in our church, Frank, began to encourage me and tell me how wonderful it was to see me play. Frank loved music and was simply delighted by my presence there. (I later found out he was almost deaf by that point, but that's beside the point.) Years later, when he was homebound by a fall, my mother asked me (forced me?) to visit him at his home. Now, I really admired Frank, but the patience of any teenager is severely tested by involuntary visits with the elderly on warm summer days. I don't recall any spiritual nuggets of life-changing wisdom. I mostly remember sitting there, feigning attention. But gradually it dawned on me that this devout man of God, who had no familial obligation to care about my existence at all,

12. Augustine, *Sermon* 108.6 (WSA III/4:130).
13. Augustine, *Sermon* 23.1–2 (WSA III/2:56).
14. Augustine, *Sermon* 134.1 (WSA III/4:341).
15. Augustine, *Sermon* 399.15 (WSA III/10:468).

thought *I* was worth sitting with. I came to know that my belonging in the family of God was bound up with his faith and love.

When I would later face my own doubts about God and the church, I knew that Frank still prayed for me and still thought of me with all the affection that he did when I was that kid playing guitar on a Wednesday night. Without knowing it, Frank's role in my life was a powerful instance of the catechesis of the broader church. I remember little explicit formal teaching from those years, but I have a strong memory of Frank's presence in my life. You can probably think of people in your own life who have played the role of unofficial catechist.

So, how does the church catechize? At the more visible level, the church's involvement in catechesis happens through sponsors or godparents. These roles form one of the oldest aspects of ancient catechetical practice.[16] In the *Apostolic Tradition* ascribed to Hippolytus (ca. third-fourth century), we learn that sponsors attended instruction with catechumens, prayed with them, and spoke on their behalf before the bishop.[17] The fourth-century *Pilgrimage of Egeria* recounts a similar process. As the catechumens are brought forward, their sponsors answer questions on their behalf. The bishop asks them questions like, "Is this person of a good life, obedient to their parents, not a drunkard or a liar?" The bishop asks about any particular vices that people struggle with. If the catechumens prove blameless in these matters, the bishop writes down their names for baptism.[18]

This practice reflects a time when evangelism was largely a practice of small-scale local networks, and sponsors served as a link between the church and the convert—a personal connection that accompanied new Christians as they journeyed into the community of the faithful. John Chrysostom presents sponsors as "spiritual fathers" who testify on behalf of their children: "If, then, those who provide surety for others in a matter of money make themselves liable for the whole sum, those who provide surety for others in matters of the spirit and on an account which involves virtue should be much more alert. They ought to show their paternal love by encouraging, counseling, and correcting those for whom they provide surety."[19]

16. For a thorough account of baptismal sponsors in the early and medieval church, see Joseph Lynch, *Godparents and Kinship in Early Medieval Europe* (Princeton: Princeton University Press, 1986).

17. See Hippolytus, *Apostolic Tradition* 15.

18. *The Pilgrimage of Egeria*, trans. Anne McGowan and Paul Bradshaw (Collegeville, MN: Liturgical Press, 2018), 188.

19. John Chrysostom, *Baptismal Instructions* 2.15 (ACW 31:49, lightly altered).

Today, the role of the godparent is almost exclusively tied to infant baptism and has become mostly sentimentalized. We attend a child's baptism and get the parents a gift. But we don't often think of testifying before God on this child's behalf. This is, in fact, what godparents do. But they not only speak for the child at baptism; they also, by the very fact of their relationship, provide a living link with the apostolic tradition. The godparent or sponsor thus plays a crucial role in how catechumens learn to follow Christ together.[20]

At a broader level, the church is involved in catechesis through ordinary relationships and through the power of the liturgy. Friendship has a major influence on our actions, our ideas, and even our tastes. As parents, we worry about our children's friends because we know that the company they keep shapes the company they become. The same is true for catechumens. We learn by imitation, or *mimesis*. We learn to reflect the image of God by first seeing it shine in the communion of saints—like Frank.

Finally, the church catechizes through liturgy and prayer; it catechizes by being the church. Every family has its own characteristics, its own certain markers that distinguish it from other families. Likewise, different cultures or regions have unique qualities or patterns of speech. The lone Canadian in an American clique is given away through a slight inflection of a word or two. The marks of faith, likewise, appear in our own words and actions. The weekly rites of confession, adoration, and thanksgiving seep into our hearts and lives, and we learn the habits of patience, humility, and justice by seeing them embodied in the lives of the saints.

Most of all, the church catechizes through those saints who, without ever making it known, pray fervently for the conversion of believers. If true transformation ultimately happens through the Holy Spirit, and the way in which Christians tap into such spiritual power is through prayer, we can do nothing more important for the renewal of catechesis than to pray. The church catechizes through simply being what it has always been called to be: a people of prayer caught up in the power of the Holy Spirit.

In Saint Thomas Aquinas's defense of prebaptismal catechesis, he appeals to a beautiful image from Saint Augustine about the role of the church "standing in" for others: "Mother Church lends other feet to the little children that they may come; another heart that they may believe; another tongue that they may confess."[21] In an individualist and entertainment-driven culture, we may tend

20. For a good example of "godparenthood" worked out in a course of letters, see Stanley Hauerwas, *The Character of Virtue: Letters to a Godchild* (Grand Rapids: Eerdmans, 2018).

21. Thomas Aquinas, *Summa Theologiae* III, q. 71, art. 1, rep. 2.

to think of catechizing as about what we do as catechists here and now. It is about *our* work and *our* ministry. But that's not the whole story. As we come to faith, as we learn to believe, "mother church" helps us learn to believe. She gives us feet to run to the cross, ears to hear the living Word, and a heart to believe in the Lord Jesus.

Becoming Citizens of the Heavenly City

"Our citizenship is in heaven," Saint Paul declares, "and from it we await a Savior, the Lord Jesus Christ, who will transform our lowly body to be like his glorious body, by the power that enables him even to subject all things to himself" (Phil. 3:20–21). To close out this chapter, I want to turn to two patristic authors who especially capture the relational dimension of catechesis well, envisioning catechesis as a process of becoming citizens of the heavenly city of God.

John Chrysostom (ca. 347–407) and Theodore of Mopsuestia (ca. 350–428 or 429) were citizens of the major city of Antioch in the late 300s. Citizenship in the ancient world was no small matter; it bestowed significant responsibilities and privileges. But John and Theodore both saw citizenship in heaven as infinitely more valuable, and they both described catechesis in precisely this way.

For John, baptism was the ultimate marker of heavenly citizenship. No matter how virtuous a catechumen is, John thought, he remained a stranger and alien among the baptized believers until baptism. John drew the lines in no uncertain terms: "For one, Christ is king, but for the other, sin and the devil." "Heaven is the city of one, earth of the other." And he encouraged catechumens to cross over into the ranks of heavenly citizenship: "How long do we tarry over the border, when we ought to reclaim our ancient country?" "Let us then give diligence that we may become citizens of the city which is above."[22] The Christian's new citizenship included not just fellow local church members but the faithful throughout the world and the company of angels in heaven, too.[23] It especially included the martyrs, who taught catechumens better than any skilled orator that the Christian's chief goal is to "seek the things that are above, where Christ is, seated at the right hand of God" (Col. 3:1).[24]

John warned them that their new citizenship would make them appear strange to the world. In their care for the poor and their lives of patience,

22. John Chrysostom, *Homilies on the Gospel of John* 25.3, in *NPNF*², 14:89.

23. Chrysostom, *Baptismal Instructions* 1.2.

24. This is the main theme of John's seventh baptismal instruction (ACW 31:104–18).

moderation, and charity, Christians proved themselves to be new creatures in Christ.[25] As John put it: "Since we have become Christ's and have put him on, . . . let us train ourselves to live as men who have nothing in common with the affairs of the present life. For we have been enrolled as citizens of another state, the heavenly Jerusalem."[26]

John used a variety of metaphors to describe citizenship in the church. He described the process of catechesis using the technical language for enrolling as a citizen of a new city: *politographēthēnai* (literally, "being written as a citizen").[27] He also described citizenship as belonging to a new family[28] and as a school where one learns the basic grammar of faith.[29] In another sermon, he describes catechumens using a range of metaphors: the catechumen is "a deserted inn and a hostel without a door, open to all without distinction; he is a lair for robbers, a refuge for wild beasts, a dwelling place for demons." And yet, John adds, in these desolate and dangerous places, Christ makes for himself a "royal palace." Teachers and catechists "prepare the inn," while the bishop's instruction makes the walls secure and the foundations strong.[30]

Perhaps John's favorite metaphor is a military one. He addresses catechumens as "soldiers of Christ" newly enlisted in "Christ's special army."[31] Prebaptismal catechesis, in turn, is "a school for training and exercise." At baptism, he tells them, "the arena stands open, the contest is at hand, the spectators have taken their seats."[32] Unlike secular contests, though, where the judge stands far off, in spiritual combat Christ the judge is entirely on our side. Christ provides sturdy armor to withstand the devil's attacks and rich sustenance (the sacraments) to nourish his troops and prepare them for their final feast in glory.[33] In another sermon to the newly baptized, John takes up the metaphor

25. See 2 Cor. 5:17; Chrysostom, *Baptismal Instructions* 4.26.

26. Chrysostom, *Baptismal Instructions* 4.29.

27. Chrysostom, *Baptismal Instructions* 1.18; 4.6; 4.29. On the citizenship language here, see Claudia Rapp, "City and Citizenship as Christian Concepts of Community in Late Antiquity," in *The City in the Classical and Post-Classical World: Changing Contexts of Power and Identity*, ed. Claudia Rapp and H. A. Drake (Cambridge: Cambridge University Press, 2014), 153–66.

28. Chrysostom, *Baptismal Instructions* 4.1–6.

29. John Chrysostom, *Homilies on Hebrews* 9.1, in *NPNF*[2], 14:408. See Everett Ferguson, "Preaching at Epiphany," *Church History* 66, no. 1 (1997): 1–17 (at 9).

30. Chrysostom, *Baptismal Instructions* 10.16.

31. Chrysostom, *Baptismal Instructions* 1.8, 18, 40; 2.1, 8; 4.6; 5.26; 12.30–35.

32. Chrysostom, *Baptismal Instructions* 3.3.

33. Chrysostom, *Baptismal Instructions* 3.12.

to stress the abundant grace of God. In an earthly army, soldiers are recruited for their strength and skill, and they must be freedmen instead of slaves. They are recruited for what they can offer. In the kingdom of heaven, however, things are different: God welcomes slaves as well as free, old as well as young, weak as well as strong. They are recruited not for what they can give to God (for God lacks nothing) but only because of God's extravagant mercy and kindness.[34]

John also emphasized the role catechumens had in teaching, praying, and caring for one another. In a beautiful phrase, John exhorts Christians to become "the cause of catechumens" among their neighbors.[35] And because their baptism puts them "in the front ranks of [God's] friends," their prayers become especially effectual, and "nothing gladdens Him so much as our fellow feeling for those who are members of the same Body, our manifestation of abundant affection for our brothers, and our great preoccupation with the salvation of our neighbors."[36]

Theodore of Mopsuestia's catechesis was also characterized by a robust vision of the church's life together.[37] He too deployed the metaphor of the Christian life as heavenly citizenship. Jesus is the king of a heavenly city, he writes—what Saint Paul and the Letter to the Hebrews describe as the "Jerusalem above" (Gal. 4:26) and "Mount Zion . . . the city of the living God, the heavenly Jerusalem" (Heb. 12:22). Citizens of this kingdom are the "firstborn" who are immortal and immutable, having "been enrolled in heaven as its inhabitants."[38]

Christians living in the world will experience the full benefits of this heavenly membership in the world to come, when they shall see God's kingdom and be free from all troubles in their enjoyment of the beatific life. But for Christians in the present age, God has ordained the church as a symbol of this heavenly reality. "It is as if [Christ] had said, I wish you to look at things

34. Chrysostom, *Baptismal Instructions* 12.30.

35. John Chrysostom, *Homilies on the Book of Acts* 18.5, cited in Benjamin Edsall, *The Reception of Paul and Early Christian Initiation: History and Hermeneutics* (Cambridge: Cambridge University Press, 2019), 178.

36. Chrysostom, *Baptismal Instructions* 2.30.

37. For Theodore's writings, see Theodore of Mopsuestia, *Commentary on the Nicene Creed*, trans. Alphonse Mingana, Woodbrooke Studies 5 (Cambridge: Heffer & Sons, 1933); *Commentary on the Lord's Prayer, Baptism and the Eucharist*, trans. Alphonse Mingana, Woodbrooke Studies 6 (Cambridge: Heffer & Sons, 1933). Because Theodore was condemned, many of his works are lost. These passages are preserved in an ancient Syrian version.

38. Theodore of Mopsuestia, *Catechetical Homilies*, in Mingana, *Commentary on the Lord's Prayer, Baptism, and the Eucharist*, 23–24.

belonging to the next world, and while you are in this world to arrange your life as much as possible as if you had been for a long time in the next world."[39] Those who desire to be citizens of the heavenly kingdom gain familiarity with this kind of life by learning to live as members of the church on earth.

Theodore expands this metaphor for the process of catechesis, especially thinking of sponsors and godparents. Those who want to become citizens of the new city see that it's a better city, and they make careful plans to prepare their arrival. But how can they do this without someone to show them the way?

> This is the reason why, as if he were a stranger to the city and to its citizenship, a specially appointed person, who is from the city in which he is going to be enrolled and who is well versed in its mode of life, conducts him to the registrar and testifies for him to the effect that he is worthy of the city and of its citizenship and that, as he is not versed in the life of the city or in the knowledge of how to behave in it, he himself would be willing to act as a guide to his inexperience.[40]

Catechesis is a deeply relational enterprise. To become citizens of the heavenly city, we need to be instructed in its way of life by those well versed in its habits and customs.

In the writings of John and Theodore, we see the importance of relationships in catechesis. They viewed the church as an outpost of the heavenly city of God, and catechesis as a process of enrolling for citizenship. To become a Christian is to learn what it means to be a part of this city—to belong to one's fellow citizens, on earth and in heaven, and to have God as king. The pathway into Christianity is not a solo journey but a pilgrimage of fellowship and friendship, a life in which my good is bound up with yours, and together we walk side by side into God's glorious city.

In the historic catechism of the Book of Common Prayer, the first question is a rather strange one: "What is your name?" It is notably different from the more grandiose question that begins the Westminster Confession: "What is the chief end of man?" But as Drew Keane has argued, the prayer-book catechism's opener tells us something important about the relational context of catechesis.[41] By opening this way, it implies a form of catechesis thoroughly

39. Theodore of Mopsuestia, *Catechetical Homilies*, 11.

40. Theodore of Mopsuestia, *Catechetical Homilies*, 24–25.

41. See Drew N. Keane, "'Let Me Heare . . . If Thou Canst Say': The Utility of the

embedded in the context of a known community. This catechism presupposes that the process of catechesis happens not just with learning but also with a communion of persons. We are joined to the Great Tradition, but that joining is mediated through *these* particular people.

While becoming Christian is deeply personal, it is not individualistic. We become citizens of heaven amid the company of saints and friends who help us know what it means to belong to Christ's body.

Prayer Book Catechism (1549–1604)," *Journal of Technical Writing and Communication* 52, no. 1 (2022): 19–56.

9

The Craft of Catechesis

The Church of the Holy Sepulchre in Jerusalem is one of the most distinguished churches from the ancient world. Dedicated in the year 339 at the behest of Emperor Constantine, the church featured a rotunda called the Anastasis (meaning "Resurrection"), built upon the site where Christ was thought to have been buried. Since the destruction of the temple in Jerusalem in AD 70 and then the city's final razing after the Bar Kokhba rebellion in AD 137, Jerusalem had held little cultural importance. But by the fourth century, hundreds of pilgrims were flocking to the revitalized city to behold this architectural wonder.

Cyril of Jerusalem was the bishop of this great city in the mid to late fourth century. And he not only had the privilege of catechizing new Christians on the physical foundations of the Christian faith. He also sought to provide a strong foundation for their lives in catechesis.

> Learn these teachings and keep them forever. Do not imagine that these are ordinary homilies, which are good and worth believing but can be learned tomorrow if neglected today. The instructions on the font of regeneration are given in order; if neglected today, when will they be made up? Imagine it is the season for planting trees. If we haven't dug deep, when else can the tree that has once been badly planted be planted properly?
>
> Imagine catechesis as a building. Unless we bind and joint the whole structure together, piece by piece, we will have dry rot and leaks, and all our prior work will be wasted. Stone must be laid upon stone in order, the corners aligned and the rough edges smoothed over: only then will the complete structure arise.
>
> In the same way, we bring you, so to speak, stones of knowledge. You must learn about the living God; you must learn about judgment; you must

> learn about Christ; you must learn about the resurrection. And many things are spoken in order, which are now being sown like seed but will later be brought into a harmonious whole. If you don't connect them as one, remembering what is first and what is second, the builder might build, but the structure will not have a solid foundation.[1]

In catechesis, we lay down each brick one at a time, in order, and in this way "stones of knowledge" are built into a dwelling place for the Holy Spirit.[2] There is a unity of design that gives catechumens a clear sense of the structure of the faith. We know where the beginning and the end are, and so can grasp its synthetic harmony.

Catechesis as craftsmanship has been a central theme of this book, and in this final chapter, we'll conclude by reflecting on four key practices for our apprenticeship: memory, the imagination, the role of questions, and the connection between knowledge and prayer. As I look over the broad history of catechesis and observe what makes for a strong practice of catechesis today, these four practices especially stand out. They aren't quick tips or easy tricks. Drawing on the best wisdom of the Christian tradition, these are habits of mind and heart that can help sustain a thriving practice of catechesis today.

The Architecture of Memory

Cyril's architectural pedagogy belongs within a tradition called the "art of memory," or *ars memorandi*, in ancient Greek and Roman education.[3] New Testament writers had already picked up on this tradition, as when Saint Paul compared himself to the "wise builder" who laid the foundation for others to build upon (1 Cor. 3:10–17) and Saint Peter described the church as "living stones" built up into a holy dwelling (1 Pet. 2:5). In antiquity, memory was understood as "locational," an idea that is still with us today in the notion of the

1. Cyril of Jerusalem, *Procatechesis* 11, in *Lectures on the Christian Sacraments*, trans. Maxwell Johnson (Crestwood, NY: St. Vladimir's Seminary Press, 2017), 74–75 (translation altered).

2. Cyril of Jerusalem, *Procatechesis* 6 (Johnson, 71): "the indwelling Spirit makes your mind into a divine house."

3. On the importance of memory, see the excellent study of Mary Carruthers, *The Craft of Thought: Meditation, Rhetoric, and the Making of Images, 400–1200* (Cambridge: Cambridge University Press, 1998), 7–24.

"memory palace" (though we often associate this with the medieval period). In this understanding, the student's memory was focused by thinking of the mind as an architectural structure: usually some kind of building with clearly arranged floors and rooms. You would then populate those mental structures with images that symbolized what you wanted to remember—and the more interesting and outlandish, the better.

Ancient memory was also understood as *recollective* and *creative*, not merely reiterative. It was not only about learning to memorize information by rote but also about forging a framework for generating new thought and action. As Mary Carruthers puts it, memory in the ancient world was a "compositional art"—among the "arts of thinking" that we today more commonly associate with the imagination and creativity.[4] Today, we are likely to see rote memory as the antithesis of imagination and creativity, but in the ancient world it was the opposite: there was no creativity—no building—unless there was a foundation already in place.

In catechesis, the tenets of the catechism serve as the chief "rooms" for the architecture of memory. Once we have these items memorized, they become placeholders where we can "store" a nearly infinite amount of additional information. Without a clear structure, though, it becomes impossible to make any progress. Catechesis is a time for building new memory structures—new mental and spiritual maps that can guide us on the path of discipleship for the rest of our lives.

Today, memorization often gets a low priority. We worry about students memorizing facts by rote without understanding their meaning. This is not a new worry. It's one we find emerging at least by the Reformation, if not earlier. I noticed this particularly clearly in a letter by evangelical theologian Jonathan Edwards in the seventeenth century. On the one hand, Edwards commended "the ancient good practice of catechizing."[5] He is "far from thinking [that catechisms] ought to be entirely neglected."[6] At the same time, Edwards worried that catechizing by rote memorization was not enough. "One of the grand defects, I humbly conceive, is . . . that children are habituated to learning without understanding."[7] Edwards knew the importance of catechesis in the

4. Carruthers, *The Craft of Thought*, 9.

5. Edwards to Rev. James Robe (May 23, 1749), in *The Works of Jonathan Edwards*, ed. George Claghorn (New Haven: Yale University Press, 1998), 16:280.

6. Edwards to Sir William Pepperrell (November 28, 1751), in *Works of Jonathan Edwards*, 16:408–9.

7. Edwards to Pepperrell, in *Works of Jonathan Edwards*, 16:407.

Christian tradition, but he was alert to new Enlightenment thinking about knowledge and pedagogy, while also emphasizing the need for a true conversion of the heart.

Skepticism about memory has only grown since then. Add the advances in digital technology, which encourage us to think of memory as something "stored" on our computers or devices, and we have a potent recipe for the neglect of memory.

Memory, though, is central to the Christian life. God calls his people again and again *to remember*. Israel is enjoined to remember the covenant, to remember God's mighty deeds, to remember their vocation to be a light to the nations. They are called to "store" God's word in their hearts. The heart is a treasure chest (Deut. 11:18; Pss. 37:31; 119:11; Prov. 6:21) and a tablet for inscribing God's word (Jer. 31:31–34; 2 Cor. 3:3; Heb. 8:10). These images are all about memory—about getting God's words *in our hearts*. And it is what comes out of the heart, Jesus tells us, that ruins or blesses (Matt. 15:18–20).

Memory is also important for the moral life. Medieval theologians like Albert the Great and Thomas Aquinas discussed memory under the broader category of virtue, particularly the virtue of prudence.[8] We can't know how to act wisely unless we can remember what wisdom is and how to avoid folly. The fool returns to his folly like a dog returns to its vomit, the proverb goes (Prov. 26:11). And because memory is formed through sensory impressions—through what we see, hear, taste, touch, and feel—we don't know how to act wisely without a well-formed memory. Prudence, then, depends on character, character on experience, and experience on *memory*. We cannot live, and we certainly cannot live wisely, without memory.

Catechesis, then, is a time for building the architecture of memory for inscribing the words of the catechism on the heart. Many church fathers, including Cyril, encouraged catechumens to write down the creed not on paper but on their hearts. They are to "engrave" it on the hearts and "keep it as a provision through the whole course of [their lives]."[9] Saint Basil adds that, since the Holy Spirit writes in proportion to the size of our hearts, we should "expand" our heart by purifying the lusts of the flesh.[10] Gregory of Nazianzus, meanwhile, describes his role as a "calligrapher" of the heart: as he teaches catechumens the creed, God is writing the new covenant on their hearts like God wrote the commandments on stone tablets for Moses. "Give me the tables of your

8. This comes from Thomas Aquinas, *Summa Theologiae* II-II, q. 49, art. 1.

9. Cyril of Jerusalem, *Catechetical Lectures* 5.12 (FC 61:146).

10. Basil of Caesarea, *Homily 17 on Psalm 44* (FC 46:281–82).

heart," Gregory implores, and "I will be your Moses."[11] Peter Chrysologus refers to the soul as a library (*bibliotheca*) for storing the creed.[12] And Augustine encourages Christians to meditate upon the creed daily to help them amid spiritual warfare. "Let your memories be your books," he tells them. "Don't write it down and then forget it. Store it in your heart so that you can recall it when you need it, when you need to confront the lies and deceptions of the Enemy."[13] Memory, then, is about much more than rote memorization. It is the beginning of the transformation of the heart. Catechesis is a time for building the architecture of memory, the library of the soul.

Practically, there are several ways to encourage this.[14] First: order. The ancient idea of the memory palace comes from the way classical authors helped students learn the "art of memory." They taught students to think of memory as a building or a book, something that was organized and had plenty of space for storage. Then, whenever a person wanted to remember something, she could quite literally "store" an image of it and recall it at ease. Order, though, was key. A good memory requires a mind in which there is, as the old saying goes, "a place for everything and everything in its place."

Second: imagery. We'll talk more about the role of the imagination in the next section, but for now, we can note that we largely remember through images, and we remember better when those images are striking or unusual. It's not the humdrum ordinary things we remember (What did you have for lunch yesterday?) but the most unusual—that breathtaking view of the Grand Canyon, that haunting image from a Flannery O'Connor story, your mother's funeral. These moments stick in the memory because they are, literally, outstanding—they stand out from the rest.

Third: repetition. There is no way around it: memory comes by repetition. Like shooting free throws in basketball or practicing scales on the piano, we memorize by repeating something over and over until gradually, like grooves on a well-worn trail, it becomes indelibly imprinted in us. A little at a time is usually best, rather than long periods of extended exposure. Recall Augustine's advice: "write it on your hearts, and say it to yourselves every day; before you go to sleep, before you go out in the morning, fortify yourselves with your symbol."[15]

11. Gregory of Nazianzus, *Oration* 40.45, in *Festal Orations*, trans. Nonna Verna Harrison (Crestwood, NY: St. Vladimir's Seminary Press, 2008), 140.

12. Peter Chrysologus, *Sermon* 58.2 (FC 109:222).

13. Augustine, *Sermon* 398.1 (WSA III/10:445).

14. For a helpful set of practical resources, see www.biblememorygoal.com.

15. Augustine, *Sermon* 398.1 (WSA III/10:445).

Finally: reflection. To memorize something, we need to think about what we are remembering and reflect on its significance and meaning. Memorization trains us to slow down and be attentive. It cultivates a contemplative, meditative posture toward knowledge. Especially in a culture that values speed, efficiency, and pragmatism, memorization works against these impulses and trains us to attend to God's word thoughtfully. Memory is, in this capacity, the seedbed of attention, and as the great Jewish mystic and philosopher Simone Weil famously put it, attention taken to its highest degree is prayer.[16]

The basic work of memory in catechesis, in short, directly aims at contemplating God in heaven. And it does so precisely by the way it trains us to slow down, to contemplate what is good and true and beautiful. Memory calls us to remember the God who creates and saves us. Ultimately, memory invites us to remember who we are by remembering God.

Image and Imagination

Memory is closely tied to the imagination. Imagination is the faculty by which we take in images through our senses and integrate them into meaningful patterns. The imagination, in particular, is related to beauty. We are not catechized merely by putting our doctrinal stones in order. We want to have a vision of the whole house, fully complete, before our eyes.

Beauty commands our attention by disclosing some aspect of the mysterious in ways we find hard to articulate. We encounter beauty in a great work of art or piece of music. What makes it great? Why do we call it beautiful? The imagination lets us see or hear more than what meets the senses. Imagination perceives this *more*. All Christian theology, not least catechesis, is concerned with beauty. It is a category, writes David Bentley Hart, that is "indispensable to Christian thought; all that theology says of the triune life of God, the gratuity of creation, the incarnation of the Word, and the salvation of the world makes room for—indeed depends upon—a thought, and a narrative, of the beautiful."[17]

At a basic level, the imagination helps us make connections between things that are unlike one another. Through metaphor, we structure every aspect of our perceived reality.[18] All the more so with spiritual knowledge, as we seek a

16. See the reflections in her famous essay "Reflections on the Right Use of School Studies," in *Waiting for God* (New York: Routledge, 2021), 61–63.

17. David Bentley Hart, *The Beauty of the Infinite: The Aesthetics of Christian Truth* (Grand Rapids: Eerdmans, 2003), 16.

18. See George Lakoff and Mark Johnson, *Metaphors We Live By* (Chicago: University of Chicago Press, 1980).

God who transcends every human image and language. Scripture piles metaphor upon metaphor to teach us who God is. God is a rock, a warrior, a door, light, life, a shepherd, a lion, a lamb. Scripture does this, in part, because this is how humans know anything at all. But it's also a part of the logic of incarnation. The God beyond all time and space takes on a *form* we can behold, drawing us by the vision of his human flesh into a vision of something that no eye has seen, no ear heard (1 Cor. 2:9). In the incarnation, we cross the threshold from the human to the divine through the imagination.

Imagination also taps into desire. Catechesis is not just about *knowing* God but also about desiring God. We *thirst* for God, as the deer pants for water (Ps. 42:1). Beauty has little to do with "disinterested" truth, which has come to dominate the meaning of knowledge in the wake of Immanuel Kant. But true knowledge always entails the *desire* for truth. The very term "philosophy" means not just wisdom (*sophia*) but a *love of wisdom* (*philo-sophia*).

But we mostly don't desire God. After the Fall, our natural desire for God becomes dissipated—spread out and cast abroad on everything that is *not* God. And so desire must be cultivated, and it is cultivated not only through visual but also through moral perception. The desire for God, then, must be cultivated, tended. The beautiful does not always overwhelm and immediately offer itself to every immediate taste. And sometimes, like with the cross, that which is truly beautiful is that which we initially find hideous. As Hart puts it, "Christ's beauty, like that of Isaiah's suffering servant, is not expressed in vacuous comeliness or shadowless glamor, but calls for a love that is charitable, that is not dismayed by distance or mystery, and that can repent of its failure to see."[19] Beauty, then, is how we know God. God is not just something beautiful but Beauty itself, and so every instance of beauty in the world is a dim reflection of the God who illumines creation. Like Moses, the encounter with the living God renders us similarly radiant. We see a small glimpse of the divine light and thirst for more. And this thirsting, in turn, is its own kind of satisfaction.

Helping catechumens discover the Beauty at the heart of the world is vital for catechesis. Many Christian educators today learn the importance of storytelling to tap into their students' imaginations. In the late medieval period, the use of image-based texts became extremely popular to teach the faith. Works like the *Speculum Vitae* ("Mirror of Life"), the *Biblia Pauperum* ("The Paupers' Bible"), and the *Speculum Humanae Salvationis* ("The Mirror of Human Salvation") are examples of how catechists brought together word and image to ground new Christians in the essentials of the faith. In earlier periods, cat-

19. Hart, *Beauty of the Infinite*, 20.

echists like Ambrose of Milan, Gregory of Nazianzus, and Ephrem the Syrian used poetry and hymnody to communicate the faith in ways that would teach, move, delight, and even "enchant" their hearers.

But there are many other ways that catechists can use words and images to tap into our love of beauty. We can use metaphor, analogy, symbol, antitheses, rhyme, and a whole host of other rhetorical tools to help the word of God stick in our memories. Teaching well does not always mean more explanation. Sometimes, clarity comes through a particular image or story that helps the students see the truth in a way different from that of a more didactic approach. The catechist can deploy images like this to help faith stick in the memory long after the teaching is over. We should not restrict ourselves to thinking that catechizing only happens during formal teaching settings. We can begin to ask ourselves new questions: How does our church's architecture teach the faith? Does it teach new people that Christianity is going to be about entertainment? Does it prime people to think of Christianity as an academic lecture? What do the sights, sounds, and smells of our teaching spaces communicate about the faith?

Through the use of poems, images, art, stories, music, architecture, and much else, we can train new Christians to perceive the true beauty at the heart of the world. Catechesis shapes our desires so that we learn to love the beauty of holiness; it enlarges our imaginations and opens us to the God who is Beauty itself.

Questions and the Quest

With memory and imagination, another key element of catechesis is the use of questions. Since the Reformation, at least, catechesis has often taken the form of a question-and-answer pedagogy. But asking and answering questions is not a neutral activity. How we think about the purpose and function of questions may look different depending on what our aims are. In their most sinister form, questions can be demonically deceptive. Think of Dostoevsky's Grand Inquisitor, or Satan in the Garden: "Did God actually say, 'You shall not eat of any tree in the garden'?" (Gen. 3:2). Questions may also serve to examine. Think of a pastor asking questions to evaluate one's readiness for baptism or confirmation. We also might see question asking within the framework of scientific inquiry—probing questions and seeking answers until I get to the right one. The *questio* was the main style of theological method in medieval scholasticism, and it was put to work beautifully in the *Summa Theologiae* of Saint Thomas Aquinas.

For some, though, the question-and-answer method is stifling. It smacks of scholastic dialectics and a quest for mastery over truth rather than humble submission to the divine mystery. For others, it just seems disingenuous to call them *questions* if the answers are ready-made. The very word "catechism" denotes for some an uncritical acceptance of truth based on authority rather than reason. Has the question-and-answer format run its course?

This format, to be sure, is not the *sine qua non* of catechesis. The church fathers did not have question-and-answer catechisms, and not even the Reformers were exclusively tied to this genre. In fact, some Christians at the time worried that the rise of printed catechisms would obscure the more personal, relational dimensions of catechesis highlighted in the dialogue between teacher and student. As one Calvinist pastor in the late sixteenth century put it, "written or printed books would help but little if there are none to teach and expound them by a lively voice."[20] Catechesis is a practice among persons, and it takes place "by a lively voice."

What is helpful about questions, though, is how they inculcate a certain posture in the Christian life. A question-based pedagogy dates at least to Socrates, who approached education through a series of carefully crafted questions to draw students into a greater awareness of the truth for themselves. Questions help the learner grasp the information from the inside, inviting a more personal and relational encounter with truth. The truth is no less objective or real for that reason, but it also doesn't remain at a distance, as something remote from us. Questions enable the truth to get deep inside of us. As George Herbert put it: "At sermons and prayers, men may sleep or wander; but when one is asked a question, he must discover what he is."[21]

Questions thus embody a certain mode of being in the world. They belong to the world of faith-seeking-understanding, of pilgrimage rather than conquering.[22] Questions are for those on a *quest*. We begin a question because we are prompted by a perplexity—some disruption in our normal day-to-day existence. Something is amiss, and we must ask questions to find out what it is.

20. Jeremias Bastingius, *Commentary on the Catechism* (Cambridge, 1549), A3^{v}. I discuss this in more detail in Alex Fogleman, "Iconoclasts of the Imagination? Image and Memory in Sixteenth-Century English Catechesis," *Church History and Religious Culture* 99, no. 1 (1999): 1–20 (at 18).

21. George Herbert, *The Country Parson*, in George Herbert, *The Complete English Works*, ed. Ann Pasternak Slater (New York: Knopf, 1995), chap. 21.

22. On this theme, see Matthew Lee Anderson, *Called into Questions: Cultivating the Love of Learning within the Life of Faith* (Chicago: Moody, 2023).

God asks Adam in the garden: "Where are you?" (Gen. 3:9). It is a question that disorients us even as it draws us into salvation. Only at the end, when faith gives way to sight, when seeking gives way to rest, does the quest end. Until then, questions beget questions. Words open to wonder. It's the only way home.

The Reformed theologian T. F. Torrance stated the importance of questions well: A catechism, he said, "not only trains [a person] to ask the right questions, but trains him to allow himself to be questioned by the Truth." It puts "questions . . . into his mouth which he could not think up on his own, and which therefore call into question his own preconceptions. In other words it is an event of real impartation of the Truth."[23] We begin with fears, doubts, hesitations. We don't know what to ask, and the questions we do ask aren't often good ones. But the catechism helps us formulate better and more productive questions. It helps get us out of ourselves and into God.

In this vein, theologian Cody Strecker describes catechesis as taking place in the "interrogative mood." If the hortatory mood is one where we are exhorted to act or think in some way, and the declaratory mood is one where we're simply told what is or isn't the case, catechesis in the interrogative mood puts us in a posture of discovery. The questions are not merely rhetorical. Nor are they a never-ending postmodern spiral to nowhere. Rather, true questions invite us into an ongoing dialogue with the church of ages past and, ultimately, with God. Questions are the first steps in a conversation that moves both catechist and catechumen deeper into the mutual indwelling of the triune life. Catechisms become "sites for dialogue," as Strecker puts it: "They combine confessional specificity in the form of answers, which present a Christian perspective on the shape of the Christian life and the God whom it desires to follow, with an affirmation of questions as properly part of the shape of Christian faith."[24] This back-and-forth response takes place, first of all, in the liturgy itself. We are called by God to worship; we answer. God speaks to us in the proclaimed Word and invitation to the table; we respond by sharing in the bread of life; we are sent out.

Questions, then, can be understood within a more contemplative framework.[25] We should not only think about questions within the framework of a

23. Thomas F. Torrance, *The School of Faith: The Catechisms of the Reformed Church* (1959; reprint, Eugene, OR: Wipf & Stock, 1996), xxvi.

24. This reflection is found in Paul Gutacker et al., "A Symposium on Teaching Virtue: Interdisciplinary Perspectives on Pedagogy, Liturgy, and Moral Formation," *International Journal of Christianity and Education* 23, no. 2 (2019): 204–30 (at 218).

25. Again, I am indebted here to Anderson, *Called into Questions*. I also have in mind

restless quest for knowledge but also as appropriate responses in the face of mystery. Here, we might consider the virgin Mary as a guide to contemplative questioning. In response to the angel Gabriel's announcement of the birth of Christ, she asks, "How will this be?" (Luke 1:34). This is somehow different than Zechariah's version of the same question about the birth of John (Luke 1:18). Materially, they are the same question, but whereas Mary's question is generative (literally and figuratively), Zechariah's question results in the inability to speak. Perhaps this is not a bad thing. Perhaps we see here a picture of the discipline of silence as a fruitful pedagogy. But it seems beyond doubt that Mary is a paragon of virtuous asking. She is our pattern of contemplative questioning. As John Henry Newman once put it, Mary "does not think it enough to accept, she dwells upon it; not enough to possess, she uses it; not enough to assent, she develops it; not enough to submit to Reason, she reasons upon it."[26]

Mary's pattern of questioning, then, can serve as a model for how we approach the question asking of catechesis. "How can this be?" we might ask. This need not be asked from a place of doubt, though many people, to be sure, will bring plenty of those questions. But part of the grace of catechetical questions is that it allows the doubting questions to be gently transformed into contemplative ones—questions that open up, not close down, questions that expand our imaginations for knowing God, not reduce them to false idols that we first came with. Mary's question is posed not from a place of doubt, nor of a relentless quest for mastery. Rather, she asks the question from a posture of stillness, of wonder. "Let it be unto me according to your Word." She poses a question, but it is a question couched in praise. It generates true contemplation, the indwelling of the Word.[27]

One of the important skills for a catechist to develop, then, is the art of asking questions. In good conversation, questions are born from a basic posture of openness, trust, humility, and a willingness to learn—to think *with* others even though you don't always agree or even understand. Again, this does not mean the catechist is shy about proclaiming the hard truths of the Scriptures. Questioning isn't just a matter of being open and accepting whatever catechumens think. Rather, it is about allowing the Holy Spirit opportunities to

---

Paul Griffiths, *The Vice of Curiosity: An Essay on Intellectual Appetite* (reprint, Eugene, OR: Wipf & Stock, 2006).

26. John Henry Newman, *University Sermons*, 312–13, quoted in Andrew Louth, *Discerning the Mystery: An Essay on the Nature of Theology* (Oxford: Clarendon, 1983), 141.

27. This way of phrasing it borrows from Louth, *Discerning the Mystery*, 142.

emerge within a back-and-forth conversation, to draw us out of our own self-contained limitations. In this way, questions are at the heart of "education"—of being "led out" (*ex* + *ducere* = to lead out).

So, we ask open-ended questions, questions that invite thought and wonder. We ask questions to which we don't know the answer. And in doing so, we embody the kind of spiritual quest that has characterized so many of the great theologians and saints throughout the ages.

Good questions open our minds to discover the truth of things. They belong in a dynamic movement of love among a company of friends journeying toward the God who calls us into salvation. Through the dialogue of catechesis, we are drawn into a journey that is at once a conversation with God. Like the disciples on the road to Emmaus, we ask, we learn, we discuss. But in the end, our questions give way to something else: We see at last in the breaking of bread. We will know then why our hearts were burning within us.

Knowledge of the Heart

Throughout this chapter, we've been exploring specific ways of understanding catechesis as the craft of discipleship. The purpose of reflecting on memory, imagination, and questions is to help us see catechesis as a process of encountering Christ, the One in whose image we are made and in whom we find true rest. Yet while catechesis trades mostly in words and images, its ultimate aim lies beyond. Catechesis goes beyond factual knowledge by laying the foundations for a knowledge of the heart. In a wonderful phrase from the fourth-century monastic theologian Evagrius of Pontus, "a theologian is one who prays, and the one who prays, truly, is a theologian."[28] The goal of catechesis is to guide others to become true theologians—those who pray truly.

The separation between theoretical and affective knowledge is perhaps one of the most devastating yet pervasive features of the modern age. Hans Urs von Balthasar once noted that in the early and medieval ages, theologians were often saints and saints were often theologians, but since then, the two offices have rarely coincided in the same person.[29] In his brilliant essay on the nature of theology, *Discerning the Mystery*, Andrew Louth calls this a "dissociation of sensibility." There is something deep in our cultural consciousness that sunders thought and feeling, mind and heart, theology and spirituality. Appealing to

28. Evagrius, *On Prayer* 61.

29. Hans Urs von Balthasar, "Theology and Sanctity," in *Explorations in Theology*, vol. 1, *The Word Made Flesh* (San Francisco: Ignatius, 1989), 181–209.

the patristic notion of *theologia*, or true knowledge of God, Louth writes: "It is not just that theology and spirituality, though different, are held together; rather *theologia* is the apprehension of God by a man restored to the image and likeness of God."[30]

Catechesis is the kind of foundation-laying work where mind and heart are reintegrated into the image and likeness of God. It is at once a form of thinking and praying, a way of loving God with all one's mind as well as body. What does this mean?

First, it means helping catechumens make the connections between, as J. I. Packer once put it, "the doctrine by which we live" and "how we live that doctrine."[31] The importance of theology does not simply lie in its practical payoff. The telos of catechesis, as I've stressed, is nothing less than seeing God face-to-face. At the same time, we should consider how to help catechumens make the connections between doctrine and spirituality that they may not automatically see.

For example, the doctrine of divine simplicity—the belief that God is not made up of composite parts—might seem esoteric and impractical. (I personally think it's both beautiful and indispensable, as will soon become clear.) But it has serious, concrete implications. Several years ago, a young woman began attending our church, having grown up in a tradition with a strong emphasis on the sovereignty and righteousness of God. She confessed that she struggled in prayer. She couldn't really relate to God as a merciful father because she believed that, fundamentally, God was not really merciful. She knew God to be just and righteous. But she could only see mercy as a contradiction—a setting aside of what God fundamentally was.

My friend is not alone in thinking about God this way, and praying to God as if this were true. But it is not. The doctrine of divine simplicity helped her see that there is no contradiction between God's mercy and God's justice. She no longer needed to second-guess God in her prayers. Is God merciful or just? Rather than getting rid of either term, we got rid of the "or." God's mercy is not simply one *part* of God, separable from other parts. Rather, God's mercy and justice are inseparable aspects of the one divine nature. God's mercy is one and the same with God's justice. For my friend, this was not just a doctrine to believe; this changed the way she prayed. This changed not only what she knew about God; this changed *how* she knew God.

30. Louth, *Discerning the Mystery*, 4.

31. I heard him say this in an online interview at Trinity Anglican Seminary (formerly Trinity School for Ministry), posted on March 20, 2014, https://tinyurl.com/unjtzuse.

Another example I often see in catechesis is how we help catechumens learn spiritual disciplines like silence, fasting, and study. When I teach about these disciplines, some people can't help but see this as a form of "works righteousness," a prideful attempt to earn salvation. In this case, a question about practice raises theological questions about salvation. How does growing in holiness relate to our justification? Do we earn salvation through such practices? Are these activities we do to merit eternal life? In this case, reflection on spiritual practices opened critical theological questions. This is why we have stressed the inseparability of doctrine, spirituality, and ethics in catechesis. They are all intertwined.

One of the best examples of this kind of knowledge of the heart comes from Gregory of Nyssa's *Life of Moses*.[32] In this text, Gregory distinguishes three successive modes of knowing God: the knowledge of light, the knowledge of "the cloud," and the knowledge of darkness. Counterintuitively, Moses's journey doesn't move from darkness to light. That's only the first step. Afterward comes the haze of the cloud and then, finally, a dazzling darkness.

First is the knowledge of light. Here, Gregory finds a paradigmatic moment in Moses removing his sandals before the burning bush (Exod. 3:1–17). This moment signals, for Gregory, our purification and illumination—the "dead and earthly covering of skins . . . [being] removed from the feet of the soul." Gregory refers here to the garments of skin given to Adam and Eve after the Fall (see Gen. 3:21). These are images of human sin and ignorance, which signify Moses's inability to recognize that God alone truly exists. Everything else in the world—all that is perceived by the senses—exists by being created and sustained by God. "It seems to me," Gregory explains, "that at the time the great Moses was instructed in the theophany he came to know that none of those things which are apprehended by sense perception and contemplated by the understanding really subsists, but that the transcendent essence and cause of the universe, on which everything depends, alone subsists." For Gregory, the knowledge of light is especially linked with baptism, when we are purified of our old selves and experience the illumination of the divine light.[33]

This is not the end of the story, however. Next comes the knowledge of the cloud (not the kind you invisibly store your electronic files in). This knowledge

32. Gregory of Nyssa, *Life of Moses*, trans. Abraham J. Malherbe and Everett Ferguson (New York: Paulist, 1978). See also Gregory's *Commentary on the Song of Songs* 11, trans. Richard A. Norris (Atlanta: SBL Press, 2012), 339–41. My account here also draws from Andrew Louth, *The Origins of the Christian Mystical Tradition*, rev. ed. (Oxford: Oxford University Press, 2007), 78–94.

33. Gregory of Nyssa, *Life of Moses* 2.22, 24 (Malherbe and Ferguson, 60).

entails a deeper understanding of God through looking at creation through the lens of Christ. Gregory sees knowledge of the cloud signified in Moses hearing the heavenly trumpets on Mount Sinai and the image of the tabernacle. From purification, the soul rises to contemplate the world and the things in the world that reveal God's almighty power. Scripture calls this the cloud, Gregory explains, because it teaches God's invisibility and incomprehensibility. One enters the cloud when one learns what it means that God is beyond all knowledge and comprehension.[34]

The word Gregory uses for "contemplation" here is the Greek word *theōria*, which is where we get the English word "theory." Yet the Greek meaning of the term is much more expansive than "theory." It was the term Plato used to describe the pure knowledge of the Forms—a kind of knowledge gained through an abiding union with the object. *Theōria*, as Andrew Louth puts it, "is not simply consideration or understanding; it is union with, participation in, the true objects of true knowledge."[35] It is not an object of knowledge that we stand "over" in a posture of mastery but one that we are enveloped in and surrounded by. We cannot attain it simply by striving for it but must receive it as a divine gift.

Gregory interprets the cloud christologically using the image of the tabernacle "not made with hands" (Heb. 9:11). This tabernacle is a figure of Christ because in his divine nature he is uncreated—not made by human hands—and in his human nature he is created for us in the incarnation by taking on flesh: he is "capable of being made when it became necessary for this tabernacle to be erected among us." This mystery, Gregory goes on to say, is the authentic teaching handed down by the apostles. While such knowledge applies to elemental instruction in the faith, we enter more deeply into this kind of knowledge of Christ through a greater contemplation of the world, which points to the One who truly exists.[36]

Finally comes the knowledge of darkness. After purification and contemplation comes an even deeper encounter with God, where one realizes even more the greater heights of God's incomprehensibility. At this point, the soul leaves behind intellectual and sensory knowledge. The knowledge of darkness, as Gregory understands it, is a "seeing that consists in not seeing." It is what happens when what is sought after "transcends all knowledge, being separated on all sides by incomprehensibility as by a kind of darkness." This expresses

34. Gregory of Nyssa, *Life of Moses* 2.168–169 (Malherbe and Ferguson, 95–96).
35. Louth, *Origins*, 3.
36. Gregory of Nyssa, *Life of Moses* 2.174 (Malherbe and Ferguson, 98).

the soul's deepest desire: to love God and be filled with his presence. "Hope always draws the soul from the beauty which is seen to what is beyond, always kindles the desire for the hidden through what is constantly perceived."[37]

Here we arrive at the final vision for God, which Gregory describes as the soul's "stretching out" (*epektasis*) in seeking to comprehend God (Phil. 3:13). Because God is infinite, not bound by any finite limits, Gregory sees the soul's journey into God as a constantly increasing desire for God. There is no limit to an infinite nature, Gregory reasons, because what is limitless cannot be understood by human minds. The result is that the vision of God is, paradoxically, a state of *not* being satisfied in one's desire to see God: "Every desire for the Good which is attracted to that ascent constantly expands as one progresses in pressing on to the Good. This truly is the vision of God: never to be satisfied in the desire to see him. But one must always, by looking at what he can see, rekindle his desire to see more."[38]

The deepest knowledge of God is knowledge transfixed by love, by an infinite longing for the God who transcends the world. Such knowledge is characterized by a vision that is never satiated. And because it is never satiated, the soul longs to know God even more. True knowledge for God, then, is not just thinking profound thoughts about God, about getting clear in your head certain propositional truths about God. It is plunging ever deeper into the divine embrace, only to discover how much more there is to know and to love. True knowledge of God is the bliss of a soul rapt before the presence of God, a presence that is ever inviting us into greater union and love.

Gregory, to my mind, was a true theologian—a theologian who prayed truly. His writing about the soul's movement into God reveals a way of understanding Christian knowledge that cuts against the modern "dissociation of sensibility." His approach cannot be categorized as either rationalism or pietism. He wouldn't understand the modern bifurcation of the head and the heart. He shows us rather how knowledge can be a form of love and virtue.

The practice of catechesis I've been developing in this chapter embodies the beatitude "Blessed are the pure in heart, for they will see God" (Matt. 5:8). If the heart is the locus of the human person, and we are formed in the image of God, then the pure heart is like a mirror we see God in. In the heart cleansed of the sin that clouds our vision of the Holy One, our soul is able to gaze upon the Lord. This is a form of theology that is, truly, prayer.

37. Gregory of Nyssa, *Life of Moses* 2.162–164, 231 (Malherbe and Ferguson, 95, 114).
38. Gregory of Nyssa, *Life of Moses* 2.238–239 (Malherbe and Ferguson, 116).

The practice of Christian catechesis is no methodological program or neat one-size-fits-all procedure. To become master catechists, we need to enroll in the school of Christ and apprentice ourselves to the true Master. Though the pull is strong, we'll need to resist the temptation to what Jacques Ellul called *la technique*—the attempt to mastery by proficiency, efficiency, and methodization. We must recover instead what Gregory of Nyssa described as learning faith in the "workshop of virtue." As an art, catechesis is a habit of mind, heart, and body. It is a way of life.

At bottom, catechesis is part of the divine pedagogy in which God himself is our teacher. And those whom we teach are taught by God through us. God is the good shepherd who guides his flock to the nourishing pastures of doctrine, which feeds their souls and converts them through the still waters of baptism. By learning from the Master Catechist, we share in a lifelong quest that finds its final rest in God's own holy embrace.

Conclusion

Three Things Needful

There is much more we could say about the history, theology, and practice of catechesis. But in closing, I want to leave you with three things I think every catechist needs, three qualities essential for a flourishing practice of catechesis. It goes without saying that catechesis needs Jesus, the foundation and master builder. And we need the Spirit, who leads us into all truth. There's no getting around the fact that the beginning and end of catechesis is the triune God.

I also hope that you will seek opportunities to learn more about the content and methods of catechizing. I would encourage any aspiring catechist to seek good training, resources, and opportunities for learning. But over the years, I've noticed that it's not those with the most degrees that make good catechists. Nor those who are the most eloquent speakers or have the sharpest answers to tough questions. Those I've seen with the most effective catechetical ministries are those who teach with humility, joy, and love.

Humility runs like a seamless thread throughout the history of catechesis. From Augustine to Luther to Herbert, many of the great luminaries of catechetical history emphasized humility. Recall Luther's lambasting of the pride associated with thinking we ever get beyond the catechism and his hope to remain a "child and pupil of the catechism." Recall Herbert's word to the country parson that in catechizing "there is a humbleness very suitable to Christian regeneration." Catechesis aids the mortification of our flesh.

Augustine went further in rooting catechesis in the humility of the eternal Word in the incarnation. If the catechist finds the work demeaning or small, we can remember the smallness of Christ in the manger and his humiliation on the cross. However far we think we "come down" to meet new believers in the simplicity of catechesis, Christ comes down infinitely more in becoming man for our sakes.[1] Humility is a beautiful quality of the Christian catechist. It is attractive in its own right, and as newcomers see the humility of the catechist, they see something of the humility of Christ. Humble catechesis imitates the way of the humble Lord, who, though he was equal to God, did not demean the humility of the cross.

Humility is the seedbed of joy. Recall again Augustine's writing to weary Deogratias, who thought his boring catechesis could be solved by fixing technical questions like how long to teach the biblical narrative or how to exhort newcomers to live the Christian life. Those issues have their place, Augustine acknowledges, but the important thing is joy: "Our greatest concern," he writes, "is how to make it possible for those who catechize to do so with joy."

The Latin noun for joy here is *hilaritas*, related to the Greek adjective *hilaros*, which Saint Paul uses in his admonition that "God loves a *cheerful* giver" (2 Cor. 9:7). If God loves a *hilaris* (the Latin adjective) giver of material goods, Augustine reasons, how much more does he love the *hilaris* giver of spiritual goods? Joy is linked to the freedom of giving, of an open-handed posture of abundant generosity. Catechesis as cheerful giving doesn't count costs but has an overflowing, out-of-the-abundance-of-the-heart attitude.

This is no sentimental facade. At the heart of Christian joy is tough, Christlike compassion. For *hilaritas* to be present at the right time, Augustine says, a teacher needs compassion. Joyful catechesis begins from mercy that goes down to the catechumen's level. Like a hen hovering over her brood, or a mother bird who chews up food for her chicks to digest, the compassionate catechist feeds catechumens with the food of Christian teaching in a form they can take in. The joy of abundant, life-giving catechesis stems from humble, Christlike compassion.

Finally, humility and joy are rooted in love. At the center of the Christian story is the God who loves us so much that he became one of us and died for us. The love of God in Christ, shed in our hearts by the Holy Spirit, is the energizing core of catechesis. And it is only in the "going down" of incarnate love that we find the true rest and quiet that our souls seek. As Augustine puts it: "The more love goes down in a spirit of service to the ranks of the lowliest people, the more surely it rediscovers the quiet that is within when its good conscience testifies that it seeks nothing of those to whom it goes down but their eternal salvation."[2]

1. Augustine, *On Catechizing the Uninstructed* 10.15, in *Instructing Beginners in the Faith*, trans. Raymond Canning (Hyde Park, NY: New City, 2006), 91–93.

2. Augustine, *On Catechizing the Uninstructed* 10.15 (Canning, 93).

The love that "goes down in a spirit of service" instills a spirit of compassion in the catechist. It also creates a deep bond between catechist and catechumen, one that echoes the coinhering love of the triune God. The teacher learns "in" the student, while the student teaches "in" the teacher. When compassion is present, the student is touched by the teacher's voice, as if the student were in the place of the teacher. Meanwhile, the teacher learns in the listening attention of the student. "We each dwell in the other, and so it is as if they speak in us what they hear while we, in some way, learn in them what it is we teach."[3]

Augustine compares catechesis to the way you might give a close friend a tour of your hometown. You drive by the fields where you played baseball, the school you attended, the streets where you once got lost. You've seen these sites hundreds of times, but now, when you show them to your friend, you experience them anew, as if for the first time. You experience them through your friend's perspective. And the deeper your compassion, Augustine writes, the newer these sites appear. "As we come together more and more through this bond of love, what had gotten old becomes new to us all over again."[4] Love makes all the difference.

No matter how skillful or masterful our teaching is, it is nothing without love. And love, ultimately, is a gift of the Holy Spirit. It is the Spirit of Truth who scatters the darkness of despair and gloom and brings light to catechesis. When the Spirit who is love dwells in our midst, Augustine says, our words "break forth vigorously and cheerfully from the rich vein of charity."[5] It is as if the words that we speak and hear are not those just from our own mouths but from the mouth of the Spirit who lives and speaks in each of us—the Spirit who is the love shed abroad in our hearts (Rom. 5:5).

At the heart of catechesis is the God of love: the God of infinite, abundant, joyful, self-giving love, who became human for our sakes, who pours his own Spirit into our hearts that we may be empowered and inspired to love God and our neighbors in return. Let us, then, lay our foundation on this Rock, take heed of his words, and be rooted and grounded in his love.

3. Augustine, *On Catechizing the Uninstructed* 12.17 (Canning, 97).
4. Augustine, *On Catechizing the Uninstructed* 12.17 (Canning, 97).
5. Augustine, *On Catechizing the Uninstructed* 12.17 (Canning, 97).

Appendix 1

Beginning Catechesis at Your Church

There is no secret trick to beginning catechesis at your church. At the very least, you can begin by picking up a catechism and gathering those in your community seeking a surer foundation in the faith. You don't need a big program, fund-raising campaign, or market strategy. All that is needed are people hungry for sound doctrine, devoted prayer, and guidance for living faithfully. You can build out a more expansive platform, but it does not need to be complicated. Begin where you are, with the people that are there, and with the tools at your disposal.

Many potential catechists worry that they don't know enough about the Bible or theology. I wholly believe in the value of good training, and there are several excellent accrediting and nonaccrediting schools and institutes to serve this purpose. But you do not need a master's degree or PhD in theology to be a catechist. Part of the utility of the catechetical method I have outlined in this book is that it looks to the structure of the catechism to guide discussion and uses questions to seek deeper understanding. If our goal is not just having right answers but modeling a contemplative *theoria* that seeks to grow deeper into life with God, then we can be free from the unnecessary burden of professionalization.

That said, pastors and church leaders should help catechists find good training! A well-trained catechist can be an immense blessing to pastors and church leaders. Having a team of trusted teachers enables the lead pastor to oversee other responsibilities in the church, while trusting that the vital ministry of catechesis is being undertaken well.

There are still many practical questions to ask: What structure will work best for our church? How long should the process of catechesis last? Will it be more formal or informal, structured or fluid? What elements of teaching, prayer, and service will be incorporated? You can begin by asking: What are the natural rhythms of the church's life? Of the community's life? What are the natural points of connection that people in your church will already have with catechesis?

Finally, you'll want to think about what kind of catechism to use. It should be clear by now that catechesis is not the same as picking the right catechism, and some churches will elect not to use one at all. Still, many will want to, and there are many out there to choose from. So how do you know which one to choose? Here are a few things you might consider.

First, theological alignment. Does the catechism align with your church tradition? How does it handle commonly agreed-upon questions versus denominational particulars? I know several Baptist churches that use the Anglican catechism *To Be a Christian*, and Anglican churches that use the Presbyterian-based *New City Catechism*, in both cases adapting it to the theological needs of their own tradition. If your church tradition has a catechism that is denominationally approved, great. But if not, there are other ways that preexisting catechisms can be adapted to fit your needs.

Second, what is the purpose? Is it to prepare young people for baptism or confirmation? Is it for teaching adult non-Christians who have never been part of a Christian tradition before? Is it for use in a Sunday school class setting or for study at home? Being clear about the purpose of catechesis can help you think about what kind of catechism to use.

Third, and related, who is the audience? Is it primarily young children? If so, a smaller catechism, such as Luther's *Small Catechism*, *Westminster Shorter Catechism*, or the children's version of the *New City Catechism* may be best. These catechisms are short—usually fewer than 50 questions—and can be easily memorized. For an older or more advanced audience, a longer catechism may be beneficial, such as the Anglican catechism *To Be a Christian*, which contains 368 questions over the course of expositing the gospel, the Apostles' Creed (which includes teaching on sacraments), the Lord's Prayer, and the Ten Commandments. The *Christian Essentials* series from Lexham Press also contain short volumes on each article of the catechism in a manner that most teenage or adult congregants could easily digest.

For more in-depth studies, there are larger volumes like Luther's *Large Catechism* and other equivalent works that engage similar topics but in a much more robust manner. Churches can develop catechetical libraries that house a range of catechisms and catechetical texts that can speak to different audiences (see appendix 2). There could be many texts that fall in varying stages of growth, but all of which are oriented in the basics of the faith and draw us into deeper life with God.

A fourth consideration is the arrangement of topics. Form affects content, medium is message, and the arrangement of topics in a catechism shapes our understanding of their meaning. If you begin with the Ten Commandments, this can present the commandments as a call to repentance. By contrast, if they come at the end of the catechism, after the creed, they serve more as a guide for holy living. Either way, the order of what is taught contains a theological judgment.

Above all, what is needed is discernment. Who are the people you serve and what do they need? Catechesis brings the ancient tradition into present contexts; it brings what is universally true into a particular setting. Catechesis is never a neutral practice, conveying timeless truths in a timeless fashion. Catechesis passes on the Christian tradition in ways attuned to this unique place and time, and it presents the faith in ways that forge Christian identity along the road of conversion and transformation.

Appendix 2

Building a Catechetical Library

In the seventeenth century, George Herbert gave the following advice to fellow pastors: "The country parson has read the Fathers, and the schoolmen, and the later writers, or a good proportion of them, out of all which he hath compiled a book and body of divinity which is the storehouse of his sermons. . . . This body he made by way of expounding the Church Catechism, to which all divinity may easily be reduced."[1] Along similar lines, the English clergyman Thomas Bray envisioned well-stocked libraries throughout England organized around the topics of the catechism—what he once referred to as a *Bibliotecha Catechetica*. The following list is only partial, but it hopefully offers a few suggestions to start building a catechetical library to assist both in teaching and providing resources for further study.

One-Volume References and Historic Catechisms

Augustine, *Enchiridion on Faith, Hope, and Love*
John Chrysostom, *Baptismal Instructions*
Thomas Aquinas, *Compendium of Theology*
Martin Luther, *Small Catechism* and *Large Catechism*
Heidelberg Catechism
Westminster Shorter Catechism and *Westminster Larger Catechism*
Chad Van Dixhoorn, *Creeds, Confessions, and Catechisms: A Reader's Edition*
The Catechism of the Catholic Church
Josef Pieper, *On Faith, Hope, and Love*
J. I. Packer, *Growing in Christ*
Joshua Strahan, *The Basics of Christian Belief: Bible, Theology, and Life's Big Questions*
Ben Myers, Wesley Hill, and Peter Leithart, *The Lexham Press Catechism*

1. George Herbert, *Priest to the Tempel* (1632), chap. 5.

On the Creed

Augustine, *On Faith and the Creed* and *Sermon to Catechumens on the Creed* (= sermon 398)
Hans Urs von Balthasar, *Credo: Meditations on the Apostles' Creed*
Karl Barth, *Credo*
Richard Baxter, *The Christian Religion Expressed*
Michael F. Bird, *What Christians Ought to Believe: An Introduction to Christian Doctrine through the Apostles' Creed*
Phillip Cary, *The Nicene Creed*
Cyril of Jerusalem, *Catechetical Lectures*
Donald Fairbairn and Ryan M. Reeves, *The Story of Creeds and Confessions: Tracing the Development of the Christian Faith*
Trevor Hart, *Confessing and Believing: The Apostles' Creed as Script for the Christian Life*
Luke Timothy Johnson, *The Creed: What Christians Believe and Why It Matters*
Alister McGrath, *I Believe: Exploring the Apostles' Creed*
Ben Myers, *The Apostles' Creed: A Guide to the Ancient Catechism*
William Perkins, *An Exposition of the Symoble or Creed of the Apostles*
Rufinus of Aquileia, *Commentary on the Creed*
Thomas Aquinas, *Exposition of the Apostles' Creed*

On the Lord's Prayer

Lancelot Andrewes, *Nineteen Sermons upon Prayer in General, and the Lord's Prayer in General* (vol. 5 of *The Sermons of Lancelot Andrewes*)
Augustine, *Letter* 130
Karl Barth, *Prayer*
C. Clifton Black, *The Lord's Prayer*, Interpretation Commentary Series
John Calvin, *Institutes* book 3, chapter 20
John Cassian, *On Prayer* (from *Conferences* book 9)
Meister Eckhart, *On the Lord's Prayer*
John Gavin, *Mysteries of the Lord's Prayer: Wisdom from the Early Church*
Justo L. González, *Teach Us to Pray: The Lord's Prayer in the Early Church and Today*
Gregory of Nyssa, *On the Lord's Prayer*
Nijay Gupta, *The Lord's Prayer*, Smyth & Helwys Bible Commentary
Stanley Hauerwas and Will Willimon, *Lord, Teach Us: The Lord's Prayer & the Christian Life*
Jacob of Sarug, *Homily on the Lord's Prayer*
F. D. Maurice, *The Lord's Prayer: Nine Sermons Preached in the Chapel of Lincoln's Inn*
Paul Murray, *Praying with Confidence: Aquinas on the Lord's Prayer*

William Perkins, *An Exposition of the Lord's Prayer*
Alexander Schmemann, *Our Father*
Kenneth W. Stevenson, *The Lord's Prayer: Text in Tradition*
Alister Stewart-Sykes, *Tertullian, Cyprian, and Origen on the Lord's Prayer*
Teresa of Ávila, *Ways of Perfection*, chapters 27–42
Thomas Aquinas, *On the Lord's Prayer*
John Wesley, *Commentary on the Lord's Prayer: The Prayer That "Contains All We Can Reasonably Pray For"*
N. T. Wright, *The Lord and His Prayer*
William Wright IV, *The Lord's Prayer: Matthew 6 and Luke 11 for the Life of the Church*

On the Ten Commandments

Klaus Bockmuehl, *The Christian Way of Living: An Ethics of the Ten Commandments*
Bonaventure, *Collations on the Ten Commandments*
Carl Braaten and Christopher Seitz, eds., *I Am the Lord Your God: Christian Reflections on the Ten Commandments*
John Calvin, *Sermons on the Ten Commandments*
Kevin DeYong, *The Ten Commandments: What They Mean, Why They Matter, and Why We Should Obey Them*
J. V. Fesko, *The Rule of Love: Broken, Fulfilled, and Applied*
Jeffrey Greenman and Timothy Larsen, *The Decalogue through the Centuries*
Stanley Hauerwas and William Willimon, *The Truth about God: The Ten Commandments in the Christian Life*
Gilbert Meilaender, *Thy Will Be Done: The Ten Commandments and the Christian Life*
J. I. Packer, *Keeping the Ten Commandments*
Philip Ryken, *Written in Stone: The Ten Commandments and Today's Moral Crisis*
Thomas Aquinas, *Explanation of the Ten Commandments*
Thomas Watson, *The Ten Commandments: Life Application of the Ten Commandments with Additional Chapters on Sin, Salvation, Prayer, and More*

On the Sacraments

Ambrose of Milan, *On the Sacraments* and *On the Mysteries*
Sarah Jean Barton, *Becoming the Baptized Body: Disability and the Practice of Christian Community*
Kimberly Belcher, *Eucharist and Receptive Ecumenism: From Thanksgiving to Communion*
Hans Boersma, *Heavenly Participation: The Weaving of a Sacramental Tapestry*

Bonaventure, *Commentary on the Sentences of Peter Lombard*
Romanus Cessario, *The Seven Sacraments of the Catholic Church*
Cyril of Jerusalem, *Lectures on the Sacraments*
Andrew Davison, *Why Sacraments?*
J. V. Fesko, *Word, Water, and Spirit: A Reformed Perspective on Baptism*
Justin Holcomb and David Johnson, *Christian Theologies of the Sacraments: A Comparative Introduction*
Robin Jensen, *Baptismal Imagery in Early Christianity: Ritual, Visual, and Theological Dimensions*
Robert Jenson, *Visible Words: The Interpretation and Practice of Christian Sacraments*
Maxwell Johnson, *Sacraments and Worship*
Aidan Kavanaugh, *The Shape of Baptism: The Rite of Christian Initiation*
John Macquarrie, *A Guide to the Sacraments*
Maximus the Confessor, *Mystagogy*
Isaac Morales, *The Bible and Baptism: The Fountain of Salvation*
John Williamson Nevin, Philip Schaff, and Emanuel Gerhart, *Born of Water and the Spirit: Essays on the Sacraments and Christian Formation*
Aidan Nichols, *The Holy Eucharist: From the New Testament to Pope John Paul II*
Ps.-Dionysius, *The Mystical Theology*
Joseph Ratzinger, *Signs of New Life: Homilies on the Church's Sacraments*
Alexander Schmemann, *For the Life of the World*
Thomas Schreiner and Shawn D. Wright, *Believer's Baptism: Sign of the New Covenant in Christ*
Thomas Aquinas, *Summa Theologiae*, book 3, questions 60–65
Leonard Vander Zee, *Christ, Baptism, and the Lord's Supper: Recovering the Sacraments for Evangelical Worship*
Edward Yarnold, *The Awe-Inspiring Rites of Initiation*

Acknowledgments

I've been thinking about the contents of this book for about seven years, ever since a conversation over enchiladas with Lee Nelson at Rufi's Cocina. Since then, I've had the great privilege of learning about catechesis from many wonderful people. My thanks go to Fr. Lee, from whom I've learned so much about catechesis, as well as the exceptional priests of Christ Church Waco over the years: Fathers Ryan Butler, Nicholas Norman-Krause, Jonathan Kanary, and Matthew Aughtry. In addition, I'm thankful to the whole parish of Christ Church, which has done so much to form our family in the faith.

I've also learned much from the many kind friends and fellows of the Catechesis Institute, especially Jonathan Bailes, Beth Conkle, Malcolm Foley, Curtis Freeman, Ethan Harrison, Kyle Hughes, Ryan Jones, Hanna Lucas, Mike Niebauer, Stephen Presley, Joel Scandrett, Cody Strecker, and Leslie Thyberg. I'm grateful, too, for several wonderful teachers whom I'm thankful now to call friends: Hans Boersma, D. H. Williams, Bruce and Carolyn Hindmarsh, and Craig and Julie Gay. A special thanks to Hans for writing the foreword (not to mention responding to dozens of other requests over the years). My academic home at Baylor's Institute for Studies of Religion, led by Byron Johnson, has been nothing short of phenomenal in its provision of a generous space to pursue research that is truly *pro ecclesia*. Having colleagues like Philip Jenkins, Thomas Kidd, and David Lyle Jeffrey to ask questions to about the Paulicians or the Puritans almost seems unreal.

Portions of this book have appeared in *Church Life Journal* and *Christian Scholar's Review*. My thanks to the editors for permission to reproduce that material here. I also had the chance to present some of this material at the Anglican Church in North America's Provincial Council in 2023 and the Forward in Faith North America conference in 2024. My thanks to Bishops Alan Hawkins and Eric Menees for their kind invitations and for their decisive championing of catechesis in the Anglican world.

Several intrepid souls read portions of the manuscript and offered astute feedback. My warmest thanks to Jake Anthony, Hans Boersma, Thomas Breedlove, Michael Distefano, Paul Gutacker, Tiffani Harris, Bruce Hindmarsh, Christina Lambert, and Chris Palmer for their labors. A special thanks to Matt Anderson for not only reading the manuscript so carefully but also opening his home to many of those said readers in a most convivial way. The wonderful team at Eerdmans has been exceptional in guiding this book to production. Thanks especially to James Ernest for taking a chance on a new writer on a not-so-hot topic, and to Andrew Knapp, Jenny Hoffman, and Tom Raabe for their studious editorial work.

It's still amazing to me that my family not only supports but even encourages my strange line of work. My parents, Jim and Mary Edna, and in-laws, Tom and Peggy, have been so generous over the years, and I'm so grateful. My grandmother, Ann Crawford, thinks I'm a genius, and I think I'm her favorite grandchild; we both may see the truth dimly, but I'm okay with that. I'm certain that I have the best siblings in the world. Will, Morgan, Rob, and Laura—I love you guys.

Molly remains my best friend and best reader. She read through the manuscript, and her words about it mean the most to me. She also gently reminded me to catechize our children along the way and, most incredibly of all, bore my distracted attention and late arrivals with (mostly) grace and humor. I dedicate this book to our boys: James, Thomas, William, and Charlie. As Augustine says (which is a phrase my kids adore), when love comes down in tender compassion, the teacher hears in the student and the student speaks in the teacher, and they indwell one another in love. I have learned more from these boys than anywhere else about the extraordinary love of our heavenly Catechist. You guys are my champions.

Select Bibliography

Ambrose. *On the Mysteries*. Translated by Roy Deferrari. FC 44. Washington, DC: Catholic University of America Press, 1963.

———. *On the Sacraments*. Translated by Roy Deferrari. FC 44. Washington, DC: Catholic University of America Press, 1963.

Anatolios, Khaled. *Deification through the Cross: An Eastern Christian Theology of Salvation*. Grand Rapids: Eerdmans, 2020.

Anderson, Matthew Lee. *Called into Questions: Cultivating the Love of Learning within the Life of Faith*. Chicago: Moody, 2023.

Arnold, Clinton E. "Early Church Catechesis and New Christians' Classes in Contemporary Evangelicalism." *Journal of the Evangelical Theological Society* 47, no. 1 (2004): 39–54.

Athanasius. *On the Incarnation*. Translated by John Behr. Crestwood, NY: St. Vladimir's Seminary Press, 2011.

Augustine. *Confessions*. Translated by Henry Chadwick. Oxford: Oxford University Press, 1991.

———. "Enchiridion on Faith, Hope, and Love." Translated by Bruce Harbert. In *On Christian Belief*, edited by Boniface Ramsey. WSA I/8. Hyde Park, NY: New City, 2005.

———. *Instructing Beginners in the Faith*. Translated by Raymond Canning. Hyde Park, NY: New City, 2006.

Balthasar, Hans Urs von. "Theology and Sanctity." In *Explorations in Theology*, vol. 1, *The Word Made Flesh*, 181–209. San Francisco: Ignatius, 1989.

Bantu, Vince. *A Multitude of All Peoples: Engaging Ancient Christianity's Global Identity*. Downers Grove, IL: IVP Academic, 2020.

Basil of Caesarea. *Hexameron*. In *Basil of Caesarea: Exegetic Writings*, translated by Agnes Way. FC 46. Washington, DC: Catholic University of America Press, 1963.

Bast, Robert. *Honor Your Fathers: Catechisms and the Emergence of a Patriarchal Ideology in Germany, 1400–1600*. Leiden: Brill, 1997.

Bastingius, Jeremias. *Commentary on the Catechism*. Cambridge, 1549.

Baucum, Tory L. *Evangelical Hospitality: Catechetical Evangelism in the Early Church and Its Recovery for Today*. Lanham, MD: Scarecrow, 2008.

Bernard, Richard. *The Faithful Shepheard; or, The Shepheards Faithfulnesse*. London, 1607.

Bingham, Jeffrey. "Paideia and Polemic in Second-Century Lyons: Irenaeus on Education." In *Pedagogy in Ancient Judaism and Early Christianity*, edited by Karina Martin Hogan, Matthew Goff, and Emma Wasserman, 323–58. Atlanta: SBL Press, 2017.

Boersma, Hans. *Catechized for Beatitude: Theology as Initiation and Discipleship*. Waco, TX: Catechesis Institute, 2023.

———. *Heavenly Participation: The Weaving of a Sacramental Tapestry*. Grand Rapids: Eerdmans, 2011.

———. *Pierced by Love: Divine Reading with the Christian Tradition*. Bellingham, WA: Lexham, 2023.

———. *Seeing God: The Beatific Vision in Christian Tradition*. Grand Rapids: Eerdmans, 2018.

Bonhoeffer, Dietrich. *Prayerbook of the Bible*. Translated by Daniel Bloesch and James Burtness. Vol. 5 of Dietrich Bonhoeffer Works. Minneapolis: Fortress, 1996.

Boyd, Jared Patrick. *Imaginative Prayer: A Yearlong Guide for Your Children's Spiritual Formation*. Downers Grove, IL: InterVarsity Press, 2017.

Bray, Thomas. *Bibliotecha catechetica; or, The country curates library: being an essay towards providing all the parochial cures of England, endow'd with not above ten pounds per annum, with a study of usefull books of like value, to enable the ministers thereof to catechise the youth, and to instruct the people in all things necessary to salvation*. London, 1699.

Calvin, John. *Commentary on the Epistles of Paul the Apostle to the Corinthians*. Translated by John Pringle. Grand Rapids: Baker Books, 1984.

———. *Institutes of the Christian Religion*. Translated by Ford Lewis Battles. Edited by John T. McNeill. 2 vols. Philadelphia: Westminster, 1960.

———. *Sermons on the Ten Commandments*. Translated by Benjamin W. Farley. Grand Rapids: Baker Books, 1980.

Cameron, Michael. *Christ Meets Me Everywhere: Augustine's Early Figurative Exegesis*. Oxford: Oxford University Press, 2012.

Carruthers, Mary. *The Craft of Thought: Meditation, Rhetoric, and the Making of Images, 400–1200*. Cambridge: Cambridge University Press, 1998.

Cavadini, John C. "Simplifying Augustine." In *Educating People of Faith*, edited by John Van Engen, 63–84. Grand Rapids: Eerdmans, 2004.

Cavalletti, Sofia. *The Religious Potential of the Child: Experiencing Scripture and Liturgy with Young Children*. Chicago: Liturgy Training Publications, 1992.

Charry, Ellen. *By the Renewing of Your Minds: The Pastoral Function of Christian Doctrine*. New York: Oxford University Press, 1997.

Colish, Marcia. *Ambrose's Patriarchs: Ethics for the Common Man*. Notre Dame: University of Notre Dame Press, 2005.

Conybeare, F. C. *The Key of Truth: A Manual of the Paulician Church of Armenia*. Oxford: Clarendon, 1898.

Crawford, Matthew. *The World beyond Your Head: On Becoming an Individual in an Age of Distraction*. New York: Farrar, Straus & Giroux, 2015.

Cyril of Jerusalem. *Catechetical Lectures*. Translated by Leo McCauley and Anthony Stephenson. 2 vols. FC 61 and 64. Washington, DC: Catholic University of America Press, 1969, 1970.

———. *Lectures on the Christian Sacraments*. Translated by Maxwell Johnson. Crestwood, NY: St. Vladimir's Seminary Press, 2017.

Daniélou, Jean. *The Bible and the Liturgy*. Notre Dame: University of Notre Dame Press, 1956.

———. "Catechesis in the Patristic Tradition." Translated by Alex Fogleman. *Communio: International Catholic Review* 47, no. 3 (2020): 617–33.

Distefano, Michael. "Embodied Theology in the Greek Apologetic Writings of the Second Century." Master's thesis, Baylor University, 2023.

Douthat, Ross. *Bad Religion: How We Became a Nation of Heretics*. New York: Free Press, 2012.

Dunkle, Brian. *Enchantment and Creed in the Hymns of Ambrose of Milan*. Oxford: Oxford University Press, 2016.

Earley, Justin Whitmel. *Habits of the Household: Practicing the Story of God in Everyday Family Rhythms*. Grand Rapids: Zondervan, 2021.

Edsall, Benjamin. *The Reception of Paul and Early Christian Initiation: History and Hermeneutics*. Cambridge: Cambridge University Press, 2019.

Egeria. *The Pilgrimage of Egeria*. Edited and translated by Anne McGowan and Paul F. Bradshaw. Collegeville, MN: Liturgical Press, 2018.

Ephrem the Syrian. *Hymns on Faith*. Translated by Jeffrey Wickes. FC 130. Washington, DC: Catholic University of America Press, 2015.

Fagerberg, David. *On Liturgical Asceticism*. Washington, DC: Catholic University of America Press, 2013.

Farey, Caroline, Waltraud Linnig, and Sr. M. Johannah Paruch, eds. *The Pedagogy of God: Its Centrality in Catechesis and Catechist Formation*. Steubenville, OH: Emmaus, 2011.

Ferguson, Everett. "Catechesis and Initiation." In *The Early Church at Work and Worship*, vol. 2, *Catechesis, Baptism, Eschatology, and Martyrdom*, 18–51. Eugene, OR: Wipf & Stock, 2014.

———. "Irenaeus' *Proof of the Apostolic Preaching* and Early Catechetical Instruction." In *The Early Church at Work and Worship*, vol. 2, *Catechesis, Baptism, Eschatology, and Martyrdom*, 1–18. Eugene, OR: Wipf & Stock, 2014.

———. *The Rule of Faith: A Guide*. Eugene, OR: Wipf & Stock, 2015.

Finn, Thomas. *Early Christian Baptism and the Catechumenate: Italy, North Africa, and Egypt*. Collegeville, MN: Liturgical Press, 1992.

———. *From Death to Rebirth: Ritual and Conversion in Antiquity*. New York: Paulist, 1997.

Fogleman, Alex. "'Build Up This Knowledge to a Spiritual Temple': George Herbert's Catechetical Poetics." *Crux* 59, no. 2 (2023): 16–27.

———. "*Confitendum et proficiendum*: Augustine on the Rule of Faith and the Christian Life." *Pro Ecclesia* 31, no. 4 (2022): 454–77.

———. "Ecclesial Enculturation: John Westerhoff's Appeal to Catechesis in Contemporary Theological Education." *Journal of Anglican Studies*, 2023. https://tinyurl.com/52byk957.

———. "The Golden Thread of Charity: Love and the Formation of Character in Origen and Augustine." *Journal of Spiritual Formation and Soul Care* 13, no. 2 (2020): 246–61.

———. "Iconoclasts of the Imagination? Image and Memory in Sixteenth-Century English Catechesis." *Church History and Religious Culture* 99, no. 1 (1999): 1–20.

———. *Knowledge, Faith, and Early Christian Initiation*. Cambridge: Cambridge University Press, 2023.

Foster, Richard. *The Celebration of Discipline: The Path to Spiritual Growth*. New York: HarperCollins, 1978.

Freeman, Curtis. *Pilgrim Journey: Instruction in the Mystery of the Gospel*. Minneapolis: Fortress, 2023.

———. *Pilgrim Letters: Instruction in the Basic Teaching of Christ*. Minneapolis: Fortress, 2021.

Gatch, Milton McC. "The Medieval Church: Basic Christian Education from the Decline of Catechesis to the Rise of the Catechisms." In *A Faithful Church: Issues in the History of Catechesis*, edited by John H. Westerhoff III and O. C. Edwards Jr., 79–108. Wilton, CT: Morehouse-Barlow, 1981.

Gavrilyuk, Paul L., and Sarah Coakley, eds. *The Spiritual Senses: Perceiving God in Western Christianity*. Cambridge: Cambridge University Press, 2012.

Green, Ian. *The Christian's ABC: Catechisms and Catechizing in England c. 1530–1740.* Oxford: Oxford University Press, 1996.

Gregory of Nyssa. *Catechetical Discourse.* Translated by Ignatius Green. Crestwood, NY: St. Vladimir's Seminary Press, 2019.

———. *Life of Moses.* Translated by Abraham J. Malherbe and Everett Ferguson. New York: Paulist, 1978.

Griffiths, Paul. *The Vice of Curiosity: An Essay on Intellectual Appetite.* Reprint. Eugene, OR: Wipf & Stock, 2006.

Hadot, Pierre. *Philosophy as a Way of Life: Spiritual Exercises from Socrates to Foucault.* Malden, MA: Blackwell, 1995.

Haile, Getatchew, ed. *The Homily of Zär'a Ya'eqob's Mäṣḥafä B̲erhan on the Rite of Baptism and Religious Instruction.* Leuven: Peeters, 2013.

Harmless, William. *Augustine and the Catechumenate.* Rev. ed. Collegeville, MN: Liturgical Press, 2014.

Harrison, Carol. *The Art of Listening in the Early Church.* Oxford: Oxford University Press, 2013.

Hart, David Bentley. *Atheist Delusions: The Christian Revolution and Its Fashionable Enemies.* New Haven: Yale University Press, 2009.

———. *The Beauty of the Infinite: The Aesthetics of Christian Truth.* Grand Rapids: Eerdmans, 2003.

Hart, Trevor. *Confessing and Believing: The Apostles' Creed as Script for the Christian Life.* Minneapolis: Fortress, 2022.

Hauerwas, Stanley. *The Character of Virtue: Letters to a Godchild.* Grand Rapids: Eerdmans, 2018.

Herbert, George. *The Complete English Works.* Edited by Ann Pasternak Slater. New York: Knopf, 1995.

Hindmarsh, Bruce. *The Spirit of Early Evangelicalism: True Religion in a Modern World.* Oxford: Oxford University Press, 2018.

Hippolytus. *On the Apostolic Tradition.* Edited by Alistair Stewart. Rev. ed. Crestwood, NY: St. Vladimir's Seminary Press, 2015.

Hitchen, Danielle, with Stephen Crotts. *Sacred Seasons: A Family Guide to Center Your Year around Jesus.* Eugene, OR: Harvest House, 2023.

Howard, Agnes Rose. "'The Blessed Echoes of Truth': Catechisms and Confirmation in Puritan New England." PhD diss., University of Virginia, 1999.

Hunter, James Davison. "The Denial of the Moral as Lived Experience." *Hedgehog Review* 26, no. 1 (Spring 2024).

Ijekeye, Julius. "St. Augustine's Epistemology and the Education Process." *Ekpoma Review* 5, no. 1 (2019): 139–56.

Irenaeus of Lyons. *On the Apostolic Preaching*. Translated by John Behr. Crestwood, NY: St. Vladimir's Seminary Press, 1997.

Jaeger, Werner. *Paideia: The Ideas of Greek Culture*. 3 vols. Oxford: Oxford University Press, 1939–1944.

Janz, Denis, ed. *Three Reformation Catechisms: Catholic, Anabaptist, Lutheran*. New York: E. Mellen Press, 1982.

Jenkins, Philip. *The Lost History of Christianity: The Thousand-Year Age of the Church in the Middle East, Africa, and Asia—and How It Died*. New York: HarperCollins, 2008.

Jennings, Willie. *The Christian Imagination: Theology and the Origins of Race*. New Haven: Yale University Press, 2010.

Jensen, Gordon A. "Shaping Piety through Catechetical Structures: The Importance of Order." *Reformation and Renaissance Review* 10, no. 2 (2008): 231–36.

John Chrysostom. *Baptismal Instructions*. Translated by Paul Harkins. ACW 31. Mahwah, NJ: Newman, 1963.

John Paul II. *Catechesi Tradendae: On Catechesis in Our Time*. Manchester, NH: Sophia Institute, 2014.

Johnson, Adam. *Atonement: A Guide for the Perplexed*. London: T&T Clark, 2015.

Johnson, Sarah Cowan. *Teach Your Children Well: A Step-by-Step Guide to Family Discipleship*. Downers Grove, IL: InterVarsity Press, 2022.

Jones, L. Gregory. "A Dramatic Journey into God's Dazzling Light: Baptismal Catechesis and the Shaping of Christian Practical Wisdom." In *Knowing the Triune God: The Work of the Spirit in the Practices of the Church*, edited by James J. Buckley and David S. Yeago, 147–77. Grand Rapids: Eerdmans, 2001.

Justin Martyr. *First Apology*. In *Justin, Philosopher and Martyr*, edited and translated by Denis Minns and Paul Parvis. Oxford: Oxford University Press, 2009.

Keane, Drew N. "'Let Me Heare . . . If Thou Canst Say': The Utility of the Prayer Book Catechism (1549–1604)." *Journal of Technical Writing and Communication* 52, no. 1 (2022): 19–56.

Keefe, Susan A. *Water and the Word: Baptism and the Education of the Clergy in the Carolingian Empire*. 2 vols. Notre Dame: University of Notre Dame Press, 2002.

Keller, Timothy. *How to Reach the West Again: Six Essential Elements of a Missionary Encounter*. New York: Redeemer City to City, 2020.

Kim, Jung. "Catechesis and Mystagogy in St. Ephrem the Syrian: The Liturgy of Baptism and the *Madrashe*." ThD diss., Boston University, 2013.

Kingdon, Robert. "Catechesis in Calvin's Geneva." In *Educating People of Faith:*

Exploring the Histories of Jewish and Christian Communities, edited by John Van Engen, 294–313. Grand Rapids: Eerdmans, 2004.

Kinzig, Wolfram, ed. *Faith in Formulae: A Collection of Early Christian Creeds and Creed-Related Texts*. 4 vols. New York: Oxford University Press, 2017.

Kreider, Alan. *The Change of Conversion and the Origin of Christendom*. Reprint. Eugene, OR: Wipf & Stock, 2006.

Leclercq, Jean. *The Love of Learning and the Desire for God: A Study of Monastic Culture*. Translated by Catharine Misrahi. 3rd ed. New York: Fordham University Press, 1982.

Levering, Matthew. *Participatory Biblical Exegesis: A Theology of Biblical Interpretation*. Notre Dame: University of Notre Dame Press, 2008.

Louth, Andrew. *Discerning the Mystery: An Essay on the Nature of Theology*. Oxford: Clarendon, 1983.

———. *The Origins of the Christian Mystical Tradition*. Rev. ed. Oxford: Oxford University Press, 2007.

Ludlow, Morwenna. "Making and Being Made: Some Preliminary Thoughts on Craft-Education as a Model for Christian Formation." *Studies in Christian Ethics* 33, no. 1 (2019): 3–14.

Luther, Martin. *The Large Catechism*. In *The Annotated Luther*, vol. 2, *Word and Faith*, translated by Kirsi Stjerna. Minneapolis: Fortress, 2015.

———. *The Small Catechism*. In *Martin Luther's Basic Theological Writings*, edited by Timothy Lull. Minneapolis: Fortress, 1989.

Lynch, Joseph. *Godparents and Kinship in Early Medieval Europe*. Princeton: Princeton University Press, 1986.

MacIntyre, Alasdair. *After Virtue*. 2nd ed. Notre Dame: University of Notre Dame Press, 1984.

Marthaler, Berard. *The Catechism Yesterday and Today: The Evolution of a Genre*. Collegeville, MN: Liturgical Press, 1995.

Mather, Cotton. *Ratio Disciplinae Fratrum Nov-Anglorum: A Faithful Account of the Discipline Professed and Practiced; in the Churches of New-England with Interspersed and Instructive Reflections on the Discipline of the Primitive Churches*. Boston, 1726.

Mather, Richard. *A Catechisme; or, The Grounds and Principles of Christian Religion, set forth by way of Question and Answer.* London, 1650.

Maximus the Confessor. *On the Cosmic Mystery of Jesus Christ: Selected Writings from St. Maximus the Confessor*. Translated by Paul M. Blowers and Robert Louis Wilken. Crestwood, NY: St. Vladimir's Seminary Press, 2003.

McLaughlin, Rebecca. *The Secular Creed: Engaging Five Contemporary Claims*. Austin, TX: Gospel Coalition, 2021.

McNall, Joshua. *The Mosaic of Atonement: An Integrated Approach to Christ's Work.* Grand Rapids: Zondervan, 2019.

McNally, Deborah Coleen. "To Secure Her Freedom: 'Dorcas Ye Blackmore,' Race, Redemption, and the Dorchester First Church." *New England Quarterly* 89, no. 4 (2016): 533–55.

Meeks, Wayne. *The Origins of Christian Morality: The First Two Centuries.* New Haven: Yale University Press, 1993.

Meilaender, Gilbert. *Thy Will Be Done: The Ten Commandments and the Christian Life.* Grand Rapids: Baker Academic, 2020.

Miskotte, Kornelis Heiko. *Biblical ABCs: The Basics of Christian Resistance.* Translated by Eleonora Hof and Collin Cornell. Lanham, MD: Lexington Books, 2022.

Morgan, John. *Godly Learning: Puritan Attitudes towards Reason, Learning, and Education, 1560–1640.* Cambridge: Cambridge University Press, 1986.

Niebauer, Michael. *Virtuous Persuasion: A Theology of Christian Mission.* Bellingham, WA: Lexham, 2022.

Noll, Mark A. *The Rise of Evangelicalism: The Age of Edwards, Whitefield, and the Wesleys.* Downers Grove, IL: IVP Academic, 2003.

———. *The Scandal of the Evangelical Mind.* Grand Rapids: Eerdmans, 1994.

O'Malley, Timothy. *Divine Blessing: Liturgical Formation in the RCIA.* Collegeville, MN: Liturgical Press, 2019.

Packer, J. I., and Gary Parrett. *Grounded in the Gospel: Building Believers the Old-Fashioned Way.* Grand Rapids: Baker Academic, 2010.

Packer, J. I., and Joel Scandrett, eds. *To Be a Christian: An Anglican Catechism,* approved ed. Wheaton, IL: Crossway, 2020.

Parker, John. "Radechesis: A Return to Radical Catechesis." In *Healing Humanity: Confronting Our Moral Crisis,* edited by Alexander F. C. Webster, Alfred K. Siewers, and David C. Ford. Jordanville, NY: Holy Trinity Seminary Press, 2020.

Pedraza, Brian. *Catechesis for the New Evangelization: Vatican II, John Paul II, and the Unity of Revelation and Experience.* Washington, DC: Catholic University of America Press, 2020.

Phelan, Owen M. "Catechising the Wild: The Continuity and Innovation of Missionary Catechesis under the Carolingians." *Journal of Ecclesiastical History* 61, no. 3 (2010): 455–74.

Pieper, Josef. *On Faith, Hope, and Love.* San Francisco: Ignatius, 1997.

Pignot, Matthieu. *The Catechumenate in Late Antique Africa (4th–6th Centuries): Augustine of Hippo, His Contemporaries and Early Reception.* Leiden: Brill, 2020.

Polanyi, Michael. *The Tacit Dimension.* Chicago: University of Chicago Press, 1966.

Presley, Stephen O. *Cultural Sanctification: Engaging the World like the Early Church.* Grand Rapids: Eerdmans, 2024.

Raboteau, Albert J. *Slave Religion: The "Invisible Institution" in the Antebellum South.* Updated ed. Oxford: Oxford University Press, 2004.

Rapp, Claudia. "City and Citizenship as Christian Concepts of Community in Late Antiquity." In *The City in the Classical and Post-Classical World: Changing Contexts of Power and Identity*, edited by Claudia Rapp and H. A. Drake, 153–66. Cambridge: Cambridge University Press, 2014.

Ratzinger, Joseph Cardinal. *Gospel, Catechesis, Catechism: Sidelights on the "Catechism of the Catholic Church."* San Francisco: Ignatius, 1997.

———. *Handing on the Faith in an Age of Disbelief.* San Francisco: Ignatius, 2006.

———. *The Spirit of the Liturgy.* Translated by John Saward. San Francisco: Ignatius, 2000.

Richmann, Christopher J., and Alex Fogleman. "Augustine's *De Catechizandis Rudibus* and the Scholarship of Teaching and Learning." *Teaching in Higher Education* 28, no. 7 (2023): 1640–55.

Ristuccia, Nathan J. *Christianization and Commonwealth in Early Medieval Europe: A Ritual Interpretation.* Oxford: Oxford University Press, 2018.

Rowe, C. Kavin. *World Upside Down: Reading Acts in the Graeco-Roman Age.* New York: Oxford University Press, 2009.

Rylaarsdam, David. *John Chrysostom on Divine Pedagogy: The Coherence of His Theology and Preaching.* Oxford: Oxford University Press, 2014.

Sanneh, Lamin. "Global Christianity and the Re-education of the West." *Christian Century*, July 19, 1995, 715–18.

Sayers, Dorothy L. "Creed or Chaos?" In *Letters to a Diminished Church: Passionate Arguments for the Relevance of Christian Doctrine.* New York: Nelson, 2004.

Scandrett, Joel. "'To Be a Christian': J. I. Packer and the Renewal of Evangelical Catechesis." *Crux* 52, no. 1 (2016): 4–12.

Scandrett, Joel, and William Witt. *Mapping Atonement.* Grand Rapids: Baker Academic, 2022.

Schmemann, Alexander. *For the Life of the World.* Rev. ed. Crestwood, NY: St. Vladimir's Seminary Press, 1973.

Sittser, Gerald. *Resilient Faith: How the Early Christian "Third Way" Changed the World.* Grand Rapids: Brazos, 2019.

Smith, Christian, and Amy Adamczyk. *Handing Down the Faith: How Parents Pass Their Religion on to the Next Generation.* Oxford: Oxford University Press, 2021.

Smith, Christian, with Melinda Lundquist Denton. *Soul Searching: The Religious and Spiritual Lives of American Teenagers.* New York: Oxford University Press, 2005.

Smith, Gordon T. *Transforming Conversion: Rethinking the Language and Contours of Christian Initiation*. Grand Rapids: Baker Academic, 2010.

Smith, J. Warren. *Christian Grace and Pagan Virtue: The Theological Foundation of Ambrose's Ethics*. New York: Oxford University Press, 2010.

Smith, James K. A. *Awaiting the King: Reforming Public Theology*. Grand Rapids: Baker Academic, 2017.

———. *Desiring the Kingdom*. Grand Rapids: Baker Academic, 2009.

———. *You Are What You Love*. Grand Rapids: Brazos, 2016.

Smith, Lesley. *The Ten Commandments: Interpreting the Bible in the Medieval World*. Leiden: Brill, 2014.

Smith, Ted A. *The End of Theological Education*. Grand Rapids: Eerdmans, 2023.

Sosler, Alex. *A Short Guide to Spiritual Formation: Finding Life in Truth, Goodness, Beauty, and Community*. Grand Rapids: Baker Academic, 2024.

Spellman, Chad. "The Drama of Discipline: Toward an Intertextual Profile of *Paideia* in Hebrews 12." *Journal of the Evangelical Theological Society* 59, no. 3 (2016): 487–506.

Stewart-Sykes, Alistair, trans. *On the Lord's Prayer: Tertullian, Cyprian, and Origen*. Crestwood, NY: St. Vladimir's Seminary Press, 2004.

Taylor, Charles. *Modern Social Imaginaries*. Durham, NC: Duke University Press, 2003.

Teresa of Ávila. *The Way of Perfection*. In *The Collected Words of St. Teresa of Avila*, vol. 2, translated by Kieran Kavanaugh, OCD, and Otilio Rodriguez, OCD. Washington, DC: Institute of Carmelite Studies, 1980.

Tertullian. *On Baptism*. Translated by Ernest Evans. London: SPCK, 1964.

Theodore of Mopsuestia. *Commentary on the Lord's Prayer, Baptism, and the Eucharist*. Translated by Alphonse Mingana. Woodbrooke Studies 6. Cambridge: Heffer & Sons, 1933.

———. *Commentary on the Nicene Creed*. Translated by Alphonse Mingana. Woodbrooke Studies 5. Cambridge: Heffer & Sons, 1933.

Thomas Aquinas. *The Aquinas Catechism: A Simple Explanation of the Catholic Faith by the Church's Greatest Theologian*. Manchester, NH: Sophia Institute Press, 2000.

Torrance, Thomas F. *The School of Faith: The Catechisms of the Reformed Church*. 1959. Reprint, Eugene, OR: Wipf & Stock, 1996.

Turner, Paul. *Hallelujah Highway: A History of the Catechumenate*. Chicago: Liturgy Training Publications, 2000.

Vanhoozer, Kevin J. *The Drama of Doctrine: A Canonical Linguistic Approach to Doctrine*. Louisville: Westminster John Knox, 2005.

———. *Hearers and Doers: A Pastor's Guide to Making Disciples through Scripture and Doctrine*. Bellingham, WA: Lexham, 2019.

Vanhoozer, Kevin, and Owen Strachen. *The Pastor as Public Theologian: Reclaiming a Lost Vision*. Grand Rapids: Baker Academic, 2015.

Walsham, Alexandra. "Wholesome Milk and Strong Meat: Peter Canisius's Catechisms and the Conversion of Protestant Britain." *British Catholic History* 32, no. 3 (2015): 293–314.

Warren, Tish Harrison. *Liturgy of the Ordinary: Sacred Practices in Ordinary Life*. Downers Grove, IL: InterVarsity Press, 2016.

Watson, Jonathan. *In the Name of Our Lord: Four Models of the Relationship between Baptism, Catechesis, and Communion*. Bellingham, WA: Lexham, 2021.

Webber, Robert. *Ancient-Future Faith: Rethinking Evangelicalism for a Postmodern World*. Grand Rapids: Baker Books, 1999.

———. *Ancient-Future Worship: Proclaiming and Enacting God's Narrative*. Grand Rapids: Baker Books, 2008.

Weil, Simone. "Reflections on the Right Use of School Studies." In *Waiting for God*. New York: Routledge, 2021.

Wengert, Timothy J. *Martin Luther's Catechisms: Forming the Faith*. Minneapolis: Fortress, 2009.

Westerhoff, John, III. *Will Our Children Have Faith?* 3rd ed. New York: Morehouse, 2012.

Westra, Liuwe. *The Apostles' Creed: Origin, History, and Some Early Commentaries*. Turnhout: Brepols, 2002.

Wickes, Jeffrey. "Between Liturgy and School: Reassessing the Performative Context of Ephrem's Madrāšê." *Journal of Early Christian Studies* 26, no. 1 (2018): 25–51.

Wilken, Robert Louis. "Alexandria: A School for Training in Virtue." In *Schools of Thought in the Christian Tradition*, edited by Patrick Henry, 15–30. Philadelphia: Fortress, 1984.

———. "The Church as Culture." *First Things* 142 (April 2004).

———. *The Spirit of Early Christian Thought: Seeking the Face of God*. New Haven: Yale University Press, 2003.

Willard, Dallas. *The Spirit of the Disciplines: Understanding How God Changes Lives*. New York: HarperCollins, 1991.

Willey, Petroc, and Scott Sollom, eds. *Speaking the Truth in Love: The Catechism and the New Evangelization*. Steubenville, OH: Emmaus, 2019.

Williams, D. H. *Retrieving the Tradition and Renewing Evangelicalism: A Primer for Suspicious Protestants*. Grand Rapids: Eerdmans, 1999.

Willis, Jonathan. *The Reformation of the Decalogue: Religious Identity and the Ten Commandments in England, c. 1485–1625*. Cambridge: Cambridge University Press, 2017.

Winner, Lauren. *The Dangers of Christian Practice: On Wayward Gifts, Characteristic Damage, and Sin*. New Haven: Yale University Press, 2018.

Witkamp, Nathan. *Tradition and Innovation: Baptismal Rite and Mystagogy in Theodore of Mopsuestia and Narsai of Nisibis*. Leiden: Brill, 2018.

Wright, N. T. *Scripture and the Authority of God*. San Francisco: HarperCollins, 2011.

Yarnold, Edward. "'The Catechumenate for Adults Is to Be Restored': Patristic Adaptation in the Rite for the Christian Initiation of Adults." *Studies in Church History* 35 (1999): 478–97.

Young, Frances. *The Making of the Creeds*. London: SCM Classics, 1991.

Index of Authors

Index of Subjects